Thompson Trophy Racers

The Pilots and Planes of
America's Air Racing
Glory Days 1929-49

Roger Huntington

Motorbooks International
Publishers & Wholesalers ®

First published in 1989 by Motorbooks International Publishers & Wholesalers, P O Box 2, 729 Prospect Avenue, Osceola, WI 54020 USA

Printed and bound in the United States of America

The information in this book is true and complete to the best of our knowledge. All recommendations are made without any guarantee on the part of the author or publisher, who also disclaim any liability incurred in connection with the use of this data or specific details

We recognize that some words, model names and designations, for example, mentioned herein are the property of the trademark holder. We use them for identification purposes only. This is not an official publication

Library of Congress Cataloging-in-Publication Data
Huntington, Roger.
    Thompson trophy racers / Roger Huntington
        p.   cm.
    ISBN 0-87938-365-8
    1. Airplane racing—United States—History—Pictorial works.
    I. Title.
    GV759.H83   1989   89-9474
    797.5′2—dc20   CIP

On the front cover: The elegant lines and racy paint scheme of the 1933 Thompson Trophy winning Wedell-Williams No. 44 were recreated on this full-size reproduction of the famous racer. *Budd Davisson*

On the back cover: The sleekest racer of them all—the highly modified P–51C named *Beguine*. The pods at the end of the wings house the radiator and oil cooler. *Aldrich*

Contents

	Acknowledgments	5
	Foreword	6
1	Roots of Thompson Trophy Racing	7
2	A new kind of air racing in America	15
3	Pylon racer design in the 1930s	23
4	Pulling to win	39
5	Horsepower for the Thompson	52
6	Pylon racing strategy	68
7	Prewar racers: the small engine school	81
8	Prewar racers: the big engine school	93
9	Prewar Thompson Trophy races	103
10	Making racers out of fighters	132
11	Great postwar racers	154
12	Postwar Thompson Trophy races	168
	Epilogue	181
	Race results	183
	Index	189

To my friend Geri Bruce, without whose help and encouragement this book would never have been written

Acknowledgments

I couldn't begin to list all the great friends in the hobby of air racing history who have contributed to this book. But I would like to extend special thanks to Truman "Pappy" Weaver, John Sunyak, Steve Hudek, Peter Bowers and Tony Yusken for access to their extensive photograph collections; to Dusty Carter, Bill Kerka and Harry Robinson for their brilliant three-view drawings; and to Don Berliner and Birch Matthews for the most elusive stuff of all, old technical literature. Thanks a million, guys. I couldn't have done it without you.

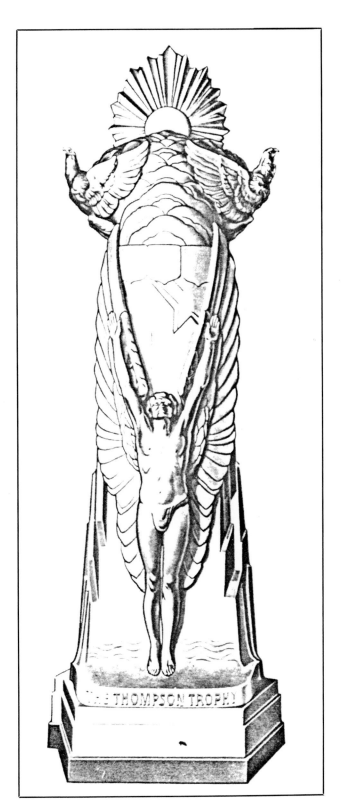

Foreword

The Thompson Trophy Races were without a doubt America's most glamorous and prestigious pylon air races. The winners became instant heroes, and their airplanes the objects of millions of modelers' dreams. Who won and who lost and at what speeds have long been thoroughly documented. But the arguments still range far into the night over why one pilot was able to leave another in his wake despite less horsepower or less fame.

At last comes Roger Huntington, a veteran motor racing writer, to lift the engine cowlings and peel back the secrets of streamlining to reveal why one airplane was so much faster than another, and why some designers swore by bulky radial engines and others were just as sold on smaller inline engines.

When you have finished reading this book, you will have a clear understanding of what it took to win and why some pilots got their names engraved on the great bronze trophy, and the rest were just also-rans.

Don Berliner
Founder, Society of Air Racing Historians

Chapter 1

Roots of Thompson Trophy racing

Several years ago, aviation historian Thomas Foxworth wrote a magnificent book on air racing in the 1920s, *The Speed Seekers* (Doubleday, 1974). The thrust of this book is that the years immediately following World War I—specifically from 1919 through 1926—saw more rapid progress in aircraft performance than did any other comparable period of aviation history.

I find no argument with this idea. Those were certainly years of great technical achievements in aviation—particularly in air racing. The world straightaway speed record was raised from 162 mph to 278 mph in this short time, and special racing planes were lapping closed pylon courses at speeds exceeding 250 mph, pulling up to 6 gs of centrifugal loading in the turns. World governments and large companies were spending millions on race plane development, and competition was international in scope. It was truly the Roaring Twenties of aviation speed progress.

However, the less sophisticated, grassroots, do-it-yourself, shoestring racing of the depression years of the 1930s can be just as intriguing. Those technical challenges were no less formidable when the

The Curtiss biplane racers that competed for the Pulitzer races in the 1920s were more advanced aerodynamically than most monoplanes of the day. Curtiss Aeroplane

amateur racer had only a few hundred dollars to build the fastest plane that he could. And the ingenuity displayed in the design and contruction of some tiny backyard bombs of the thirties, aimed at winning the Thompson Trophy, rivaled the finest Schneider and Pulitzer racers of the twenties that were designed by graduate engineers and built in fully equipped factories.

Early air racing in America

Perhaps it's a little ironic that although the science of flying was born in America, the infant of high-speed flying grew more quickly in Europe. Americans Orville and Wilbur Wright are universally credited with the first sustained flight of a heavier-than-air craft in 1903. In 1909, wealthy New York newspaperman James Gordon Bennett established the first series of international closed course air races: two laps around a 6.2 mile course for a $5,000 prize and the Bennett trophy. American Glenn Curtiss handily won the first race in a crude 50 hp open biplane at an average speed of 47.7 mph.

But that victory was just about the end of any American leadership in air racing for many years. The 1910 International Air Meet in Belmont Park, New York, was won by a French plane, and thereafter most development and racing of early high-speed aircraft was concentrated in France. Pre–World War I speed planes from French manufacturers like Antoinette, Nieuport and Deperdussin were years ahead of their time in streamlining and power-to-weight ratio. We had nothing in America to remotely compare with them. It wasn't until another wealthy American newspaperman, Ralph Pulitzer, established a strictly American series of closed circuit air races after World War I that this country's aircraft industry began to think seriously about speed development.

The first Pulitzer Trophy race was held at Mitchell Field, Long Island, on Thanksgiving Day 1920. It was a free-for-all race, four laps around a twenty-nine mile triangular course, for a prize of $5,000. Entrants showed up from all over the East—thirty-seven of them: most were surplus World War I training planes, but a few were special speed planes developed by the air wings of the US Army and Navy for experimental purposes. One of these, an Army biplane with a big 640 hp Packard V-12 liquid cooled engine, won the race at an average speed of 156.5 mph.

What the Pulitzer did for American aviation

It would be easy to assume that the early Pulitzer races put America right back on track in aircraft performance development. But it wasn't quite that easy. At the time of the first Pulitzer race, when our fastest planes were hitting 180 mph, the official world straightaway speed record was held by a French plane at 192.1 mph. Within a few months, another French plane and pilot put the record over 200 mph. Aviation development was red hot in France after World War I. The French government was heavily involved with military aviation, and dozens of small private companies were working on light sport planes for public consumption. Speed records and race victories were considered a relatively easy way to enhance national pride and company image. The major world landplane speed records stayed right in France through the 1920s.

But the Pulitzer Trophy races certainly did have a tremendous impact on aircraft development in this country, primarily because they attracted relatively large federal development budgets through our military services. Or perhaps it would be more accurate to say that the races attracted the interest of the contemporary commanding officers of those military wings. Gen. Billy Mitchell of the Army Air Service and Adm. William Moffett of the Navy air wing were interested in air racing and were convinced that it could be an effective tool for the development of combat planes that required high maneuverability. They were convinced enough to lobby in Congress for extra budget funds to support modest race plane development programs in the early 1920s. They didn't get anywhere near what they wanted, needless to say, and it was sometimes necessary to trade funds and loan planes to keep viable racing programs going in both services. But certainly progress would have been much slower with only private sportsmen to support development.

A few numbers illustrate the speed progress made in the six short years of the Pulitzer series, 1920 through 1925. The winning average speed of the races went up from 156.5 mph in 1920 to 248.9 mph in 1925. Corresponding maximum straightaway speeds of these planes rose from 185 to 265 mph. Perhaps a more convincing barometer of the progress was the fact that the horsepower of the winning planes was about the same in the first and last races, at 600–650 hp. This emphasizes the great improvements in streamlining and drag reduction in these six years.

Technical lessons from the Pulitzer races

It's to the credit of the US military men, both Army and Navy, who directed the experimental efforts of their respective Pulitzer programs, that they covered as much design territory as possible with the funds they had to work with. They tried to look objectively at most general high-speed airframe layouts of the day. If their findings were perhaps weighted in some areas, it was because individual designers in some private supplier companies did such a good job. For example, the brilliant Curtiss designers made biplanes look awfully good.

Out of the Pulitzer races came several obvious beneficial technical developments.
• The liquid cooled Curtiss D-12 engine introduced wet sleeve monobloc construction and seven main bearings for durability in the V-12 engine.
• The Curtiss-Reed metal propeller showed efficiency figures up to eighty-six percent at 1,100 feet per second tip speed and gave top speed increases up to 20 mph over the performance of wood props on some planes.
• Aerodynamic refinement included attention to fillets at joining surfaces to reduce interference drag.
• Introduction of the retractible landing gear reduced drag.
• First experiments were made with cantilever wing construction, for maximum strength and minimum weight.
• Development of all-wood fuselage and wing construction with plywood covering that started the trend to modern monocoque construction.

Were we misled by the Pulitzer?

In one way, though, the Pulitzer races may have done a definite disservice to the American military aviation establishment by perpetuating the belief

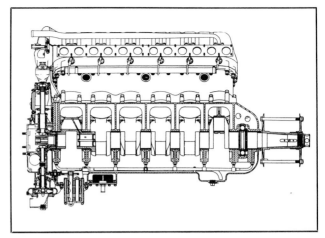

The Pulitzer races of the early 1920s were largely responsible for development of the milestone Curtiss D-12 liquid cooled engine. Its unique monobloc construction with wet cylinder sleeves was a breakthrough.

that the biplane configuration had more potential for high-speed fighter aircraft than did the monoplane. This might have put America as much as five years behind Europe in development of the monoplane.

It's true that our military aviation people were careful to develop several examples of biplane and monoplane layouts for the various races over the

The United States was able to dominate the international Schneider Trophy seaplane races in the early twenties by merely putting floats on the Curtiss Pulitzer racers. Curtiss Aeroplane

9

The US military studied most major aircraft design alternatives during Pulitzer research. This Verville R-3 racer of 1922 featured retractable landing gear and cantilever wing construction. Weaver Collection

Lt. Cyrus Bettis won the last Pulitzer race in 1925 with a Curtiss R3C-1 biplane entered by the Army Air Service. This was the peak of biplane performance development in the United States. Curtiss Aeroplane

six-year period. They wanted to have a good objective look at both. But, the monoplanes never made a very good showing. A cantilever monoplane won the 1924 Pulitzer, but all the fast biplanes that year had been withdrawn for one reason or another, and the monoplane's winning average speed was some 27 mph slower than was a biplane's winning average the year before. That wasn't very impressive.

Admittedly, aircraft designers in the 1920s didn't know enough about structural framework inside a wing to make it strong enough for combat flight maneuvers without external bracing struts and wires. The last Curtiss Pulitzer racer of 1925 was designed for a load factor of 12.5. This meant that the wing structure was strong enough to support 12.5 times the weight of the plane without breakage or permanent buckling (as when pulling out of a high-speed dive). So high a load factor would have been unthinkable with a cantilever monoplane of that day.

One other important factor that helped to perpetuate the biplane in our military was the lack of efficient hydraulic arresting gear on our very early Navy aircraft carriers. This encouraged the low wing loading and slow landing speeds of the biplane.

On to Cleveland

The Pulitzer air races were never just one-shot events. They were always the feature event of a whole program of contemporary aviation performance demonstrations—from pylon races to precision parachute jumping and stunt flying. The later Pulitzers capped off three- and four-day national meets with twenty or thirty separate events for various classes of military and civilian aircraft. They were a natural for showing off new designs, public relations demonstrations by the military and just plain making money off a curious public intrigued with the new sport of air racing.

So it's not surprising that when the last Pulitzer race was over in 1925, there was a groundswell of demand within the American aviation community to keep a series of national air races going, with or without the support and attraction of the heavily financed military racers. A year later, the National Aeronautic Association (NAA) was formed, affiliated with the Federation Aeronautique Internationale (FAI) in Paris, and their first job was to organize and sanction a big national air show in Philadelphia that fall. It was a booming success. The 1927 show was hosted in Seattle, Washington—and the National Air Races (NAR) were off and running.

While the NAA was launching the new series of National Air Races at various cities around the country, a group of aviation loving businessmen in Cleveland, Ohio, became equally dedicated to nailing down this blockbuster air circus as a permanent annual event at their beautiful new Hopkins Airport on the west edge of town. The group was headed by Fred Crawford, vice president of Thompson Products, and Louis Greve, head of the Cleveland Pneumatic Tool Company. Both companies were deeply involved in developing advanced equipment for the fledgling aircraft industry, and their leaders were air racing enthusiasts, pure and simple. But more important, they believed that a continuing series of industry-wide shows at one fixed location could do great things for the aviation sport as well as for the infant industry—not to mention promoting the city

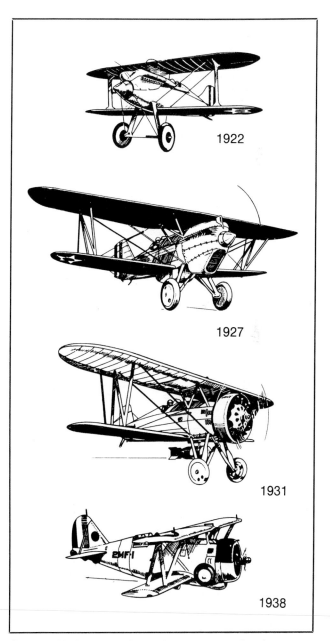

One possible disservice of the Pulitzer races was that they encouraged the US military to develop biplanes, when the world trend was monoplanes. Rolfe

11

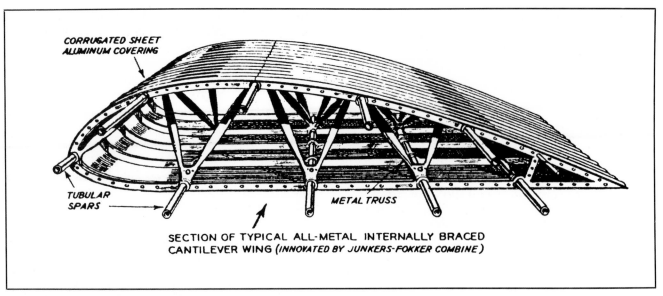

CORRUGATED SHEET
ALUMINUM COVERING

TUBULAR
SPARS

METAL TRUSS

SECTION OF TYPICAL ALL-METAL INTERNALLY BRACED
CANTILEVER WING (INNOVATED BY JUNKERS-FOKKER COMBINE)

The technology of cantilever wing construction was very crude in the 1920s, and the primitive results added weight to the planes and discouraged a trend toward monoplanes. Rolfe

of Cleveland as the hub of aviation in the United States.

Late in 1928, the Cleveland businessmen formed a committee and hired freewheeling pro-moters Cliff and Phil Henderson to manage the show details. Crawford and Greve actually did much of the legwork that first year, convincing local merchants, hotels and manufacturers to put up prizes

The TravelAir Model R stunned US aviation experts by beating our fastest military fighters in first Thompson Cup race in 1929. Beech

and sponsor the event. They got solid backing right up to the city mayor, and within weeks they were able to present to the NAA a package of events, facilities and prizes for the 1929 Labor Day weekend that was hard to turn down. It promised to be the most impressive and lucrative air meet the world had seen.

The NAA officials were sold. It was necessary to move the show to other host cities from time to time, as major construction work was done on the Cleveland airport. But the facilities and organization promised for Cleveland were impressive enough so that the NAA gave the assurances that this would be the "permanent" home of the NAR.

The new committee undertook a tremendous job to get those facilities ready. Hopkins was just a big airport in the 1920s, not a circus arena. In less than three months, the contractors had to move some 150,000 yards of dirt, build a 3,000 foot grandstand, construct fourteen new hangars to house the contesting planes and arrange parking for 40,000 cars. The job was done in the nick of time for those first 1929 Nationals in September.

It's history now that the meet more than met expectations. Over 100,000 people showed up for the opening of the ten-day program. Some 300 contestants filed entries and competed in every type of air competition. The Army and Navy air services used the races as a showcase for their latest hardware, even sponsoring some of the races. In fact, the annual Mitchell Trophy race was continued to showcase the popular Curtiss Hawk pursuit planes. Everybody got in the act. The Cleveland National Air Races of 1929 made previous national air events seem like local shows by comparison.

A race that rattled the industry

The feature event of the 1929 races was a fifty-mile free-for-all over a five-mile pylon course for a modest trophy and purse put up by none other than Fred Crawford and the Thompson Products Company, the major spark plug behind the Cleveland Nationals. But that first Thompson Cup race was perhaps most significant for its technical overtones: It was the only all-out speed contest on the program, open to the best of both military and civilian aircraft, where free modifications were allowed to get all the speed possible. Today we would call it a performance shootout between military and civilian aviation.

To make a long story short, Doug Davis won that race in a commercial sport monoplane, the TravelAir R model, powered by a 400 hp Wright Whirlwind radial engine—against a field of classic Army fighter biplanes with liquid cooled V-12s. The winning plane's top speed of 235 mph was some 50 mph faster than our fastest military fighter planes of

the day. Although a couple of modified fighter planes in the race could go as fast, they didn't hold up for the distance and were nowhere near production specifications. Needless to say, it was a race that caused some head scratching in Army and Navy air force offices the next day.

Launching the Thompson Trophy

The Thompson people were overjoyed with the success of that first event under their name, from a standpoint of institutional public relations as well as for the fun it provided for everybody concerned. Within days, Fred Crawford and his boss Charles Thompson contacted the NAA with a proposition to sponsor a feature event for future annual National Air Races: a pylon race of at least 100 miles, open to aircraft of unlimited specifications, with sizeable cash prizes and an impressive Thompson Trophy for the winner. They guaranteed a purse of $10,000 for the initial 1930 race—winner to get $5,000—with assurances of regular purse increases in future years, as conditions permitted. That was a lot of money in depression years when twenty cents an hour was a living wage.

Also, by establishing the purse nearly a year in advance, the race organizers gained plenty of time

The TravelAir R of 1929 was powered by 400 hp Wright air cooled radial engine that gave excellent performance and reliability. Most high performance aircraft used liquid cooled engines. Weaver Collection

to use that purse as bait to draw a fascinating field of commercial, military and homebuilt planes for the 1930 race. The prize money didn't rival the money in great auto races like the Indianapolis 500, and earlier international air races for wealthy sportsmen, like the Gordon Bennett, equaled these purse figures. But it was a treasure trove for backyard plane builders who were operating on a shoestring and were eager for any race competition that promised enough prize money to pay back some of their investment in a special purpose plane. American private aviation desperately needed a big league

race with some big time prize money. The Thompson Trophy series was it.

The trophy itself was an impressive thing. Thompson vice president Crawford commissioned a well-known local sculptor, Walter Sinz, to give him something besides just the usual "naked lady waving a flag." An accompanying picture shows the beauty of the thirty-inch-tall trophy presented at the 1930 races at Chicago. For the next twenty years, the Thompson trophy was destined to attract some of the greatest pylon air racing of all time.

Charles Thompson, left, presenting the beautiful Thompson Trophy to Lowell Bayles, winner of the 1931 race in the Gee Bee Z. Western Reserve Historical

Chapter 2

A new kind of air racing in America

Unlike the Pulitzer races of the 1920s, the Thompson Trophy series of the thirties was established with no thought of any substantial participation by military aircraft. It was unlikely then because both Army and Navy air services were reasonably satisfied with what had been learned in the earlier races. Racing was no longer a primary research and development concern. Further, Congress was getting tighter with military budgets in the late twenties. And of course the topper was the Wall Street crash in October 1929—which put a sudden squeeze on money in every sector of the economy.

By the time of the first Thompson race in September of 1930 it was cast in stone that this racing would be a "grassroots, do-it-yourself, tight budget" sport.

Three kinds of racing planes

As this new low budget air racing sport emerged at the 1930 Nationals, there were three distinct types of aircraft that showed up to contest for the Trophy:

Commercial aircraft

Some pilots felt they could have some fun and be reasonably competitive with certain models of

The Seversky P-35 fighter plane, released for private sale in a civilian version in 1937, was raced successfully in several Bendix and Thompson races. Weaver Collection

commercial sport planes. These were planes produced in small numbers by legitimate aircraft manufacturers—planes with better-than-average performance—but ones which met Department of Commerce (DOC) standards for structural strength, and carried the usual "NC" (commercial) designation in their license numbers. An example of this type of plane would be the Lockheed Altair.

It was predictable that these DOC legal sport planes would be barely competitive at best. But there were several aircraft companies in the early thirties that produced special series of out-and-out racing planes for "commercial" buyers. The TravelAir R model of 1929 could be considered in this category, since five more or less identical planes were built over a three year period, though there was no attempt to certify them for DOC NC licenses.

Matty Laird in Chicago produced certified sport biplanes for a variety of customers in the late twenties. Then his famous "Solution" and "Super Solution" biplanes of the 1930-1931 period were strictly racing planes, and were eventually sold to private buyers. Also the first products of the famous Granville brothers of Springfield, Mass.—the "Gee Bee" people—were licensed single seat sport planes. Both their sport models and specials showed up in early Thompson races.

This business of commercial aircraft vs. custom racers took a new twist in the late 1930s, and Frank Fuller was the catalyst. He was the wealthy heir to the Fuller Paint fortune, and a man fascinated with the idea of flying in the Bendix cross country race. But he didn't want to contest it in a "homebuilt" uncertified pylon racer of questionable structural integrity. His chance came in 1937 when the Seversky Airplane Co. won an Army contract with a Twin Wasp powered, all metal pursuit ship, designated the P-35. Fuller knew deSeversky, and somehow talked him into approaching the War Dept. for permission to build a couple of "executive" versions of the P-35 for public relations purposes. The deal went through, and Fuller bought the first Model "SEV-S2" for a reported $35,000; Jimmy Doolittle got the second one for Shell Oil promotions; and we believe one was retained by Seversky for private promotional use. (They also produced 76 planes for the Air Force before the company was absorbed by Republic.)

Anyway Frank Fuller won the 1937 and 1939 Bendix races with his job, and he flew competitively in the 1937 Thompson.

Military aircraft

There was actually only one serious attempt by a military group to win the Thompson Trophy—either prewar or postwar. That was the project by Capt. Arthur Page and US Navy technicians to enter a highly modified Curtiss Hawk fighter in the first contest in Chicago in 1930. That was an unbudgeted project from a financing standpoint. But when you consider the elaborate facilities, tools, equipment and expertise available to construct a special airplane at a naval air station—with the possibility of "borrowing" advanced experimental components—it's no surprise that a rather sophisticated racer resulted that was far and away the fastest plane entered in that race. Unfortunately an unforeseen design flaw caused a crash that resulted in Capt. Page's death, while he was leading the race.

To describe that plane very briefly, an original stock Curtiss P-1 biplane was modified by completely removing the lower wing, re-bracing the upper wing with streamlined struts, and cowling in the landing gear. The original cellular coolant radiator below the engine was replaced by fluted copper surface radiators over most of the main wing. The original Curtiss D-12 engine of 435 hp was replaced with an experimental supercharged Conqueror of 700 hp, and the entire engine cowling was redone with smoothly curved sheet aluminum squeezed in closely around the larger engine for minimum frontal area. The overall result was an apparent sixty percent reduction in parasite drag with a sixty percent increase in power, while gross weight was held within a few hundred pounds of the original 2,900 lb. And in raw racing terms, top speed went up nearly 100 mph, from 155 mph to 240–250 mph. That was effective modifying!

Do-it-yourself custom racers

Of course, the great bulk of competing planes in the prewar Thompson races were one-of-a-kind specials produced by private individuals who raced more or less as a sport, and had some source of income other than prize money. Or in some cases the builder would produce custom planes for other sportsmen, so he might be considered a small manufacturer. From a legal standpoint these were considered experimental planes, with an "R" or "X" in their DOC license designation, so had to meet no standards other than a cursory inspection by a DOC field rep. And the one common denominator in almost every design was *limited funding*. None of these specials were designed and constructed from a cost-no-object standpoint. So usually every technical decision was in some way a compromise of the speed/cost equation.

Chapters 7 and 8 detail the design and construction of a dozen or so of these specials. Just about every idea for going fast on limited funds is represented there. But we want to emphasize that these little budget built planes could not have been competitive if there had been any substantial interest in Thompson racing by the larger, better funded

The US Navy entered a highly modified 700 hp Curtiss Hawk fighter in the first Thompson race in 1930. It was the fastest plane in the race by far. Weaver Collection

Art Chester's tiny Jeep was typical of the homebuilt pylon racers of the thirties. Many early grassroots racers designed, built and flew their own planes. Repla-Tech

aircraft manufacturers or the military services. This was proved when the French Caudron "commercial" racer literally blew the other competitors away in 1936.

You might almost say that money would have spoiled prewar air racing!

The new racing brotherhood

In the Pulitzer and Schneider days of the 1920s, America's air racing heros—the names hyped in the newspapers and magazines—were military men, men usually with World War I combat records, or men who had set world air records for speed or altitude or long distances. Lt. Jimmy Doolittle of the Army Air Service was a household word in the twenties—and he went on to write some records in the Thompson races of the early thirties, as a retired officer and private employee of the Shell Oil Company. In World War II, he rejoined the Air Force and organized the famed Tokyo air raid by B-25 bombers from the aircraft carrier *Hornet*. Doolittle, a big, big name in US aviation for forty years, was the stuff racing legends are made of.

But in the lean years of the 1930s, the big racing names were those of private flyers who could somehow scare up enough money to build or buy a successful plane. And these guys ran the gamut of charisma, piloting ability and technical talent.

Roscoe Turner was by far the best-known name. Turner wasn't a mechanic, and could do little more than tighten a bolt to build a plane. But, he was a flamboyant, confident, garrulous promoter who could usually get somebody else to finance his racing dreams. He cultivated a bizarre image by traveling around with a trained lion cub and by often dressing in a snappy military uniform and polished boots, an outfit legitimatized by some vague honorary title as a colonel in a state National Guard.

Yet even Roscoe Turner was utterly dedicated to the sport. There were times in the thirties when he stayed only one jump ahead of a sheriff out to repossess a plane or car. He spent his last dollars on racing planes and would gladly loan his last dollar to help a fellow racer keep going. And winning was food and drink to Turner. He paid his dues.

Just the opposite of Turner was Art Chester. Art was quiet, reserved, secretive, and a constant thinker about race plane design. He learned to fly while in his teens and immediately set out on a career of full-time charter flying by stunting at local air shows and county fairs and instructing—any flying that could earn a buck. In 1928, he was able to build a small airport near Joliet, Illinois, and that became the base for his early racing efforts. He designed and built his own planes entirely and usually managed to win enough prize money from racing all

Keith Rider was a designer and builder who hired other pilots to demonstrate his planes for prospective buyers. Roger Don Rae climbed into a new Model R-4 in 1936. Repla-Tech

18

over the country to finance them, with a little besides. But Art didn't have the outgoing personality that it took to promote sponsorship money in those days. He had to scratch for everything. In 1936, he accepted a position with Al Menasco in Los Angeles, to work on engine development, and his impact in the late thirties was more in innovative design. But he did it on his own, without direct financial support for his racing from Menasco. Art Chester's kind was the glue that held grassroots air racing together in the 1930s.

Another distinct and vital class of contestant from the early Thompson era was the small custom builder, such as Keith Rider, who supplied the hardware but never flew his own planes in competition. Rider set up shop in an abandoned casket factory in Santa Monica, California, and took orders for one-of-a-kind racing planes from individuals or groups with enough money for a decent deposit. Some of Rider's planes were started without sponsorship, hoping that a sponsor could be found during construction. This strategy backfired more than once, and Rider ended up having to enter the plane himself for prize money, usually on a 60–40 percent split deal with an available pilot.

These pioneers did anything that they could do to keep racing. The relatively healthy Thompson prize money kept egging them on. But most of the brotherhood would have showed up at Cleveland each year anyway, just for the fun of it.

Obtaining sponsorship

Today very few big time racing drivers or pilots own the vehicles that they race. Usually, owners are able to get one or more sponsors to pay most costs, in return for the sponsor's name on the race vehicle and maybe some public relations appearances by the driver. Racing today is a complex combination of sport, business, personalities and publicity hype.

It was a different world in the 1930s. It would be untrue to say there was no money that could be hustled to help finance racing planes. Even though the depression economy had dried up many potential sources of sponsorship money, some wealthy people and booming businesses still could be considered promising targets for diplomatic approaches for financial help. It was just much tougher to squeeze it out then.

Prime targets were wealthy persons who were intrigued with the early aviation scene and welcomed the opportunity to get involved to the extent of owning or sponsoring a major racing effort. As far back as 1919, a Texas oil man, S. J. Cox, plunked down $100,000 for the Curtiss Aeroplane people to design and build him not one, but two, all-out racing planes with all the latest equipment and features for

the last Gordon Bennett race. That money meant quite a lot to Curtiss at the time, when the lush military contracts of World War I had suddenly dried up.

Wealthy widows seemed particularly susceptible to the blandishments of money-short aircraft designers with impressive plans for speed planes that would beat the world record, especially when assured that they would be contributing importantly to the broad sweep of aviation history. The story is well-known of how Lady Houston of London saved the 1931 Schneider race, thus securing the trophy permanently for Britain, by putting up £100,000 after the Air Ministry withdrew their promised support at the last minute.

Closer to home, Marion Guggenheim of New York ordered the construction of Robert Hall's *Bulldog* racer of 1932, with the idea of having the family's private pilot, Russell Thaw, fly it in the Thompson—with the Guggenheim coat of arms prominently displayed on the side. Thaw never liked the plane though, and it was never perfected.

Then there was the Santa Monica, California, widow Edith Boydston Clark: She was fascinated with aviation and air racing, and the Keith Rider team convinced her that an advanced speed plane could be a prudent investment, that potential prize winnings would cover the original cost with generous interest. She put up the money for the Rider R-3 of 1934, originally designed for the MacRobertson race to Australia, and for the Pearson-Williams pylon racer of 1938—the latter to the tune of some $16,000. Neither plane turned out to be a lucrative investment, though the R-3 placed well in several Thompsons. The Pearson-Williams failed to qualify in its only Thompson try. Mrs. Clark was rather thoroughly cured of that particular strain of investment fever.

A number of planes were financed by small groups of businessmen, interested in air racing, who were willing to pool a few hundred apiece just for the kicks of rooting for their own plane on the pylons. Keith Rider's R-1 and R-2 models of 1931 were financed by a group of San Francisco businessmen, headed by Robert Clampett. He was also a pilot and flew the planes in a few minor races, though professional pilots were brought in on prize-splitting deals for the big races.

Potentially there was a lot of sponsorship money in various businesses, for the purpose of public and press exposure—image enhancement as we'd say today. Nobody was better at promoting this type of support than the fast-talking Roscoe Turner. His primary business as a high-speed charter service for big names in Hollywood and business circles put him in a unique position to make the contacts, and

19

Keith Rider was famed for selling his racing planes to wealthy sportsmen who could afford to dabble. His midget Model R-2 in 1933 was sold to Charles McGrew, right, husband of movie star Jean Harlow, center. George Hague, left, was hired to fly it. Weaver Collection

he took full advantage. In various years, he was at least partially financed by the Gilmore Oil Company, MacMillan Ring-Free Products, Heinz 57 Varieties, Twentieth Century Studios, Pesco fuel pumps and Champion Spark Plugs. Furthermore, the Pratt & Whitney engine people were willing to loan him an engine now and then. The fact that Turner still had to put every spare cent he had into his planes,

The colorful Roscoe Turner was best of all at promoting sponsorship money. The Gilmore Oil Company paid for his first Wedell-Williams racer in 1932. Weaver Collection

and borrow to the hilt, tells you something about the cost of any serious commitment to a racing effort even in the lean depression years.

Jim Wedell may have had the best sponsorship deal of all. Jim was a penniless, self-taught barnstorming pilot and charter flyer who happened to be in the right place at the right time. He became fast friends with wealthy Louisiana lumberman Harry Williams, taught him to fly and sold him on the dream of founding a flying service in the small bayou town of Patterson. Williams went all the way by backing Wedell with a $2 million airport, a fleet of twenty or so planes and elaborate construction facilities. Jim was given a free hand to hire a crew, design and build racing and sport planes for all takers, with backing to fly his own planes in the nation's great air races—all with no worries about money. Several *Wedell-Williams* planes wrote a significant part of the Thompson history in the 1930s.

Racing without sponsorship

After all the wealthy individuals, aviation people or others, who put money into pylon racing in the thirties, the ordinary low-budget, uneducated, diehard home builder still formed the backbone of the sport in those early years. The guy who learned to fly out of a pasture with an old World War I Curtiss Jenny, maybe honing his skills by barnstorming at county fairs or charter flying anything or anybody and by doing his own building and mechanical work. Men who wanted more than anything to race in the great Thompson and who were willing to invest their last nickel in an attempt. Many were just chasing a rainbow, hoping to win even a few hundred dollars in one of the lower places. To the adventuresome young pilot of the thirties, just the thought of flying in the Thompson was like driving at Indianapolis to the young car racer. The pot of gold was never the compelling force. Winning would have only paid the bills for a new and faster plane for the next year.

There were a lot more Art Chesters than there were Frank Fullers in American air racing in the 1930s.

Making it legal

No big problem, really. The federal Department of Commerce, which had the responsibility of

Jim Wedell's benefactor, wealthy Harry Williams, bankrolled a complete airport and factory facility with $2 million. Weaver Collection

21

Benny Howard made it a goal to design all his racers with sufficient airworthiness to meet US Department of Commerce *NC license standards. They were often used for stunting demonstrations.* Weaver Collection

inspecting and certifying commercial aircraft in the early 1930s, didn't have any hard-and-fast standards

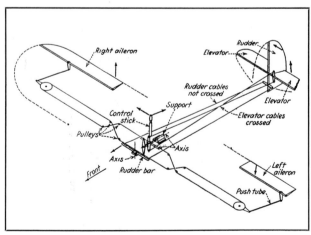

Most early pylon racers used conventional cable and lever control systems. But action needed to be very snug, friction-free and responsive. DOC inspectors checked them carefully.

for custom racing craft that weren't sold to the public and didn't carry paying passengers. A cursory inspection by a DOC field representative was about all that was required to get an R or X license number.

Certification was upgraded somewhat when the CAA took over in the mid-thirties and began using NR and NX numbers. But I know of no new design that was refused certification. By that time, construction techniques had matured naturally, and the later Thompson designs—those built in the last half of the 1930s—were considerably better, stronger planes than some of the early thirties jobs.

The inspectors were also quite critical of control systems, checking that control linkages were strong and friction-free, with no appreciable play in the response between the pilot and the control surface. Most early Thompson racers used the usual cables and levers, though a few used aluminum tubing for push-pull or torsion action where convenient to the particular design.

22

Chapter 3

Pylon racer design in the 1930s

There was a lot of good, solid science as well as art seen in the Thompson Trophy races, both prewar and postwar. It's too easy to wink at some of the speed secrets of those early days; it's important that we consider them from a standpoint of the technology that was known at the time. This is the only logical way to study technical history.

Design factors that make a good pylon racer
Maximum horsepower per sq.ft. of parasite area

Trying to achieve maximum pylon speed, builders came smack up against the question of whether to use a big, high power engine in a big plane or a small, lower power engine in a small

plane. If the two types of planes had a similar figure for hp per sq.ft. of parasite area, they should have had just about equal top speeds.

Consider the concept of parasite area. Very simply, this is the area of an imaginary flat plate that would have the same air drag as the entire plane at zero lift. The figure is calculated from an equation derived by W. B. Oswald in a 1932 NACA paper, using several parameters of the plane's design (engine hp, propeller efficiency, weight, shape factor, wing span, and so on), and is invaluable in comparing various aircraft designs for aerodynamic efficiency. Obviously the less the parasite area, the better the streamlining. And of course, the more horsepower that's available in relation to parasite area, the higher the top speed.

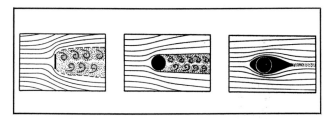

The aerodynamic drag of an object depends largely on the amount of air turbulence left in its wake, much like the wake behind a ship.

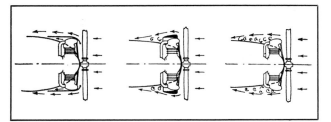

There are three ways of cowling a radial engine: no cowl at all, a simple ring cowl or a full NACA type cowl. The NACA type reduced drag by three-fourths.

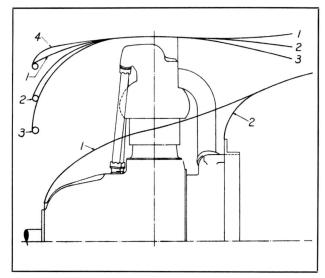

The NACA agency tested many radial engine cowling designs in 1930s, searching for minimum drag with maximum cooling efficiency.

To compare some real parasite area numbers, the smaller 1930s racers with inline Menasco engines had areas ranging from roughly 1.3 to 2.0 sq. ft. The larger prewar racers with big Pratt & Whitney radials ranged usually from 2.7 to 4.0 sq.ft. And the big WW II fighter planes ranged generally from 3.2 to 6.5 sq.ft.

Thus a small Menasco engined plane with, say, 300 hp and 1.5 sq.ft. of parasite area would have 200 hp per sq.ft. of parasite area. A large radial engine plane with 700 hp and 3.5 sq.ft. of parasite area would have the same power per sq.ft.—thus both planes theoretically should have the same top speed.

Designing a pylon racing plane posed several ticklish compromises in this area of parasite drag. For instance, some designers used extremely thin wings with minimum "profile" drag. But in doing so they often compromised the lift and stall characteristics. And the spars had to be so shallow that additional external wiring bracing was necessary. It was a bad tradeoff because profile drag is only a very small fraction of the total drag; they gave up a lot to gain practically nothing. A little wind tunnel work here would have set them straight.

Low drag landing gear

Then there was the question of retractible landing gear. The potential reduction in total parasite drag was certainly very attractive—an average of around twenty percent on those small prewar racers—but there was the additional weight to consider. Not to mention the space required in the tiny fuselages or thin wing panels. And most of those prewar retractable gears required the pilot to crank up the gear mechanism immediately after takeoff. In the heat of a racehorse start, that could be a hazardous exercise. Pilots needed to focus all their attention on just staying away from trouble.

So it's probably no wonder that the majority of prewar Thompson specials had well—cowled fixed landing gears.

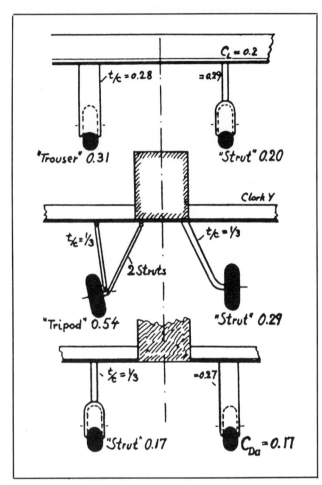

Aerodynamic efficiency of various types of fixed landing gears. The coefficients are based on exposed wheel area (black).

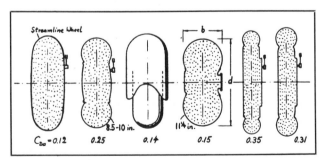

Drag coefficients for various shapes and sizes of landing gear wheels and tires, based on frontal area. (The cowled wheel is for reference only.)

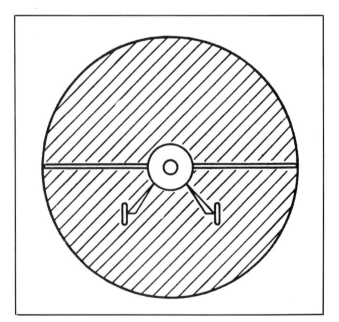

The Prandtl theory of induced drag assumes that the wing deflects a cylindrical column of air with a diameter equal to the wing span. A wider span is more efficient. Beware of wing clipping!

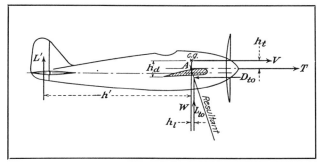

Lines of force acting on an aircraft in normal straight, level flight. Note that the distance between wing and tail surfaces (h') figures prominently in stability. Short tail leverage was the problem with the stubby Gee Bee racers.

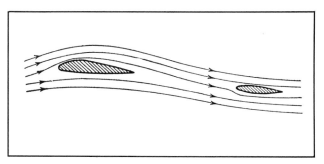

Some early race plane designers discredited the midwing monoplane layout because of the detrimental effect of front wing downwash on tail surface efficiency.

Maximum power-to-weight ratio

Newton's law of gravity states that one pound of force on one pound of mass will accelerate that mass at a rate of one gravity, or 32.16 feet per second per second. Put very simply, a plane with more horsepower in relation to weight has quicker acceleration.

This is important in pylon racing for two reasons. The most obvious is that any plane will slow down considerably when it goes around a pylon, due to the extra wing lift that must be generated to overcome centrifugal force. This increases the induced drag—drag due to lift—which literally drags down the speed of the plane. A high power-to-weight ratio will give quick acceleration back up to the top speed on the next straightaway.

A less obvious advantage of quick acceleration was apparent during the racehorse start. All the Thompson Trophy races, except the first one, were started by lining up the planes side by side on the ground and flagging them all off together. They had to take off, head for a scattering pylon about a mile away, round that pylon, then head back onto the main course. The location of the flag-off line depended on the amount of wind and its direction at start time. A high power-to-weight ratio gave a plane a quicker takeoff.

Minimum induced drag

The total drag on an aircraft in flight is made up of two parts: parasite drag and induced drag. The induced drag is that drag caused by the lift generated by the wings (and a little by the fuselage). At high speeds, induced drag makes up only a very small portion of the total drag, maybe two or three percent. But this increases at lower speeds, so at takeoff it could be ninety percent of the total.

Induced drag was important in a pylon racer because the wings had to generate extra lift to counteract centrifugal force when going around the pylons. The tighter the turn and the higher the plane's speed, the greater the centrifugal force—and the greater the lift that had to be generated. This sud-

den increase in induced drag felt much like putting on the brakes in a car. It was not at all unusual for Thompson planes to drop 30, 40 or 50 mph going around a pylon.

According to Prandtl's momentum theory of wing lift, the moving wing deflects a mass of air downward; the equal and opposite reaction is an upward lift. The theory assumes the column of air deflected has a circular cross section with a diameter equal to the wing span. What this means, in effect, is that other factors equal, induced drag is inversely proportional to the square of the wing span. So our ideal pylon race plane would have the widest possible span.

But we know that this is contrary to other requirements. A wider wing span means more wing surface area, and thus more parasite drag. Also a wide span requires more wing structure and bracing to prevent high speed flutter and possible failure in tight, high-g pylon turns, which means more weight. It seems that just about every design requirement except reduction of induced drag calls for less wing span.

Obviously, compromise was necessary. The Thompson racers usually compromised on the side of less wing span. A favorite air racing speed secret was to clip inches or feet off the ends of the wings. The reduced wing surface area often increased top speed a few miles per hour. But I wonder if many times the Thompson racers didn't clip past the point of diminishing returns; that is, the reduced span increased induced drag, which slowed the planes down in the turns more than the reduced parasite drag raised the peak speed down the straightaways. This is a bench racing question that will never be settled.

Good stability and responsive controls

Any good pylon racer should have good stability and quick response to the pilot's control. From the design standpoint, these factors were pretty cut-and-dried matters of proper center of gravity location on the wing chord, leverage length of the tail surfaces, distribution of mass about the center of gravity, area of control surfaces, slack in the control cables, and so on.

A few early pylon racers had enough book learning to work out crude relationships on paper before the plane was built. Most designed by what looked right. Either way, after the plane was built, that first flight test was always an adventure. Often grassroots builders had to do a lot of tuning of their control setups to get things the way that they wanted. More than once a twenty-pound slug of lead in the tail solved a stability problem that might otherwise have required a complete rebuilding of the plane! Such was budget building in the thirties.

One controversial design theory among pylon racing people in the thirties held that the mid-wing monoplane configuration was not safe. It was proposed that the natural downwash of air from the main wing tended to neutralize the bite of the horizontal tail surfaces, causing the plane to have marginal horizontal stability—especially in tight, high-g pylon turns. The solution was that the main wing should be either low or high, but never in the middle of the plane.

The theory was never proved or disproved either way. There were good and bad planes of all wing configurations. Study them in this book, and then you be the judge.

Variable pitch propellers

In any air race like the Thompson that took off from a standing start on the ground, it helped a lot to have a propeller that could change its pitch, or blade angle, in flight. Then a racer could flatten the blade pitch for quick takeoff and fast acceleration after liftoff, and then switch to a deeper pitch for higher speeds—rather like shifting gears with a car transmission. Such a device could shave many seconds off a plane's total time for the first lap.

But believe it or not, a study of the winning Thompson planes of the 1930s shows no consistent pattern in this use of variable pitch propellers. The first winner in 1930 had a propeller whose blades could be adjusted when standing still on the ground, but couldn't be changed in flight. The 1931 Gee Bee had a primitive fixed-pitch forged aluminum prop. Then Doolittle's 1932 Gee Bee had a Smith prop that could have the pitch varied from the cockpit.

The best handling racing planes had very conventional relationships between wing and tail areas, tail leverage and so on.
T. Chester

26

But the 1933 and 1934 winning Wedells had fixed pitch. Howard's Mulligan cabin plane that won in 1935 had a Smith controllable propeller like Doolittle's. The French Caudron that won in '36 had the famous Ratier switch pitch propeller that automatically went into high pitch at 140 mph. In 1937 Kling's speedy little Folkerts had a classic fixed pitch wooden prop that would have been in style in the twenties. Only in the last two races in 1938 and '39 did Roscoe Turner have a state-of-the-art hydraulic constant speed propeller.

Obviously it didn't take a variable-pitch propeller to win the Thompson Trophy race.

Designing it right

It may seem amazing to us now, but it didn't require a college degree in aeronautic engineering to sketch out a reasonable layout for a speed plane in the relatively primitive technological climate of the 1930s. Aerodynamics was not a complex science then. The teardrop was acknowledged as the ideal aerodynamic shape, and designing for minimum air drag was no more than freehand drawing of smooth, flowing lines on a layout sketch. The NACA research on radial engine cowlings was widely published and well known by most of the sharper backyard designers. And there were dozens of basic textbooks and handbooks available with recommended ranges for wing loading, span proportion, location of the center of gravity on thte wing chord, length of tail leverage, desired aspect ratios, rudder and elevator area, etc. Any enterprising home builder who was willing to do a litte reading could come up with at least a reasonable plane *layout*. He could not have done the detailed stress analysis calculations necessary to satisfy DOC load factor recommendations—or even for maximum possible strength with minimum weight, but at least he could draw a good basic layout.

When studying the detail design of those early homebuilt pylon racers we have to keep always in mind the ever present compromise between speed

The infamous Gee Bee R racers were designed to simulate the ideal streamline teardrop shape. But their short length made directional and torque stability hazardous. McGrath

and cost—and we must always view this compromise within the context of the technology of the times. Those early racers never had unlimited funds to work with, nor the finest tools and facilities. They had to use engines, propellers, instruments, tires, and other basic parts that they could afford to buy. What they couldn't buy they had to make. And what they had to make had to be crafted from materials, techniques and facilities they could afford, or had available to them. We've listed the five most important design goals for a good pylon racer above. How the early builders pursued these elusive goals with limited funds and facilities is outlined in subsequent chapters.

Of course there was what we would call today a "downside" to this largely unprofessional, speed oriented approach to design. We got a few marginal designs like the Gee Bee's. Those short, stubby planes were all wrong from a standpoint of longitudinal and directional stability and torque control. Any simple aeronautic textbook would have condemned them from the first page. They were literally accidents looking for a place to happen. One wonders, if they had been built in the late thirties, if they would've been certified by more particular CAA inspectors.

It's a wonder there weren't more "Gee Bee's"—what with the relatively unrestricted design climate of racing planes in the 1930s. The great bulk of the layout design of the early Thompson racers was no more than a matter of rule of thumb, and does it look right. It was common practice to check positive load factors by piling sand bags on the wings, to verify some degree of structural integrity in pylon turns. But there probably weren't more than two or three of the homebuilt designs that were ever model-tested in a small-scale wind tunnel. It's really a wonder the racers had the decent safety record they did.

Groping for structural strength

To describe in detail how these grassroots racers built competitive planes would be impossible; the planes were as individual as the pilots. Each racer had his methods, his supposed speed secrets. Every conceivable means of construction and combination of materials was tried, always in pursuit of minimum weight with maximum strength. If there was a clear choice between weight and strength, weight usually got the nod. And money was always a determining factor in carrying out design ideas.

Jimmy Wedell was at the well-funded end of the sophistication spectrum of builders. Wedell had a beautiful sponsorship deal, being fully financed and equipped by wealthy Lousiana lumberman Frank Williams. But perhaps Williams had more confidence in Wedell's genius than was fully warranted.

Wedell had no formal training in any segment of aerodynamic or structural science, nor even in the manual skills like welding. He was a very sharp,

Harry Crosby's racers were some of the very few that enjoyed wind tunnel testing. He was an instructor at the Aero Industries Technical Institute and had access to facilities. Kemp

Some original racer designs were later modified radically to improve flight characteristics. Ralph Bushy added some dorsal fin area to this Rider design to improve directional stability. Sunyak

very capable self-taught flyer and mechanic. Wedell used to joke about laying out fuselages and wings from chalk marks on his hangar floor. Blueprints were drawn after the plane was built, if ever. He lived by what looked right.

And of course, Jim had little knowledge of the relative strength of materials, alloys and heat-treating methods. For instance, he liked to use easy working mild steel tubing for tight forming situations like the tail assembly. But then he liked stronger chrome-moly tubing for the fuselage framework. Attaching them was the bug. Where one normally attached dissimilar alloys by bolting and brackets, Jim would try to gas-weld them. The high heat would alter the heat-treat effect, and he'd end up with a possible weak spot where strength was needed most.

Needless to say, Jim Wedell's planes were not noted for great structural integrity. The first plane that he built for Roscoe Turner in 1932 developed wing flutter and came apart in the air on an early test flight, forcing Jim to take to his parachute. Fortunately private engineering consultant Howard Barlow offered to save the design by a scientific stress analysis—an offer Wedell and Harry Williams gladly accepted. The redesigned racer performed reliably for many years after. It wasn't that Jim Wedell didn't trust engineers; he just did the best he could with what he had to work with.

But it's interesting that Jim didn't incorporate a lot of the Barlow modifications on his own No. 44 racer. This was a great and successful racer for three or four years. Then in the 1934 Thompson, when the plane was being flown by Doug Davis with an oversize 800 hp Wasp engine, the tail assembly reportedly broke off in a tight, high-g pylon turn (when Davis had come around to recircle after cutting), and the whole thing crashed in a heap on the ground. Davis was fatally injured.

Pilot error? Metal fatigue? Too much engine? Poor construction? Who knows for sure?

Not all design and construction shortcomings of the early homebuilt racers had quite as dramatic consequences as did the Wedell planes. Only a few early Thompson racers came apart in the air. More often, the pilots would notice gradual buckling or bending at some point in the structure during inspections and make beef-up repairs on the spot.

At the opposite end of the construction spectrum was Roscoe Turner's No. 29 *Meteor* racer of the 1937–1939 period. This was far from a seat-of-the-pants, homebuilt design. After Howard Barlow had done such a neat fix-up job on Turner's original Wedell of 1932, Turner dreamed of having Barlow design him a pylon racer from a clean sheet of paper. Meanwhile Barlow had made the switch from Washington, D.C. consultant to aeronautical engineering faculty at the University of Minnesota. When Turner finally rounded up the necessary funds to get started on his "ultimate answer to the Thompson problem," he worked on Barlow until he got him interested enough to make the plane's detail design a credit-earning project for one of his undergraduate classes in engineering at the university.

Under Barlow's supervision, and working with just rough sketches from Turner, a dozen or more eager young college students ground out blueprints for a gorgeous midwing monoplane, with fixed landing gear, stressed for a new Pratt & Whitney Twin Wasp of 1,000–1,200 hp, with a hoped-for top speed of 380 mph. In a matter of weeks, the kids delivered a package that included complete stress analysis calculations, wiring diagrams, hydraulic routing, control details and so on. Turner won the 1938 and 1939 Thompson races with the plane and set several national speed records. And the design work didn't cost Roscoe a dime.

Somewhere in between these two extremes was a racer like Benny Howard. Benny was not a college-educated engineer, but he had somehow soaked up enough textbook learning over the years to perform some basic stress calculations to submit an airplane design for a DOC NC license. It should also be emphasized that Benny Howard secured the services of Gordon Israel for all four of his race planes from 1930 on. Israel was also a knowledge-able designer with some technical school training, as well as being a skilled welder and fabricator. The two men designed and built the planes together, with added help from Eddie Fisher, an excellent metalworker and mechanic.

So even though there wasn't a college degree among the men who made Benny Howard's racers, they designed and built them to meet commercial stress requirements. They were beautifully executed, structurally sound, yet not excessively heavy. Admittedly, none could ever be licensed with the NC designation because the builders bypassed certain regulations to save weight and drag or to increase engine power to win races. But the fact that some were used for violent stunt flying at air shows is good evidence that they had plenty of structural strength.

One more example of "educated" race plane design was the Gee Bee program, under the Granville brothers in Springfield, Massachusetts. These

Gordon Israel, right, was one of few early pylon racers with technical training. Craftsman Eddie Fisher, left, usually worked with him. Benny Howard used the team to build most of his race planes. Weaver Collection

boys were essentially enthusiasts who wanted to build sporty, fun planes for the public and to eventually get military contracts, while following the pylon sport for kicks, publicity and what prize money they could get. But the head of the clan, Zantford Granville, felt strongly about also having their all-out racing planes designed with commercial structural strength. They needed a college-trained engineer to design and stress-analyze structures to meet DOC standards. In the late twenties, they hired young Robert Hall, who helped with the Model Z Gee Bee that won the 1931 Thompson. When Hall left to design his own planes, the Granvilles immediately hired Howell Miller, a recent graduate of the prestigious Guggenheim School of Aeronautics at New York University (NYU). Miller laid out the Gee Bee R-1 model that won the 1932 Thompson. His contacts at NYU made it possible to model-test the later Gee Bees in the university's wind tunnel.

It's ironic that these stubby Gee Bee designs that proved to be such man-killers had more "educated" design in them than many more conventional ships. But much controversy exists about whether Hall and Miller fully went along with the unorthodox layout of the planes. The Granvilles mostly wanted their expertise to design structures.

Just about every degree of educated and uneducated design went into the early Thompson racers.

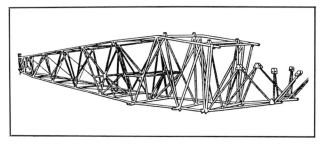

Most fuselages in the 1930s used basic framework of welded chrome-moly steel tubing.

Constructing on a shoestring

The early Thompson builders tried just about every known aircraft construction technique in their attempts to get maximum strength with minimum weight, at reasonable cost. Keith Rider built two planes in 1931 with all-aluminum fuselages. The construction didn't prove to save as much weight as expected. And since flush riveting was not yet known, the hundreds of projecting rivet heads increased skin friction air drag significantly. Even though Rider used retracting landing gears on these planes, their performance was no better than that of many racers with fixed landing gears. They were a general disappointment.

Most early Thompson racers didn't deviate significantly from common construction practices of

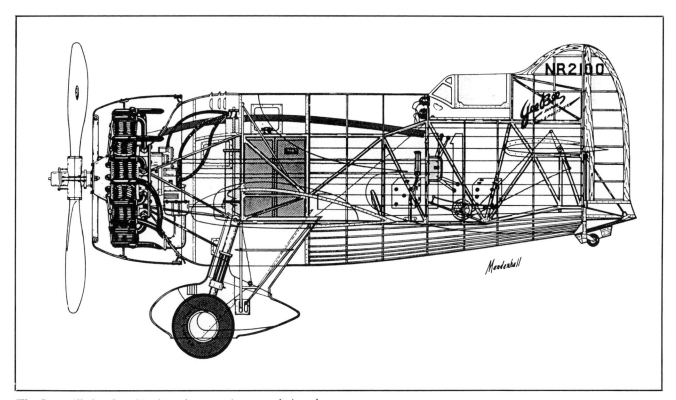

The Granville brothers hired graduate engineers to design the structures of their Gee Bee racers, to assure adequate strength in high-g maneuvers. Mendenhall

Clayton Folkerts achieved unusually light weight by using less steel tubing and more wood stringers in his fuselage construction. Sunyak

their day. The fuselage framework was welded chrome-moly steel tubing, with plywood formers and wood stringers. Wing structure was usually all wood, with spruce spars, either boxed or solid, and plywood ribs. Fuselage and wing covering were usually doped fabric, but with sheet aluminum for the front half and engine cowling. Quite often the wing leading edge was plywood, to eliminate the gradual

Some race plane builders sought better strength-to-weight ratio with all-wood construction and plywood covering, including

Keith Rider with his Model R-6 of 1938–1939. Weaver Collection loss of lift due to warpage of a fabric covering. This general construction seemed to be a good compromise between cost, ease of construction and light weight.

Plywood became a more attractive material in the mid-thirties, with the appearance of a quality Spruce plywood known as Haskelite. This had an excellent strength-to-weight ratio, and it gave an opportunity to build a fuselage and/or wing structure where the outer skin carried some of the loading (known as monocoque construction). A few late prewar Thompson racers had all plywood covering.

But there was no general trend to all-metal construction in the prewar period. Even after flush riveting techniques were perfected in the mid-thirties, all-metal construction was considered heavier than a combination of wood, fabric and metal. Even Roscoe Turner's state-of-the-art *Meteor* of 1936 used a lot of wood and fabric in the construction. As always, it was a matter of results versus cost.

A special structural problem: landing gear

You wouldn't normally think of the landing gear as a structural problem. But in the case of the early Thompson racers, there were several complicating factors. For one thing, high wing loadings

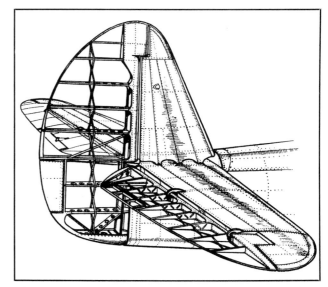

All-metal construction of the late 1930s most often used fabricated aluminum framework with sheet aluminum covering riveted on. Flush riveting was introduced in 1935.

meant high landing speeds of 60, 70 and 80 mph. These high landing speeds inherently meant higher shock loads on the landing gear assembly, other factors equal.

Rough grass fields and high landing speeds made landing gears a serious problem on tiny pylon racers. A Rider racer of the late thirties had a crank-up retracting gear. Kemp

Then you have to remember that most airfields in the 1930s had rough grass runways. Paved runways were the exception—and smooth paved runways a rarity. Even at the excellent Cleveland airport, most of the famous racehorse starts were on dirt or grass. And if there had been any amount of rain before the race, that surface could be soft and slippery.

These problems wouldn't have been so critical for larger aircraft with large diameter tires. But these little racing planes had the smallest wheels and tires possible, to keep down air drag. This restricted their ability to roll over bumps and obstructions. And if the wheel was streamlined with some form of cowling or pant, there was the problem of mud clogging up inside the pant. When you combine all these special circumstances with the ever-present need to design for minimum weight, it's no wonder there were lots of noseovers and collapsed gears on landings and takeoffs with the early Thompson racers.

Retractable landing gear presented the designers with even greater challenges. We've mentioned earlier the demands on weight, space and pilot attention to get the reduced air drag of this feature. But a retractible gear was also more of a structural problem than a fixed gear. The necessity for low-friction swiveling joints, locking devices and some form of hand cranking mechanism were added complications. Pilots would tell you the designers always compromised on pilot cranking leverage to save weight. They dreaded cranking up those gears in the heat of a racehorse start. It's fortunate, though, that a few persistent designers stuck with the problem, and managed to come up with reasonably light, reliable, compact retracting mechanisms.

Two schools of pylon racer design

Any student of American air racing history will notice right away that there were two very distinct design schools in the grassroots days of the 1930s. One school advocated the concept of a large air cooled radial engine in a relatively large, heavy plane—though of course no larger or no heavier than absolutely necessary to handle the power. The other school was based on much smaller, lighter inverted inline engines—with the size and weight of the airframe scaled down proportionally.

The big engine school accepted that a big radial engine plane would be heavier and have more aerodynamic drag, and it might be less

Folkerts used narrow-track retracting landing gears that cranked up into belly of the fuselage. They were very light, but hazardous at high landing speeds. Kemp

34

The Hughes H-1 speed record plane of 1935. Wigton

maneuverable in the turns. But they felt superior acceleration and straightaway speed should more than offset any lack of maneuverability in the turns. The small engine proponents grudgingly admitted it was pretty hard to beat brute horsepower; but there was a definite core of designers who were apparently willing to bet a life's savings that a smaller, lighter, more maneuverable plane could be made to match the pounds-per-hp and hp-per-sq. ft. factors of the large planes—and still have the advantage of maneuverability.

It's interesting to compare these performance factors for several of the faster Thompson prewar entries in both categories. Any analysis from this standpoint, however, is complicated by the odd fact that the fastest and most advanced pure racing

The Laird-Turner Meteor *of 1938.* Sunyak

The Marcoux-Bromberg Rider R-3 of 1938. Sunyak

plane built in America in the 1930s never raced in a Bendix or Thompson. This, of course, was Howard Hughes' Model H-1 monoplane with the 800 hp Pratt & Whitney Twin Wasp Junior that he used to set the world landplane 3-km record at 352.39 mph in 1935. Hughes apparently had every intention of entering this plane in the 1936 Bendix and Thompson races at Los Angeles. He even had

The French Caudron C-460 of 1936. Whittington

separate wing designs made for the two events—(a 32 ft. span for the Bendix and stubby 25 ft. wing for the Thompson). But they say he lost his stomach for man-to-man competition at the last minute, and the plane was withdrawn.

But just to keep the record straight, let's include the Hughes racer in this comparison. Let's compare these calculated performance parameters—the maximum horsepower per sq. ft. of parasite area, and the pounds per horsepower—for several of the most potent Thompson racers of the late thirties. These aren't hard to pick. Representing the large radial engine planes could be the Turner *Meteor* and the Marcoux-Bromberg Rider R-3 with the Twin Wasp Junior. The three top inline engine lightweights could be the Schoenfeldt *Firecracker* (Rider R-4) in thirty-eight-thirty-nine configuration with modified Menasco, the Folkerts SK-3 (with full available 400 hp), and the French Caudron C-460.

Here's how the numbers stack up:

Plane	hp	Weight	sq. ft.	hp/ sq.ft.	lbs./ hp
Hughes H-1	1000	4400	2.2	454	4.40
Turner *Meteor*	1200	4900	3.5	343	4.08
Rider R-3	1000	3200	3.6	278	3.20
Firecracker	500	1550	1.4	358	3.10
Folkerts SK-3	400	1380	1.3	308	3.45
Caudron C-460	400	1650	1.3	308	4.12

It would seem clear from these numbers that there was no conclusive theoretical advantage for either general type of Thompson racer—the big radial engine plane or the small inline engine plane. Either one could potentially be made into a winner. The real key to this controversy probably lies in the relative engine stresses required to maintain the quoted power levels. As we'll learn later, the big air cooled radials could maintain their required power levels with lower rpm's and manifold pressures than the small inlines. In a 200 or 300 mile race this was critical.

So the smart money was usually on the big radials.

A maverick in their midst

We can't fairly close this analysis without mentioning Steve Wittman's unique attempt to beat the system with a Curtiss D-12 liquid cooled engine in a plane that was just as light, clean and compact as could be built around that engine. It was an out-and-

The Schoenfeldt Firecracker *Rider R-4 of 1938.* Kemp

out attempt to get radial engine speed at a cost of even less than a small Menasco powered racer.

From that standpoint it was an unquestioned success. With just an old 435 hp used D-12 that cost less than $100, Steve got 475 hp with reasonable one hour reliability. Top speed of the plane with the unusual leaf spring open landing gear was an impressive 325 mph. That speed might have won him the Thompson in 1937, though Wittman had to drop out of the lead due to an oil leak. And by 1938 the plane was no longer fast enough. Also Wittman had continual cooling problems with the combination—getting enough radiator to cool the engine without causing excessive parasite drag. It is not known if he could have maintained a flying speed over 300 mph for more than a few minutes. But is was certainly a very clever, well-thought-out combination. And *Bonzo* did win considerable prize money for Steve in the four years he raced it.

He was the very epitome of grassroots racing in the 1930s.

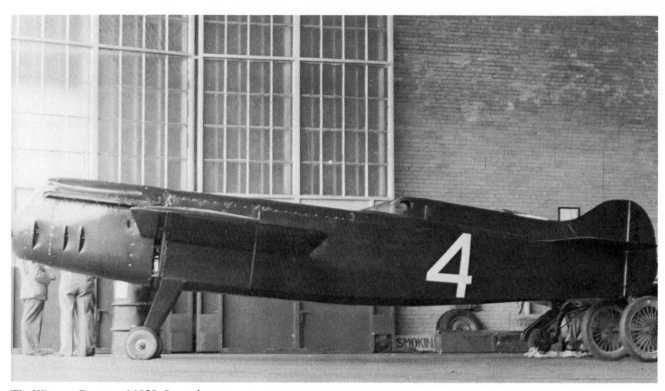

The Wittman Bonzo *of 1938.* Sunyak

Chapter 4

Pulling to win

To win races took brute horsepower and an efficient propeller, getting the maximum possible forward thrust to pull the plane through the air and around the pylons. There was as much science in this quest for horsepower as in any other area of race plane design—not just generating the power in the first place, but knowing how much of it to use at a given time in a given race. Pulling more power from an engine meant more fuel and oil consumption, more heat to get rid of—and it put the racer that much closer to the ragged edge of engine failure. Very few races have ever been won by just jamming the throttle to the stop and going for broke from the starting flag. More than one successful racing plane never flew one full lap at wide open throttle in its entire racing life, believe it or not.

In the case of the propeller, just a few percentage points lost in efficiency could be the difference

Commercial aircraft engines adapted for 1930s air racing led a hard life. No specially made engines were available. A well-used

Pratt & Whitney Wasp powers this Rider R-3. Weaver Collection

between winning and losing. At 250 mph, for instance, a 400 hp engine would deliver 492 lb. of forward thrust with eighty-two percent propeller efficiency—but only 468 lb. with seventy-eight percent. The theoretical loss in speed would be 6 mph. The propeller was just as important as the engine.

Factors that determine horsepower

Three general factors determine the horsepower delivered by a piston engine: the piston displacement of the cylinders, or the volume swept by the pistons from top to bottom stroke; the speed, or revolutions per minute, the engine is turning; and the average combustion gas pressure on the pistons during the power strokes. This latter is known as the brake mean effective pressure, or BMEP. It's determined by the breathing efficiency of the engine, the compression ratio, the amount of supercharge, and so on.

All three factors are related by a simple formula:

$$hp = ci \times rpm \times BMEP / 792,000$$

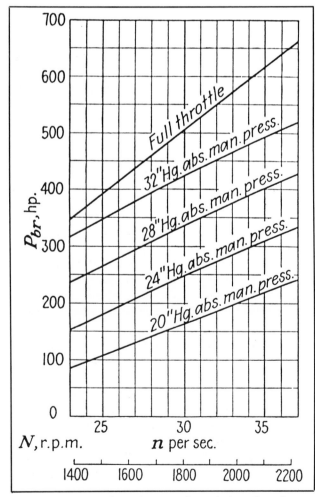

The horsepower output of a supercharged aircraft engine was roughly proportional to rpm and manifold pressure.

Thus, for example, a Pratt & Whitney Wasp with 1,344 ci displacement, turning 2400 rpm, with a BMEP of 156 psi would deliver 635 hp.

The important thing to learn from this relationship is that if a racer wanted maximum possible hosepower for his plane, he needed the biggest possible engine in terms of cubic inches. He needed to turn up as many rpm as he dared, and he needed to raise cylinder pressures with a high compression ratio, a high supercharge pressure—or any way he could.

Commercial engine power rating

Starting in 1928, the US Department of Commerce required that commercial aircraft engines, ones sold to the public or used for public transportation, had to pass certain rigid durability tests on a laboratory dynamometer to give some proof of their safety and reliability in normal flight use. When these tests were passed, the engine received its Approved Type Certificate or ATC number and could be sold to aircraft manufacturers for civilian use. The tests were quite strict. For instance, the engine had to run at takeoff power—which the manufacturer usually limited to five minutes—for ten hours to receive its ATC rating.

The particular engine could not legally be operated above these rated power levels in civilian commercial applications. But with the racer, the limit was how much punishment he was willing to inflict on his engine.

The RPM factor

Raising the crankshaft speed of an engine was especially effective in getting more power because most commercial engines were ATC rated far below the peak of their power curve, almost in the middle of the curve. This meant a ten percent increase in rpm would bring just about a ten percent increase in horsepower. If the engine developed 650 hp at 2400 rpm, power might increase to about 700 hp at 2600 rpm.

The only bug was the inertia forces inside the crankcase due to the whirling crankshaft and pistons and rods whacking up and down, these forces increased as the square of rpm. Increasing crankshaft speed from 2200 rpm to 2600 rpm would increase these internal forces by some forty percent. If bearings, rods and other parts were already loaded to near capacity, raising rpm just a little was asking for big trouble.

Large radial engines were much less tolerant of rpm increases than inline engines. This was because all the rods in a radial engine pivoted on the one main master rod assembly. This put all the main bearing loading on the single crankshaft throw (or two throws in a twin row radial)—and the bearings

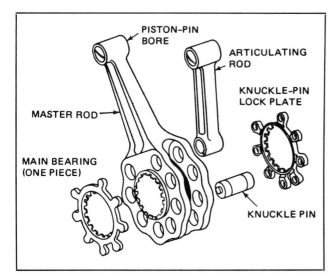

PISTON-PIN BORE

ARTICULATING ROD

KNUCKLE-PIN LOCK PLATE

MASTER ROD

MAIN BEARING (ONE PIECE)

KNUCKLE PIN

Radial engines could not be overspeeded much because of stresses on the master connecting rod assembly. There are only the two main bearings and the small link bearings to carry all the loads.

on each side of that main throw. (See drawings.) This added up to some horrific unit bearing loads.

Result: While the usable speed of a small inline Menasco engine might increase by 800 to 1000 rpm, an additional 500 rpm might throw apart a big radial.

The manifold pressure factor

Most engines in the Thompson races from the very beginning were supercharged. This means, very simply, that the fuel-air mixture, or charge, from the carburetor was forced into the cylinders under pressure by some form of rotary compressor, rather than being drawn in by suction as on a conventional engine. The cylinders were supercharged, or charged above atmospheric pressure.

The main purpose of supercharging was to maintain sea-level power in the thin air at high altitudes by compressing the air to normal sea-level density. But at ground level, this effect was to multiply power by pumping a positive boost pressure in the manifold.

The supercharger itself was a small gear-driven rotary pump on the back of the crankcase, usually a flat impeller disc with radial vanes, turning at high speed in a spiral-like housing. The fuel-air mixture was scooped in at the center of the impeller and whirled off the tips of the vanes at velocities usually between 700 and 1,100 fps. The momentum of the mass of fuel and air at this high velocity was converted to pressure as it slowed down in the outlet scroll. Some superchargers used diffuser vanes around the outlet scroll to smooth the flow off the tips of the vanes, and thus increased compression efficiency.

In US aircraft work, unlike in auto racing, supercharge pressure in the intake manifold of an

A centrifugal supercharger compressed by accelerating air mass to high velocity with the impeller (A), then converting velocity energy into pressure (B) with diffuser vanes (C).

engine is expressed in terms of inches of mercury absolute (in. Hg., which is often shortened to in.) rather than lb per sq. in. above atmospheric (which is the boost pressure referred to with British engines). To understand this, remember that standard atmospheric pressure at sea level supports a 29.92 in. column of mercury. Thus an engine with no supercharge at all, at sea level, would have a pressure in its manifold of around 29.9 in. Hg., with the throttle open (though there is some suction loss through the carburetor). With about fifty percent supercharge, this pressure would be multiplied by roughly 1.5 and increase to 45 in. Hg. A supercharger that doubled the pressure would bring it up to around 60 in. manifold pressure.

Most commercial aircraft engines of the 1930s had takeoff manifold pressures in the range of 34 to 46 in. Hg. But these pressures went as high as 75 in. on some World War II combat engines and over 100 in. under racing conditions.

Increasing manifold pressure had a profound effect on the horsepower output of an engine. Tests have showed that, within reasonable limits, engine power was just about directly proportional to manifold pressure. Raise manifold pressure ten percent and horsepower increases ten percent, much like the effect of raising crankshaft rpm. For example, if an engine developed 600 hp with 40 in. manifold pressure, with 44 in. it should develop 660 hp. Simple as that.

Supercharged aircraft engines differ from supercharged automotive, marine or industrial engines:

the aircraft engine is invariably rated at sea level at some manifold pressure that is less than the maximum with wide-open throttle. This is so the engine can maintain this sea-level rating up to some higher altitude, by merely opening the throttle wider and wider as the plane climbs. The highest altitude where the rated power can be delivered is known as the critical altitude. At this point, the throttle is wide open and the supercharger is pumping its full capacity.

As an example, let's say an engine has a rating of 600 hp at 2300 rpm at 40 in. manifold pressure, up to a critical altitude of 8,000 ft. If the pilot were to open the throttle wide at sea level, the manifold pressure would go way over 40 in. In round numbers, it should go to 52 in., and the horsepower at 2300 rpm should go up to about 780 (allowing for the difference in air density between sea level and 8,000 ft).

Imagine some of the problems involved in using higher manifold pressures at low levels for racing. The extra supercharging increases cylinder pressures and temperatures radically. This invites a phenomenon known as detonation: a sudden explosion of the fuel-air mixture ahead of the normal flame front. (We've all heard the distinctive rattling, or knocking, sound in an automotive engine.) If severe enough, detonation can work all kinds of destruction inside the engine within just seconds:

burned valves, broken piston rings, cracked head castings, burned bearings.

The fuel factor

To solve the detonation problem, racers need fuel that burns evenly under these high pressures and temperatures. And I am not referring to well-known anti-knock racing fuels like benzol and alcohol. Benzol had been successfully used in the Pulitzer races in the 1920s. But just the problem of transporting several barrels of a special chemical compound would have stopped most of the low-budget racers in the thirties. No, the only viable answer for the early Thompson racer was to use what gasoline he could readily buy at the airport hosting the race, and then maybe dope it up with some additives.

Aviation fuel in the 1920s was more like kerosene than gasoline. It knocked and rattled even at very low compression pressures. But several vital discoveries in those years gave a glimmer of hope for much improved fuels in the early thirties. One discovery was the octane scale for rating the detonation resistance of various fuels, by comparing the test fuel with a mixture of isooctane, which had very high knock resistance, and heptane, which had very low resistance. If the test fuel matched the performance of a 76–24 mixture of octane and heptane, it was rated 76 octane.

Standardized leaded aviation gas of uniform 87 octane became available from all major oil companies in 1931. Extra lead was *frequently added by racers to allow higher manifold pressure.* Shell

The first experimental batch of 100 octane gasoline in racing was supplied by Shell for Mae Haizlip's women's speed record of

255 mph in 1934, set with Wedell-Williams No. 92. Weaver Collection

Also, workers in General Motors laboratories discovered that small additions of tetraethyl lead to most gasolines slowed down the rate of combustion and helped to prevent the explosion that caused detonation. This breakthrough was destined to revolutionize aviation in a few years.

In 1930, the American Society for Testing Materials (ASTM) got together with the oil companies to standardize specifications on several grades of commercial aviation gas, based on refining techniques that were in place at that time. Three standard grades showed up at airports in 1931: 73 octane, which was an inexpensive straight run gas with no lead added; 80 octane, which contained 2 cc of lead per gallon; and 87 octane, a premium fuel with 3 cc of lead.

The favorite trick for zipping up a basic gasoline fuel for racing in the early thirties was to dope it with extra lead. The Ethyl Corporation, producers of the lead fluid, always sent one of their technicians to the Nationals—usually old "Doc" Kincade—and he was a familiar figure around the flight line, with his little bottles of the magic fluid, ready to add a few cc to your gas if a pilot was having detonation problems. But Doc knew not to use a total of more than 6 or 7 cc per gallon—or the pilot could be down with fouled plugs. Now and then, Doc guessed wrong on an engine with especially cool running plugs. With lead, the racers always had to walk a tight line between octane boost and plug fouling.

Jimmy Doolittle's decision to retire from the Army and go to work for Shell Oil in 1930 was a lucky day for Shell. He was a major driving force behind the development of true 100 octane aviation gas by Shell in the next few years. That early stuff was a 50–50 blend of straight-run gasoline and isooctane, with 3 cc of lead per gallon. The early experimental batches cost $4.50 a gallon to make. Most was delivered to military technicians at Wright Field. Their early testing showed that 100 octane gas would allow 20–25 percent higher manifold pressures in a given engine than commercial 87 octane, other factors equal. Some engine designers wouldn't believe the results until they tested the stuff on their own dynos.

Shell brought small quantities of the laboratory curiosity to Cleveland in 1934. It's said that the first civilian use of 100 octane gas was in the Wasp Junior engine in the Wedell No. 92 racer used by Mae Haizlip to set the US speed record for women that year at 255 mph.

That incident didn't turn the racing fuel picture around overnight, though. Higher octane fuels available in commercial quantities at practical prices had to wait for revolutionary new refining techniques. In 1936, the ASTM standardized a fourth grade of commercial aviation gas, at 95 octane, which gave at least 10 percent more power than 87 octane by allowing higher manifold pressures. Then finally in 1938, true 100 octane gas was made

Genuine 100 octane aviation gas was first commercially available at Cleveland in 1938. Art Chester's Goon *was fueled in 1939. Shayock*

available to all comers at Cleveland. This was good for another 10–15 percent increase in power over 95 octane, again by using higher manifold boost. Available to the racers was a dreamed-of power that they hardly knew how to handle. Some, in fact, never did take advantage of what was available.

There was a small amount of interest in exotic racing fuels such as alcohol, benzol, toluene and so on in the late 1930s. But these special fuels had little bearing on the overall flow of Thompson history. They didn't make bombs out of the engines they were used in, and so attracted little attention. For all practical purposes, American pylon racing in the

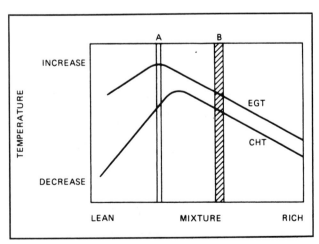

Maximum cylinder head temperatures (CHT) came with fuel-air mixtures on the lean side of ideal combustion (shaded area). "Leaning out" to save gas could burn pistons in a hurry.

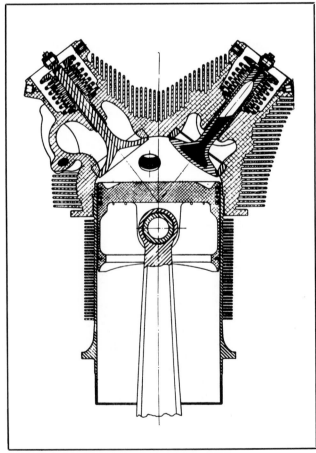

Thompson Products, sponsors of the races, invented a sodium cooled exhaust valve for air cooled engines. Liquid sodium sloshed up and down in hollow valve stem, transferring heat to the head fins.

1930s grew up on the commercial aviation gasolines the racers could buy at the pump.

The cooling factor

Any time racers pull more horsepower from an engine they burned more fuel, which meant that more heat was generated. Since most piston engines were only 20–25 percent efficient, the great bulk of this extra heat energy was going into the cooling fins and lubricating oil in the crankcase. This is why efficient cooling was doubly important for a racing engine.

Radial engines were never any big problem to cool, as long as they were properly baffled and the fuel had sufficient octane to prevent detonation and preignition. But those inline Menascos were something else. There were a dozen ways that a builder could screw up. The factory always quoted the potential buyer a ballpark figure for minimum recommended square inches of frontal inlet and rear outlet opening. And it usually supplied a set of sheet metal baffles to direct air around the cylinders. But this science assumed rated power conditions and plenty of room for air to circulate around the engine. When the pilot started running higher revs and manifold pressures, with the engine squeezed into a tiny compartment, the trouble started.

Many Menasco engine installations had marginal cooling, and pilots could never use high power for more than a few seconds at a time without hitting excessive head or oil temperatures. And yet the Menasco teams seemed very reluctant to sacrifice weight and drag to fit a special oil cooler. Usually the best they did was to expose one side of the oil tank to

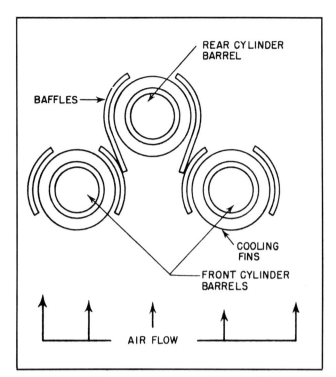

Twin row radial engines required careful air baffling to properly cool the rear row of cylinders.

the outside air stream. One wonders what records a well cooled Menasco might have set in 1930s pylon racing!

The science of hopping up engines

In the automotive world, the practice of hopping up stock production engines for more power and performance has grown into a national sport and a multimillion-dollar industry. Even back in the 1930s, car lovers often tinkered with aftermarket

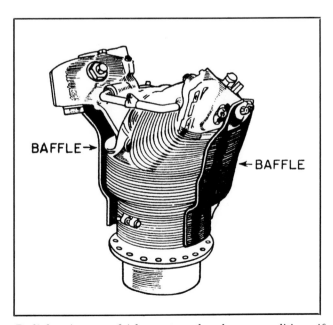

Radial engines were fairly easy to cool under race conditions, if the right baffles maintained the air flow around the fins.

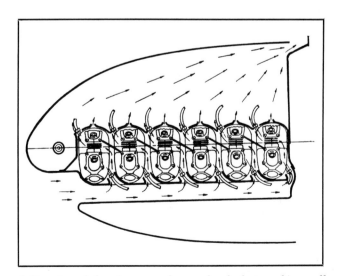

Inline air cooled engines were always a headache to cool in small race planes. They needed a lot of baffling, positioned exactly right, with proper inlet and outlet ducts.

high compression cylinder heads, hot camshafts, bolt-on superchargers and so on.

There were no such challenging possibilities with commercial aircraft engines. Due to federal ATC laws, it was not legal to tamper with factory specifications on engines for normal flying. And racers who might want to modify their engines for more power had no ready source of special parts and equipment to help the job along, unlike the car fans. As a result, there was probably much less hopping up of those old Thompson race engines than you may have assumed. Very few modifications— like going down inside the engine with reground camshafts, special high compression pistons, larger valves and special supercharger gears to give more boost—were made.

To qualify this last statement, there were a number of instances in the 1930s when Pratt & Whitney engineers modified a factory test engine with high-compression pistons and higher ratio blower gears, and then loaned or leased that engine to a promising Thompson racer under the guise of high stress testing. Everybody benefited this way. The racer got extra power, and the Pratt & Whitney people learned lessons about high-stress engine durability. Very often, that higher compression ratio and higher supercharger ratio turned up on a later Pratt & Whitney production model.

The situation differed with the smaller inline Menasco engines. For one thing, their manufacturer, Al Menasco, was dead set against any outside amateurs modifying the engines that he had so carefully engineered to give the very best compromise between performance, weight and reliability. If there was any hopping up for racing, he wanted to do it himself in his own shops and then have that engine operated according to his instructions. He did this on several occasions, as we'll see.

It was common practice with Menasco powered race planes to wrap the oil tank around top of the crankcase, to expose it to the cool outer surface of the engine cowl, as was done on this Folkerts SK-2. Weaver Collection

Art Chester was one of the few with the confidence and know-how to hop up a Menasco engine. For his 1938 Goon, he reversed *rotation by switching inlet and exhaust sides of a C6S-4 model. Chester also made many internal modifications. Sunyak*

On the other hand, since these inline Menasco engines were similar to automotive engines in general layout, popular hot rod technology could be directly applied. The problem was the lack of special parts. You could count on one hand the specialty shops in the country with the know-how, tools and equipment to make special parts from scratch. Outstanding in the mid-thirties were the shops of Fred Offenhauser and Ed Winfield, both in Los Angeles, and Floyd "Pop" Dreyer in Indianapolis. These guys could take a blueprint, or even just a sketch, and make just about any kind of special engine part. Further, they had the machinery to regrind the lobes on a camshaft to change the valve lift and timing to your specifications—or to grind a custom camshaft.

Records indicate that the only people to do extensive private modifications on Menasco engines in the 1930s were Art Chester and the team of Bill Schoenfeldt and Tony LeVier. Modification of the original commercial versions of the various engines used in prewar Thompson Trophy races was not an important factor in race results. More important was the use of instruments to get maximum safe performance from standard commercial engines.

The power of instruments

Every sharp Thompson racer had a few basic instruments on his panel to monitor engine operating conditions, to try to determine when he was on that ragged edge so that he could cut back before he blew his engine. Money spent on quality engine instruments saved many an expensive overhaul—not to mention assuring a finishing place in the list of prize money. Five instruments were definitely needed.

Tachometer

This instrument indicated the crankshaft rpm of the engine. In racers with fixed pitch or adjustable pitch props, the rpm peaked out at some fixed value with a wide open throttle (or at maximum safe manifold pressure) in level flight. But since the racers rarely ever flew at top speed, the tachometer was important as a speed gauge. With a fixed pitch prop, the rpm dropped off in roughly the same proportion as did airspeed. Lots of racers who turned, say, 2600 rpm at top speed did most of their racing at 2300–2400 rpm.

Manifold pressure gauge

This gauge read absolute manifold pressure in inches of mercury, with scales usually ranging from 12 to 60 in. In the broadest sense, a manifold pressure gauge indicated the load on the engine or the relative pressures and temperatures in the cylinders. This pressure was adjusted by opening and closing the throttle.

Manifold pressure readings varied all over the place. From maybe only 15 in. with the engine idling

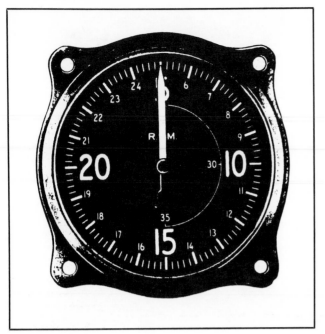

Tachometer gauge.

Oil pressure gauge.

with closed throttle to 50 or 60 in. at full super-charge. With a fixed pitch prop, manifold pressure dropped off very quickly with rpm. Where you might show 45 in. with full throttle at 2600 rpm, throttle back to 2300 rpm, the manifold might drop way back to 30 in.

This hints at how some racers with variable pitch propellers tried to save their engines in a race, since horsepower was directly proportional to both rpm and manifold pressure. They adjusted the prop

pitch to hold engine rpm down, but used a bit higher manifold pressure to maintain the power. An engine turning 2600 rpm with 34 in. manifold pressure developed about the same power as when turning 2400 rpm with 38 in. But at the lower rpm, the fuel consumption was less, and there should have been less wear and tear on the cylinders and bearings. Maximum safe manifold pressure was determined by monitoring critical engine temperatures. Pilots learned all this with years of bitter experience.

Oil pressure gauge

The oil pressure gauge showed the pressure at which the oil was being pumped around through

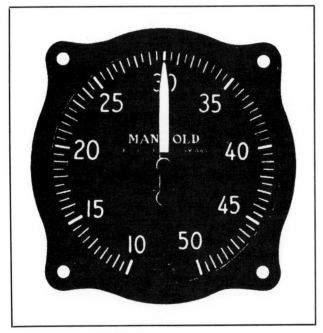

Manifold pressure gauge.

Oil temperature gauge.

48

the various passages inside the engine. Normal oil pressures in aircraft engines usually ranged from 40 to 100 pounds per square inch (psi). Obviously any sudden, radical drop in oil pressure indicated anything from a burned bearing to a depleted oil supply. In any case, the pilot had no choice but to drop out of the race and land as quickly as possible. The tougher choice was when the oil pressure started dropping off gradually; then it was a question of whether to try to nurse the engine through the race or to land.

Oil temperature gauge

Oil loses its viscosity, or it becomes thinner, as it heats up. This, in turn, reduces its film strength, or its ability to resist high rubbing pressures in a bearing without allowing metal-to-metal contact. Also the oxidation rate of oil increases rapidly with temperature, which also reduces lubricating ability and produces a residue of gummy sludge inside the engine.

In the 1930s, before the day of oil additives, oil temperature was a much more critical factor in engine safety. When we can safely run an oil at well over 200 degrees Fahrenheit today, in those days running over 180 degrees was time to throttle back. Oil temp gauges usually indicated up to 200 degrees, and pilots didn't have to worry about reading it above that!

Many Thompson racers required separate oil radiators to keep within these temperature limits, especially if pulling more than rated power from the

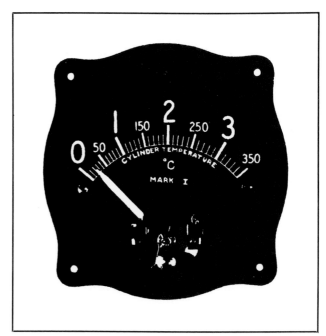

Cylinder head temperature gauge.

engine. This meant extra cost, weight and drag that nobody wanted. Some builders tried to scrimp, with tragic results.

Cylinder head temperature gauge

This was perhaps the most important gauge on the panel. On an air cooled aircraft engine, the temperature thermocouple pickup usually was a ring adjacent to a spark plug gasket, so it got a

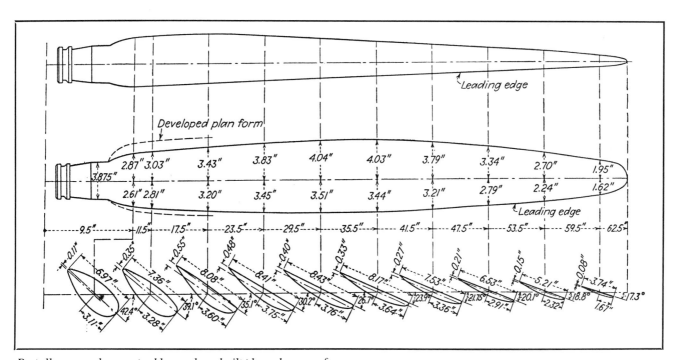

Propellers were always a problem on homebuilt planes because of the high cost of custom-engineered designs. Blade angles and diameter had to be just so for optimum efficiency.

reliable reading deep in the head casting. This reading would instantly indicate the start of detonation, or just as important, an excessively lean fuel mixture. Either one could burn a piston or valve or break a ring in a few seconds.

As for specific temperature limits, most engine manufacturers in the 1930s recommended a maximum of 475–500 degrees at any time, with 525 degrees maximum for five minutes. A reading of 550 degrees was considered maximum for even a few seconds, and 600 degrees was definitely time to shut down.

Getting the right propeller

Propellers were another major cost problem to early low-budget Thompson hopefuls. There were a lot of used props around at salvage prices, but as any student of aircraft design knows, the propeller for a given plane/engine combination must have precisely the right diameter and blade area, with the right blade angle (or pitch) distribution in order to turn the available engine horsepower into useful forward thrust. The quality is referred to as propeller efficiency and is expressed as a percentage. Unfortunately, the chances of finding a used prop that came anywhere near meeting all the parameters for any given plane/engine combination were pretty slim.

There were several possible alternatives:
• One could settle for a laminated wood propeller. Due to the necessary thicker blades for strength, thrust efficiency was about 10 percent less than with an equivalent thin metal prop. But prices were minimum for a custom-made wood prop.
• A custom fixed pitch metal prop could gain back that ten percent in efficiency and increase the top speed of a plane 5 or 10 mph, but at a price two or three times that of a wood prop. One had to decide cost versus speed.
• One could scrounge the aircraft salvage yards for a metal prop somewhere near the calculated diameter and pitch (as determined from an elementary aeronautics handbook). With a lot of luck, one found something that would be more efficient than a wood prop, at a fairly reasonable price.
• A better deal was to look for a used ground adjustable pitch metal prop of approximately the right diameter. The price was significantly more, but by cut-and-try flight testing, the builder could adjust the pitch for optimum race performance.
• Some better financed Thompson efforts in the thirties used various types of commercial props that could have their pitch, or blade angles, changed in flight, either automatically or by a lever control in the cockpit. The famous French Ratier propeller used by the 1936 Caudron, and which Art Chester

played with, was this type. These more sophisticated variable pitch props could cost up to $3,000, but gave optimum performance for any plane and engine combination.

More than one Thompson racer lived its entire life without ever getting within 10 mph of its true potential top speed because of being saddled with a budget compromise propeller. And just as many low-budget Thompson racers had to pay half as much for their propellers as they did for their engines.

The propeller was vitally important in the overall performance of any racing plane. Even if a pilot had a custom prop with just the right diameter, blade contour and pitch for top speed, it would be a great advantage to be able to vary the pitch from the cockpit while in flight. Even a ground adjustable prop could be a part of race strategy and planning.

For example, if the engine had detonation problems and ran better at a little higher rpm, but with a bit lower manifold pressure. No problem. Just reset the prop blades to a slightly lower pitch, to let the engine rev up 200–300 rpm more on the straights. The manifold pressure might drop 5–8 in. at the same airspeed!

Or for example, a pilot was qualifying on a tight five-mile course with very short straightaways and wanted maximum acceleration off the corners. Same deal. He just needed to slip the prop blades 1 or 2 degrees and come off the turns at 2400 rpm instead of 2100 rpm. He might have had to throttle back a tad at the end of the straight to keep from over-revving, but the gain in acceleration might have more than offset the loss of top speed. Documented experiments by Jimmy Doolittle in the 1920s showed that a difference of only 3 degrees in prop blade angle could change engine speed by 300–350 rpm and speed by 5 mph.

Then there was the switch pitch propeller that would automatically switch from a low takeoff pitch to a higher flight pitch sometime after takeoff. This was invaluable in the racehorse start used in the Thompson races, where all the planes were flagged off from a standing start on the ground. Being able to use a lower blade pitch for takeoff could radically shorten the takeoff run as well as the initial acceleration and climb after getaway. A competitor sometimes gained several miles on his fixed pitch opposition this way.

The well-known French Ratier prop used on the Caudron in 1936 and by Art Chester in later years was a switch pitch. A rubber air bladder in the hub was inflated on the ground to around 100 psi air pressure, which held the blades in low pitch against a spring load. A little plate on the nose of the prop was pressed back by air from the forward motion of

The French Caudron of 1936 had its propeller pitch, engine starter and retractable landing gear operated by compressed air.

The internal air storage bottle had to be charged before each flight. Whittington

the plane. At about 140 mph, this ram pressure tripped a valve to deflate the bladder, and the spring acted on a cam to increase the blade pitch about 12 degrees. The effect was to shorten the takeoff run by nearly half, with no sacrifice in top speed.

The Smith controllable pitch prop was used on a number of race planes in the 1930s. This design used a worm gear pinion carried by an adaptor on the engine crankcase, which could be momentarily meshed with a corresponding worm thread on the rotating propeller hub, which in turn twisted the blades through a system of worm gears inside the hub. The control pinion could be engaged by cable and lever or by electric solenoid. An indicator on the instrument panel showed the exact blade angle at all times.

A number of clever variable pitch propellers were available in various price ranges in the 1930s. And the smart Thompson racer would try to use one much as an auto racer uses different transmission gear ratios.

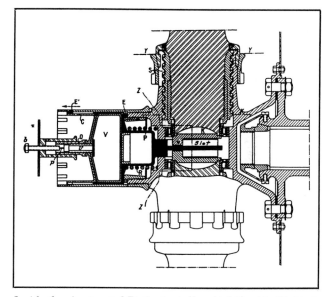

Inside the air operated Ratier propeller: At 140 mph, flight air pressure on the plate (b) deflated air pressure from the rubber bladder (V), allowing the coil spring (R) to move the cam (K) in its slot and increase blade pitch 12 degrees.

Chapter 5

Horsepower for the Thompson

American air racing in the 1930s had to feed primarily on stock commercial aircraft engines that were available both new and used at reasonable prices, and for which repair parts were readily available. Perhaps a dozen established US manufacturers made aircraft engines of various types and sizes in those years. And yet, only two names dominated the entry lists of the high-speed events like the Thompson. They were Pratt & Whitney in East Hartford, Connecticut, for the big radial engines, and little Menasco Manufacturing in Burbank, California, for the inverted inlines.

There were good reasons for this interesting phenomenon. In the case of giant Pratt & Whitney, a modest involvement in the racing sport was considered good institutional public relations and a vehicle for some high stress research and development work. It was a viable and ongoing part of corporate policy. This interest included making custom modifications on certain models for racing and loaning or leasing some engines to selected teams that showed special promise. It also included free technical help for the racers, both at the factory and in the field.

With economic conditions what they were in the thirties and with the high price of large radial engines, about the only way there could have been a substantial Pratt & Whitney presence in racing was via this lend/lease program. Pratt & Whitney reaped a priceless legacy of image and publicity in return for a relatively small expenditure on racing. It was probably the best advertising money the company ever spent.

In the case of Menasco Manufacturing, this company was really the only supplier in the early 1930s of inverted inline engines with reasonably high power—and with ready availability of complete engines and repair parts. (An Indianapolis

company, Chevrolair, was working on this type of engine in the late twenties, but they never really got off the ground.) So we could say this Menasco involvement in racing, sparked by Al Menasco's intense interest in the sport, created the small engine school of design. A specific type of racing plane was designed around Menasco engines.

Scrounging for engines

A few months before the first Thompson Trophy race in 1930, Russell Snowberger won eighth place in the Indianapolis 500 mile auto race with a hopped-up Studebaker passenger car engine that cost him $300. He then went on to finish third in points on the AAA Championship circuit that summer, using less than ten dollars worth of spare parts! His total prize winnings for the season were six or seven times the cost of the whole car.

Solving the engine problem wasn't quite that simple in early Thompson air races. Aircraft engines have always been a different world from automotive engines. For one thing, they're produced in much smaller numbers, with more precise manufacturing techniques and better materials, for ultimate reliability—so a new one cost a lot more. Repair parts cost more for the same reasons. Further, there wasn't a huge pool of junkyard parts as there is with mass-produced automotive stuff. Aircraft engines were often kept in operation for years by periodic overhauls because it was cheaper than buying a new replacement engine.

The early Thompson engine picture was complicated by the fact that there were no rules on the size, or piston displacement, of the engine. Initially, this narrowed the choice to the biggest, most powerful engine one could squeeze into his particular type of plane. Later, it boiled down to a choice of a

52

smaller engine in a very small, light plane—or a big radial or liquid cooled V-12 engine in a bigger, heavier plane. This choice was one of the great controversies in early Thompson design.

Furthermore, the aircraft builders couldn't go out and buy an engine designed specially for racing, as one could for an Indianapolis car. The tooling costs would have been prohibitive in relation to potential sales. They had to make do with available commercial engines, with possible modifications. And even here, the choice of engines that had a fighting chance of winning the Thompson race was quite restricted. Surplus World War I engines like the liquid cooled Hispano-Suiza V-8s and Liberty V-12s were much too big and heavy in relation to power. Curtiss D-12 variants from the early 1920s had some potential—as proved by Steve Wittman—but weight and size were still excessive, as they were with the supercharged Curtiss Conqueror of the late twenties (plus it was a very expensive engine).

This left the early Wright and Pratt & Whitney nine-cylinder air cooled radials, with displacements generally from 975 to 1830 ci, as the best bets for larger planes. These would include the Wright Whirlwind and Cyclone designs and the Pratt & Whitney Wasp, Wasp Junior and Hornet. Their practical horsepower range was roughly between 400 and 900 hp with 1930 technology and fuels—and they weighed about 1.5 pounds per horsepower. Prices ranged up to $15,000 new, though rebuildable used units could be had for a fraction of that.

For the racer who couldn't afford to build a big engine plane—or who wanted a plane that could race for prizes in small displacement classes as well as the Thompson—the field was even more limited. About the only practical configuration was an inline air cooled inverted engine. The inline cylinders were desirable to get a small, narrow, sleek fuselage of minimum drag. And of course, the cylinders needed to be inverted (turned upside down) to get

Menasco inverted inline engines were ideal as a basis for very small, clean monoplanes with fairly large propeller diameters.
Weaver Collection

53

the propeller shaft up high enough to allow enough prop diameter to absorb a decent amount of power— and still have room for a small, light, compact landing gear. Unfortunately, inverted engine technology was just coming on the scene in the late twenties. Only one viable US company made them in 1930, Menasco Manufacturing in Burbank, California.

But really, none of these early inverted engines would have had any chance in the Thompson: too small, and not enough power. It wasn't until Al Menasco offered special handmade supercharged six-cylinder inverted engines in 1931 that this type could be seriously considered for placing high in the Thompson. His early C6S model, rated 260 hp at 2500 rpm, was priced at $3,200. Menasco also offered supercharged four-cylinder engines during this same period, with a potential of 175–200 hp, but

these hardly had a chance to place high in a Thompson, regardless of how tiny and light the accompanying aircraft.

Lightweight power from Menasco

Albert Menasco, pioneer stunt flyer and master mechanic, first got involved in the aircraft engine business in 1926, when he bought surplus French Salmson radial engines from World War I and converted them for American budget builders. His association with an early Northrup flying wing project in the late twenties convinced him of the need for a radical new configuration of aircraft engine: an inverted inline air cooled layout that would have the propeller shaft on top, thus giving minimum frontal area and allowing a larger propeller diameter without requiring a high, heavy landing gear

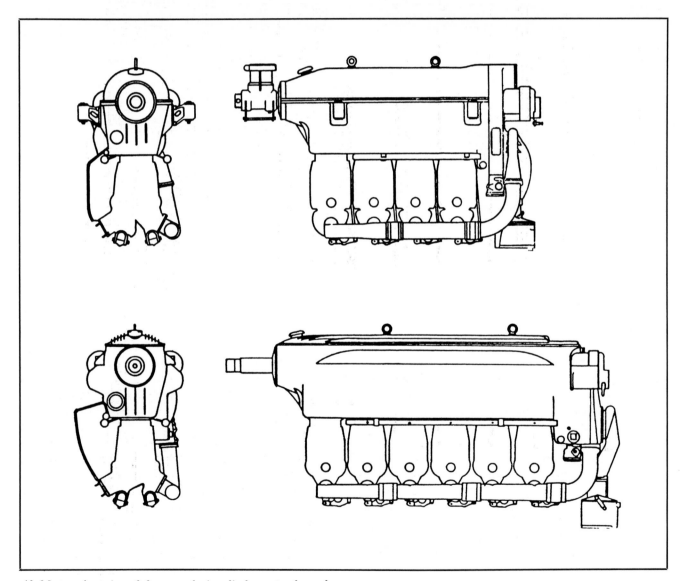

Al Menasco's series of four- and six-cylinder supercharged inverted engines in the early thirties, with power range from 150 to 300 hp, formed the basis for a new school of race plane design.

The late four-cylinder Menasco Model C4S, weighing 320 pounds, delivered up to 230 hp at 3400 rpm, using a small supercharger. Early models gave 185 hp with milder camshaft timing. Smithsonian Institution

(essentially just an inline engine turned upside down).

When Al Menasco introduced his unusual inverted engine in 1930, he probably had no idea that his products would eventually become world famous in air racing. Menasco saw a definite commercial need for the design. But he had been a racer at heart from early youth. Before he ever thought of producing engines, he was variously involved in racing motorcycle engined midget cars, World War I airplanes and Model T track jalopies. It was a natural step for Menasco to promote his new lightweight inverted engine among builders of small pylon racing planes on the West Coast.

One of the less obvious benefits Menasco offered was simply his willingness to build custom engine combinations to fit special planes for very reasonable prices. Menasco was interested enough in the sport of air racing to go far out of his way and often to forget his profit on a job. It's been said of the whole Menasco operation of the thirties that Al made more money on custom machining, casting and prototype work than on aircraft engines!

Another important advantage of Menasco engines was Al's appreciation of the economies of interchangeable parts. He could bolt together an engine to meet almost any need by scrambling various off-the-shelf parts. For instance, all his early inverted engines used the same stroke length (5⅛ inch) and a common connecting rod design. All used pushrod operated overhead valves, with many interchangeable valve train parts. There were three sizes of cylinder assemblies: A, B and C. There were four- and six-cylinder crankcases and a large and small supercharger. Also, Al liked to play around with camshaft timing to adjust a power curve; he had four or five favorite cam grinds that he scrambled.

Add to all this the fact that Menasco had one of the best-equipped small manufacturing facilities on the West Coast. He had not only a complete

55

machine shop, but cam and gear grinding equipment, the latest welding rigs plus his own pattern shop and casting foundry, as well as dynamometer facilities to verify power and durability. Al could build practically a complete engine in house, using his own craftsmen and equipment.

It's no wonder that the air racers were drawn to the Menasco shops like flies to honey in those tight money days of the 1930s.

Early Menascos

Menasco built his first custom race engines in late 1930 for twin midget monoplanes built by Keith Rider for a group of San Francisco businessmen—a four-cylinder and a six, both supercharged. Whether it was Rider who sought out Menasco or whether it was the other way around, the record isn't clear. But that first union of Menasco engines with those

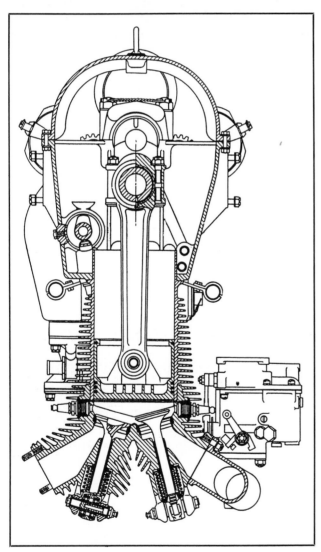

The Model C4 Menasco used a single camshaft in the crankcase, with pushrods and rocker arms to operate the inclined overhead valves. But the open valve gear spattered around quite a bit of oil.

tiny Rider racers rocketed both manufacturers into the national pylon racing spotlight practically overnight.

These early Menasco engines were in no way production ATC certified designs but were an interesting scrambling of stock and prototype parts. The four-cylinder used the large C-size cylinders to get 363 ci, moderate cam timing, with the small prototype supercharger driven at 9.6 times crankshaft speed. These early C4S engines offered up to about 200 hp at 3000 rpm on 40 in. manifold pressure, depending on cam timing, and weighed 305 lb. Several of them were sold in the next two or three years for such planes as the Miles & Atwood and Art Chester Specials.

The first C6S engine for the Rider R-1 was essentially a combination of large C4 cylinders on a B6 crankcase, 544 ci, with a prototype B6 supercharger driven at 8.75 times crank speed and mild camshaft timing. This engine tested to 272 hp at 2800 rpm on 50 in. pressure, and weighed about 480 lb (though Menasco recommended a maximum of 260 hp at 2500 rpm). Several more of these were sold in the early 1930s.

Al Menasco's next major race engine project was an upgrade of the C6S combination for Lawrence Brown's beautiful new B-2 monoplane in 1934. A primary aim this time was to take as much weight out of the engine as possible, by substituting magnesium castings for many of the aluminum parts. (Remember, Menasco could do these castings in his own shop.) These parts included the rear accessory housing, supercharger casing, induction pipe and even the main bearing caps in the crankcase. The total weight reduction was over 60 lb, bringing the engine down to a total of 418 lb.

Other changes included an increase in blower gear ratio from 8.75:1 to 10.4:1, a slight drop in compression to compensate for the higher boost, and a larger carburetor. The result was an increase in peak output to 320 hp at 2800 rpm on 55 in. manifold pressure at full throttle.

This special lightweight C6S engine for Lawrence Brown was probably written off as an experimental project; there is no record of a sale. And it was likely an expensive experiment. Magnesium casting was a touchy art in those days, with usually more than a 50 percent scrap rate. This is hinted when Menasco also made one of these engines for Harry Crosby for his CR-3 racer in 1936 because it apparently didn't have all the magnesium parts of the earlier Brown build-up.

Perhaps we should mention some of the weak points of these early Menasco supercharged engines. There were plenty. Some engines had too much supercharge pressure and compression ratio

56

for the available fuels. Detonation and preignition were constant problems at higher speeds, using the best available 87 octane commercial aviation gas of the day. One apparent factor in the detonation problem was uneven fuel distribution between cylinders with the straight log type intake manifold, fed from the back. The lean cylinders ran hotter and detonated. A simple fix would have been a split-flow Y-type manifold as used on later Ranger inverted engines. The Schoenfeldt team experimented with something like this on their modified Menasco. Menasco never admitted it was a problem.

Other problems included aluminum alloy connecting rods, which weren't strong enough for the application. Sometimes Al got carried away with his passion to save weight. Also the thrust bearing in the front of the B6 crankcase frequently failed because it tended to pick up heat from the front cylinder. Supercharger casings were prone to crack at thin sections, losing supercharge pressure. And there was a weakness that only a few mechanics ever caught onto: The two magnetos on the back of the engine tended to absorb heat through their mountings and short out, causing misfiring. Any magneto temp over 160 degrees Fahrenheit was asking for trouble. Efficient air circulation around the mags was vital.

Because of these weak points many of the early Menascos did most of their racing at 2200–2600 rpm with 30–40 in. manifold pressure—and with the planes running 20–40 mph below their potential top speeds!

The improved Menascos

Al Menasco was well aware of all these bugs in his early supercharged engines. He was on a learning curve just like everybody else. Remember, none of those early supercharged combinations were really production designs with ATC ratings. Actual production of C4S and B6S engines started in 1936, to fill several national and overseas commercial contracts. At this time, a number of design changes

The Brown B-2 racer of 1934 was designed around a new lightweight C6S Menasco engine. Both Brown and Menasco were hoping to attract military contracts. Whittington

57

were made that greatly improved durability and power.

For instance, compression ratios were reduced to 5.5:1 across the board, forged steel connecting rods were adopted, and camshaft timing was lengthened to bring the peak of the torque curves up from around 2000 to 2600 rpm. This reduced BMEP in the lower speed range where the engines were ATC rated and permitted them to be rated on inexpensive 73 octane fuel. It also served to help the racers, by bringing the power peaks up to 3200–3400 rpm. The little C4S was said to develop 220–230 hp at 3400 rpm with the late camshaft and improved supercharger. The late B6S pulled upwards of 290 hp. Several racers bought these upgraded production engines in 1936 or brought the new parts to rebuild their early engines.

It should be noted that Al Menasco hired Art Chester for research and development work in 1936. Chester had a strong reputation for getting lots of reliable horses out of his four-cylinder Menasco, and Al wanted to tap some of that direct-from-the-pylons know-how. During Chester's later work for Menasco, it was said he once pulled 309 hp at 3600 rpm from a C4S by adapting a larger B6 supercharger on it. If this engine ever flew on the pylons is not known.

An entirely new engine appeared in 1937: the six-cylinder C6S-4 model, and it was the first

Menasco that really had the power potential to win the Thompson Trophy outright. This engine was a complete redesign of the C6S configuration. Very few parts were carried over, though it had the same bore and stroke (544 ci displacement). It was a bigger and stronger engine from top to bottom, weighing nearly 70 lb more than the C6S.

Internally the C6S-4 had twin camshafts, operating overhead intake and exhaust valves separately, with the pushrods and overhead gear enclosed for better lubrication. Valves and ports were much larger for better breathing. Cylinder fins were modified for better cooling. The bottom end had bigger bearings and a beefier crankcase, and forged steel crankshaft and connecting rods. The crankcase had an eight-inch front housing to provide space for a reduction gear that was planned for a later model. The supercharger had more air capacity than the B6S design and was driven at 10.9 times crank speed. The accessory drive at the back of the engine was also completely redesigned for better cooling and reliability. A substantially larger Stromberg updraft carburetor was used.

When evaluating the performance of the new C6S-4, it's important to remember that camshaft timing had a major effect. The first prototype of the engine, supplied to Rudy Kling for his new Folkerts SK-3 racer in early 1937, had relatively long-duration camshaft timing. This put the power peak at a lusty

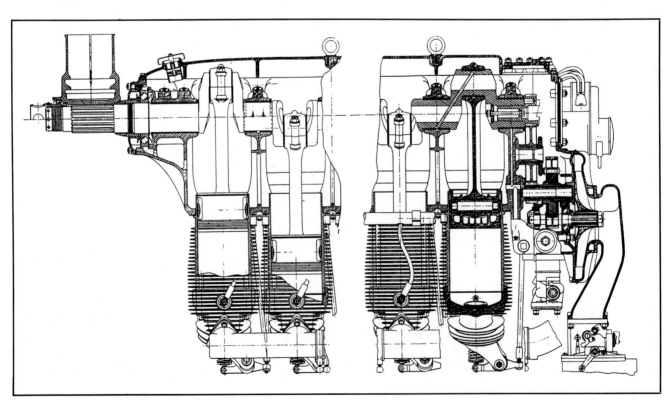

The six-cylinder Menasco B6 engine, available with or without supercharger, was very similar to C4 design. Improved production models in 1936 had forged steel connecting rods and could turn 3200 rpm.

The epitome of Menasco engine development was the C6S-4 model of 1937. Featuring twin camshafts, enclosed valve gear, large ports and improved supercharger, it could deliver up to 400 hp at 3300 rpm. Smithsonian Institution

The Menasco C6S-4 engine in Harry Crosby's racer used a long log type exhaust manifold, to eliminate any turbulence restriction around the engine cowling. Sunyak

400 hp at 3300 rpm on 70 in. manifold pressure. However, Menasco recommended a maximum of 350 hp at 2600 rpm on 55 in. for extended operation, and this is what Kling actually used. Either output required 95 octane fuel, which was just becoming available.

The commercial version of the C6S-4 that was ATC-certified in 1938 at 260 hp, the one seen in old aviation books, had milder camshaft timing and a lower peak power. It was never raced or produced in any volume, but several units were sold for prototype aircraft in the late 1930s.

Two of the most successful C6S-4 engines in the late thirties—the units in the Schoenfeldt *Firecracker* (Rider R-4) and Art Chester's *Goon* racer—were highly modified from factory specs. This variety of specifications for cam timing, compression, blower gear ratio and so on made it difficult to closely evaluate Menasco power levels in specific aircraft.

The reliable inline Renault

A discussion of inverted inline engines for the Thompson is not complete without mentioning the magnificent six-cylinder Renault Coupe Deutsch

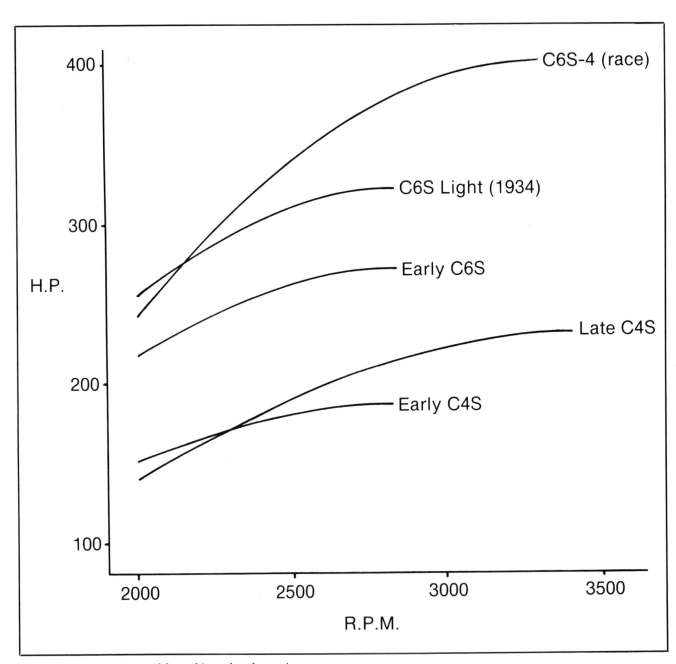

Several Menasco engine models used in early pylon racing gave these full throttle power curves. A rev limit of 2500–2600 rpm was usually recommended.

engine that powered the French Caudron to that runaway win in 1936. This engine was certainly the closest to a custom-built factory racing design ever to fly the Thompson pylons, either prewar or postwar. The huge Renault industrial conglomerate in France committed considerable resources to develop an eight-liter engine for the Deutsch racers that not only delivered a lot of horsepower in relation to its size and weight, but delivered this power with great reliability. When fitted in the highly refined Caudron airframe, the combination literally overwhelmed our grassroots guys, even the big Pratt & Whitney radial engine racers.

Just as important as this engine performance was the reliability of this performance: The particular unit used at Los Angeles, judging from the timed speeds and pilot Detroyat's later statements, operated with wide open throttle at 3250 rpm and 50-plus in. manifold pressure for at least two, and possibly three, consecutive ten-mile laps. And world light-plane speed records set in France at that time suggest lower compression versions were capable of turning 3200 rpm at 45–50 in. pressure for several

hours with excellent reliability. The inline Renault was one of the first engines to use forged pistons, and these pistons were a major factor in the Renault's reliability.

Brute power from Pratt & Whitney

Pratt & Whitney radials became the engines of choice in the big Thompson racers simply because the company chose to use the sport as a laboratory for durability development and as a showcase for institutional public relations. Pratt & Whitney offered custom modifications and convenient lend/lease accommodations for specific racing teams. A fact not quite so well-known is that the company supplied two factory technicians at each major pylon racing event across the country from 1930 through 1939. These men, Tiny Flynn and Ray Peck, were as familiar around the hangars at Cleveland as the racers themselves. They were the first to arrive and the last to leave, and sixteen-hour working days were the norm. Whether you needed a replacement piston or just some advice on spark timing, Tiny or Ray had the answer.

The Renault Coupe Deutsch engine won the 1936 Thompson in a Caudron racer by combining power with unusual high rpm durability. Note the efficient ram air scoop to feed the carburetor.

Pratt & Whitney did not take its racing lightly in the 1930s. And these two experts were a big factor in the company's success.

Early Pratt & Whitneys

Illustrative of this big company promotion program in the thirties was the saga of Wasp Junior production engine No. 2, which came off the assembly line in the summer of 1930. It was a brand-new design, and Pratt & Whitney wanted to get one into some heavy-duty use right away for observation. The company agreed to loan it to Matty Laird in Chicago for his new *Solution* racing biplane, which was then under construction for the first Thompson race coming up in September.

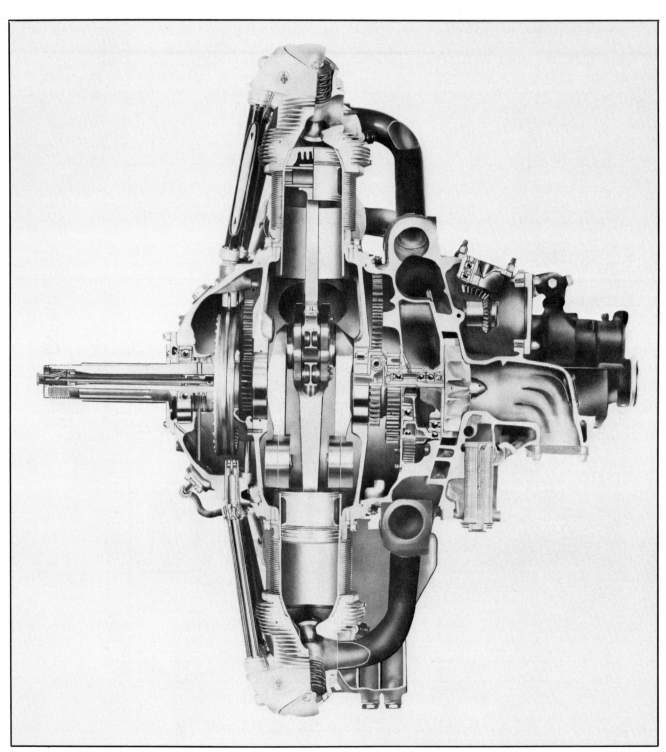

The Pratt & Whitney Wasp nine-cylinder radial engine was the main source of power for large engine Thompson racers of the 1930s. *It could develop up to 800 hp, depending on compression, rpm, supercharger gear and fuel.* United Technologies

It was a crash thrash from the word go. Technician Ray Peck and the engine didn't get away from the factory and on the train to Chicago until a week before the race. He and the Laird crew worked on the installation up to two hours before race time. Pilot "Speed" Holman actually had to trim the plane and work in the controls on the ten-minute hop from the Laird factory over to the Reynolds Airport,

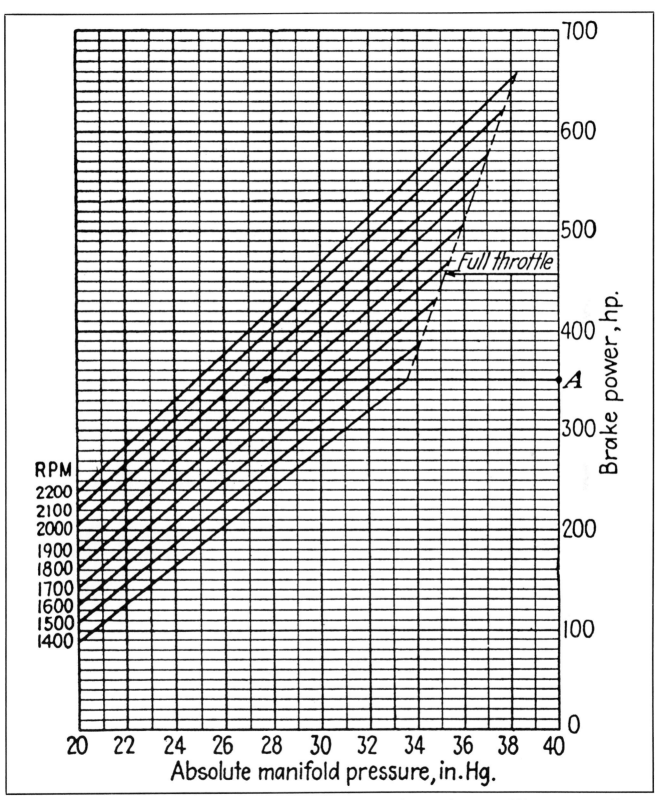

Sea-level power curves for typical Pratt & Whitney Wasp, with 6:1 compression and 10:1 blower gears. Takeoff rating was 550 hp at 2200 rpm on 34 in. manifold pressure, using 80 octane gasoline.

where he pulled up to the line for the start only minutes before the first plane was flagged off. (There was no required qualifying flight in 1930.) The engine never missed a beat, though, and Holman won the race at a record speed.

But that was only the beginning. That same engine was then rebuilt and shipped to the Granville brothers in Springfield, Massachusetts, for the Gee Bee Model Z being prepared for the 1931 Thompson. We know it won that race with ease. The Pratt & Whitney people were apparently impressed with the Granville plans for 1932, so they left the engine for another year, for use in the new Gee Bee R-2 model aimed at long distance racing in the Bendix. This combination didn't turn out quite so well. The best that pilot Lee Gehlbach could do with the R-2 was fourth in the Bendix and fifth in the Thompson, which apparently wasn't quite good enough to satisfy anxious Pratt & Whitney officials. Wasp Junior No. 2 finally ended up with stock specs in Martin and Osa Johnson's Sikorsky amphibian, exploring Africa for their travel lecture circuit! Pratt & Whitney made engines available where they would do the company the most good.

When we examine the evolution of Pratt & Whitney's technical involvement in racing, we find that first Wasp Junior engine for the 1930 Laird *Solution* was actually stock—in the sense that the combination of 5:1 compression ratio and 8:1 supercharger gear ratio was in the process of being tested for an ATC rating. That rating of 400 hp at 2300 rpm was issued a few months later. But for the Thompson race, Pratt & Whitney engineers approved of one hour at 2400 rpm and wide open throttle, which gave 470 hp at 37 in. manifold pressure.

Incidentally this output called for a gasoline with 2 or 3 cc of lead per gallon, with an octane value over 80, which wasn't generally available at airports in 1930. Standard Oil supplied such fuel at the Nationals in Chicago, though, and "Speed" Holman used it in his Wasp Junior to win the 1930 Thompson.

By the time this same engine was being prepared by Pratt & Whitney engineers for the *Gee Bee Z* in 1931, the new standardized fuel specifications were in force and the top 87 octane grade with 3 cc of lead seemed adequate for a boost in compression ratio to 6:1 and the blower gear ratio to 10:1. This combination raised the full throttle output to 535 hp at 2400 rpm at 43 in. manifold pressure. Sponsors of the Laird *Super Solution* racer for Jimmy Doolittle that year bought him a geared version of the same engine, which turned 2500 rpm without excessive propeller tip speed, and thus developed 560 hp (though Doolittle decided not to use it in the race because of prop torque handling problems).

Admittedly all these Wasp Junior engines with 6:1 compression and 10:1 blower gears were marginal on detonation when using full throttle with standard 87 octane gas. Doolittle wrote of using an extra 2 cc of lead per gallon—which tested to 89 octane in the Shell labs—and this lowered his cylinder head temperature and smoothed the engine right out. But he burned a piston in the 1931 Thompson, possibly because of preignition caused by lead deposits on the spark plugs. This business of adding lead to cure detonation was always critical in those early days because of plug fouling.

For the 1932 Thompson, Pratt & Whitney loaned the Granville boys a larger Wasp R-1340 engine for the formidable Gee Bee R-1 that was being prepared specifically for that race. (The twin Junior powered R-2 was intended basically for the Bendix.) This big Wasp engine had 6:1 compression and 12:1 blower gears, a combination not yet ATC rated, and developed about 770 hp at 2350 rpm on 45 in. manifold pressure with full throttle. This output not only required doped gas, but also required considerably richened carburetion to let the fuel do some internal cooling—and the R-1 was noted for its trail of heavy black smoke when running hard.

This famous engine not only won the Thompson in 1932 in the Gee Bee, but pushed the world landplane speed record to 294.38 mph during qualifying trials. Then Jim Wedell used it a year later to up that record to 304.98 mph in his Wedell 44. This Wasp had some real muscle.

Another interesting custom Wasp configuration by Pratt & Whitney engineers was the high-altitude modification for Benny Howard's unusual *Mr. Mulligan* cabin monoplane in 1933–1936. They made up a one-of-a-kind set of 13.85:1 blower gears for this engine, so that it could deliver a continuous 500 hp at 2200 rpm clear up to 11,000 ft altitude, running on the usual 87 octane pump fuel. This was intended to give fast, economical cruising at high altitudes for the cross country Bendix races.

The bug was that these high ratio gears were quite inefficient at sea level, causing excessive mixture heating and blower power loss. This compromised the power available for pylon racing. Since two-speed superchargers were unknown, Pratt & Whitney engineers had no choice but to clamp on a limit of only 34 in. manifold pressure at 2200 rpm with the available 87 octane. This was only around 500 hp. Pilot Harold Neumann tried to exceed this on a doped fuel when qualifying for the 1935 Thompson, but burned a piston. In the race, he didn't use more than about 480 hp.

Improved Pratt & Whitneys

Pratt & Whitney's only special race project involving the big Hornet R-1690 engine was for

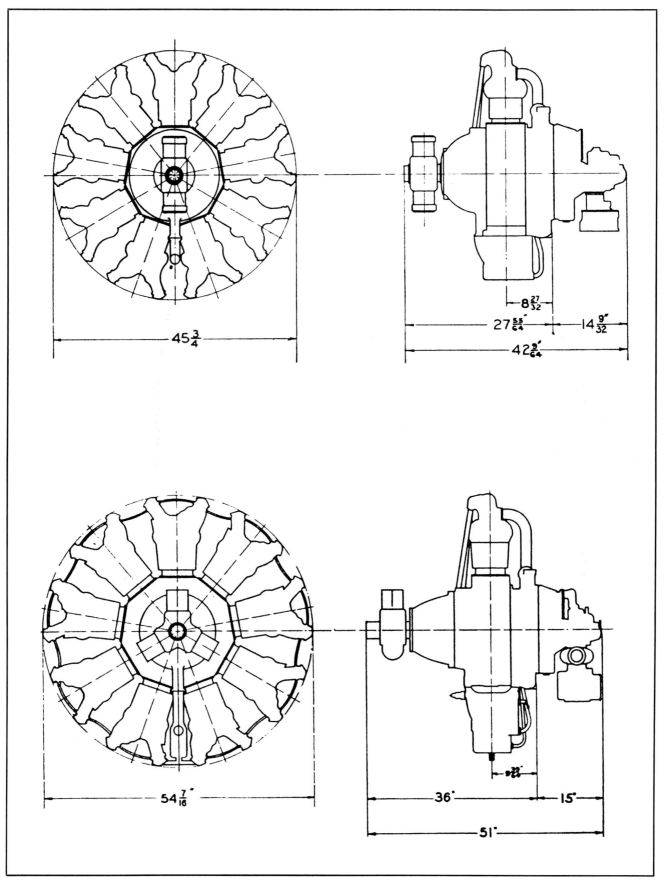

The largest nine-cylinder Pratt & Whitney Hornet engine was almost ten inches larger in diameter than was the small Wasp Junior model. This increased frontal area offset much of the additional power in a small plane.

When Roscoe Turner put a big Pratt & Whitney Hornet engine in his Wedell racer in 1934, the huge cowl and extra drag practically canceled any increase in top speed. Weaver Collection

Roscoe Turner in 1934. This one had the usual 6:1 compression ratio, but special 13:1 supercharger gears were made up to give a reasonably high manifold pressure at the relatively low rev limit of 2200 rpm.

The basic problem with the Hornet was inadequate capacity of the oil scavenger pumps. At sustained crank speeds above about 2250 rpm, the oil just accumulated in the crankcase and was eventually pumped out of the breather pipes. Since Pratt & Whitney had no need to run the engine at higher speeds commercially, there was no urgent need to fix the scavenging problem. But more than one overeager racer found his Hornet pumped dry of oil after a run of several hours at speeds in the 2300–2400 rpm range.

This special Hornet engine for Roscoe Turner was said to develop 1030 hp at 2200 rpm with full throttle at sea level. But this performance would have required 100 octane fuel, which wasn't available until late in the plane's career. Pratt & Whitney engineers rated the original version 825 hp at 2200 on 40 in. manifold pressure for the available 87 octane. Turner always called that Hornet a "1,000 hp engine." But there is no record that he ever operated it at that level.

The two last known prewar example of custom Pratt & Whitney race engines were the fourteen-cylinder Twin Wasp and Twin Wasp Junior for use in the late thirties by Roscoe Turner and Earl Ortman respectively. These were basically military engines at the time and were not yet ATC rated. Pratt & Whitney engineers merely quoted maximum rpm and manifold pressure figures that they felt would be reasonably safe for an hour's racing on the new standardized 95 octane avgas grade that became available in 1936.

In the case of Ortman's R-1535 Twin Wasp Junior, this race rating was set at 1000 hp at 2675 rpm on 48 in. pressure. For the big R-1830 Twin Wasp for Turner's *Meteor,* they quoted 1,200 hp at 2650 rpm on 47 in. Simple as that. There is reason to believe, however, that neither pilot used these full outputs until genuine 100 octane fuel was released in 1938. In many ways, race pilots were more conservative than factory enginers about pushing their engines. For the racers, finishing a race was a matter of bread and butter—or under certain circumstances, life and death—while to the Pratt & Whitney engineers a blown engine was just another simple rebuild!

All these specific engine setups were by no means all the Pratt & Whitney engines that raced in the prewar Thompsons. There were many others, mostly Wasp and Wasp Junior models. And undoubtedly some were ordered new with special high compression pistons and/or special blower gears. And it is likely that some older stock engines were returned to the factory for special pistons or gears, after word got around about who had what. Pratt & Whitney made these modifications for the usual rebuild fees, though always with no warranty when used in non-ATC-rated applications.

66

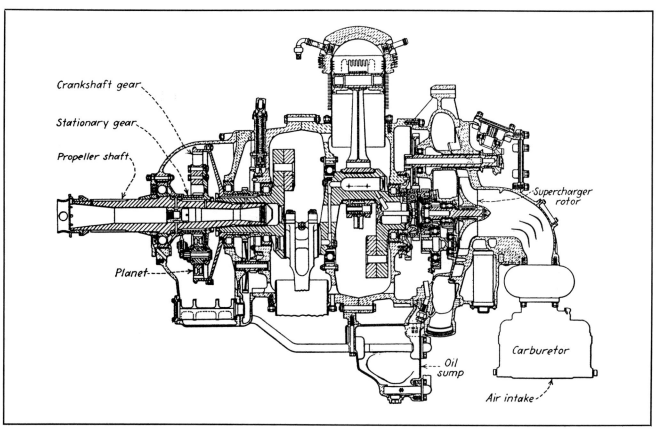

The Pratt & Whitney Twin Wasp Junior engine of late 1930s, with fourteen cylinders in two rows, had very small diameter, but offered up to 1,000 hp on 95 octane fuel. It was a good racing engine.

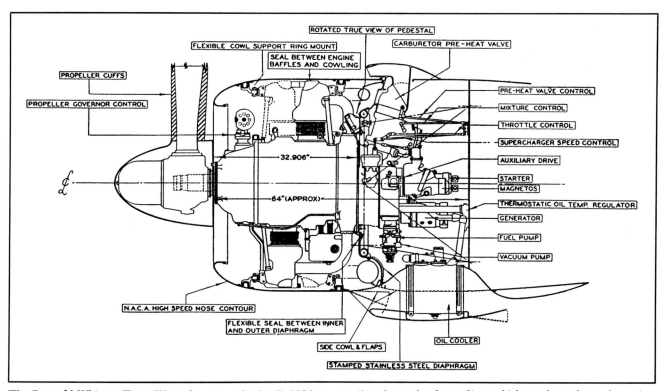

The Pratt & Whitney Twin Wasp fourteen-cylinder R-1830, was approved for 1,200 hp on 95 octane fuel. Roscoe Turner's original Laird Meteor used this "factory" installation, with an oil cooler under the cowling, which was later changed to reduce air drag.

Chapter 6

Pylon racing strategy

To win a race, you must first finish. This is where thorough race preparation and sound racing strategy enter the picture. The really successful pilots all knew that most of the effort necessary to win a race is done before it even begins. They left little to chance because they prepared their planes to withstand the rigors of a long race, and took care to learn the limits of their planes so that they did not exceed them.

Race preparation

For the serious Thompson racer, there was a never-ending list of jobs to do and items to check when getting ready for the big race. First was an overhaul of the engine. It's common practice in auto racing to go through the engine several times in a season of racing, replacing even mildly worn parts, and many other key parts, in case they might be close to some form of fatigue failure.

No such luxuries existed in early grassroots air racing. The one reason was money. With aircraft engine parts costing three or four times that of auto parts, even a semi overhaul often took over $300 worth of parts. No, in low budget air racing about the best you could hope for was an engine overhaul

Many smaller pylon racers were designed with removable wings, so that they could be trailered around the country behind a car. Art Chester's Goon *arrived at Cleveland in 1938.* Sunyak

once a season. And more often than not a pilot flew until something broke.

Even time was a critical preparation factor at the National Air Races. Many times a component failed during practice or qualifying. Then it came down to the all-night wrench thrashing session to replace a piston or seal up a supercharger case or repair a landing gear. An experienced crew of mechanics was invaluable here. But they were an expensive luxury that most pilots could not afford. Who could afford to pay food and hotel bills for three or four guys for a week before the race, like the big teams do today?

Budgets were always tight. Sleeping accommodations were often blankets and cots beside the plane in a hangar, and the menu was rarely more than hot dogs and beans. Pickup crews were easy to recruit on the spot at Cleveland, because a lot of race fans planned their vacations at that time, and made a pilgrimage to the Nationals. One time Jimmy Wedell, who had to fly his plane in, enjoyed the help of three friends who rode motorcycles up from Louisiana! With roads and motorcycles as they were in 1932 . . . well, they must have been real friends. (They sold their 'cycles and used the money to buy train tickets back.) Only a few big name racers like Roscoe Turner could afford the luxury of a full time mechanic and posh accommodations.

Where the racing plane was small and light, the usual practice was to design it with detachable wings and transport it on a trailer behind a car. (These tiny planes didn't have large enough gas tanks for any practical cross-country flying anyway.) But then the pilot could bring one or two fellows with him to Cleveland to help out, plus a reasonable choice of tools in the trunk. This simplified the transport problem. Racers like Art Chester and Steve Wittman trailered their little planes all over the country.

Once settled at Cleveland, there was plenty to do to get ready to race. Most early Thompson racers felt a smoothly polished surface on a plane's fuselage and wings helped reduce skin friction drag. Often you'd see them, hours before the race, rubbing and polishing on their planes. They apparently considered it well worth the time and effort if it gained them even one mph of speed.

Though it doesn't sound like a particular preparation problem, Thompson teams had to be careful about loading up with an adequate amount of fuel and oil for a given race distance. Sometimes unexpected race conditions forced a racer to run a little harder than planned—and thus use extra gas and oil. Or a less obvious trap was having to richen the fuel-air mixture a bit to help cool the cylinders internally on a specially hot day. That manual carburetor mixture lever on the panel was a temptation

Installing the wing on the Brown B-2 racer, after the plane was hauled to Cleveland on a trailer. These small racers didn't have enough fuel capacity for practical ferry flying. Sunyak

69

Few grassroots racers could afford the luxury of large ground crews at the Nationals. Friends were often recruited on the spot. Repla-Tech

The infamous racehorse start added excitement—and danger— to the Thompson races. Planes were lined up in order of their qualifying times. McReynolds

to use as a means to control cylinder head temperature with extra fuel. More than one Thompson race was lost when the leader ran low on fuel or oil and had to drop back.

Surviving the racehorse start

Without question, the racehorse start was the most exciting and dangerous part of any Thompson Trophy race. When you think of eight or ten planes lined up side by side, gunning their throttles together at the drop of a flag and heading for a single pylon turning point only a mile away—well, there's no way it could have been anything else but exciting and dangerous. That there were only two or three start mishaps in the twenty-year history of the Thompson is probably a miracle.

Why was the racehorse start necessary anyway? It wasn't. It was strictly an invention of promoter Cliff Henderson to create excitement for the spectators. A rolling start could have been arranged. This type start is used in many forms of auto racing. It's used in powerboat racing: the boats come down to the starting line at some particular time, as indicated by a sweep second hand on a large clock display; if a boat crosses the line before the hand hits zero, the driver's penalized. And of course, they use a moving lineup start with modern 500 mph Unlimited air racers at Reno.

The first Thompson race at Chicago in 1930 was started by flagging off the individual planes at ten-second intervals and timing them from the standing start. In effect, the planes were racing against the clock, rather than each other. The fans didn't like it. In response, the racehorse start was introduced, for the second race at Cleveland in 1931. The fans went wild, and it stuck from then on.

Starting from a standstill on the ground called for some method for determining the order of lineup. Since most closed course pylon racing was in a counterclockwise direction and all the turns were to the left, theoretically planes lined up on the left end, or inside end, of the row had a slight advantage over planes on the other end—since they were a few feet closer to the first pylon. The difference was admittedly small, but it did start the practice of qualifying the competing planes, and then lining them up with the fastest qualifier on the left end of the start line. On the pole, as they say in auto racing.

Qualifying flights were necessary anyway, to verify the performance of both plane and pilot, and to prevent excessively slow planes from entering the race and obstructing the faster ones. Minimum prewar qualifying speeds varied from 175 to 240 mph. The list of qualifying averages was just a convenient classification for lining up the start.

The role of the "scattering" pylon should also be mentioned. This was an extra moveable pylon that could be specially positioned to allow the planes a long upwind, or into-the-wind, takeoff run in front of the main grandstand. They would take off toward the scattering pylon, round it and then fan out onto the main race course. Its position, of course, depended on wind direction. And it wasn't always necessary, if the wind was blowing from the direction of the first race pylon. But the presence of that scattering pylon only 5,000 ft or so from the starting line, which had to be rounded without full flying speed, always added an extra challenge to the start.

It was one breathtaking scene when the green flag fell. With all the planes having different rates of acceleration and different degrees of ground control, they were all over the place, in the air and still on the ground. Just getting into the air without hitting somebody was an accomplishment. Then once in the air, a racer had to try to stabilize control and get set up for the scattering pylon. Often he had to be cranking up a retractable landing gear at this same time, and always watching in every direction for other planes. There was not a second to relax.

A very interesting and exciting description of this process came from recent correspondence with Tony LeVier, a first-rate pilot of the late thirties and early postwar Thompson races. In preparation for the 1939 Thompson the Schoenfeldt team had switched Tony's Menasco powered Rider R-4 *Firecracker* racer to an alcohol base fuel—which greatly increased the fuel consumption rate, and required an additional 35-gal. tank behind the pilot's seat. This not only added 250 lb of weight to the tiny airplane, but also added the mass where it would move the center of gravity back several inches, and screw up the longitudinal stability. Takeoff and initial climb were bound to be a handful, even flying alone. And LeVier had no chance to test the plane beforehand with that loading configuration. To make things worse, the 1939 Thompson was flagged off after a hard rain, on a soft, wet, muddy grass field. But let Tony tell about that memorable racehorse start:

"The flag drops and my crew gives me a lusty shove. It doesn't leap forward as in previous races, and I can feel the effect of the soft ground. My throttle is wide open and the control stick full forward. I feel my knuckles against the forward fuel tank. I glance right and left, and notice the other racers only slightly ahead—no one is burning up the ground today. They are all running heavy, and the soft ground isn't helping. My speed continues to increase, but my tail skid is hard against the ground, with no sign of lightening. The ground is far from smooth, causing the *Firecracker* to lurch from side to side. Still no feel of lightness. I find myself using more rudder than usual because of the rearward center of gravity.

"We pass the mid-point of the Cleveland airport, and I'm still not airborne. I venture a glance at my airspeed and it reads 110 m.p.h. The main wheels start bouncing off the ground, but my tail skid is still on the ground with full forward stick. I think of aborting. But at this point I'd never get it stopped short of a thousand people in my path.

"Finally the wheels leave the ground, and the nose rises at an alarming angle—then suddenly the tail clears. The *Firecracker* is now very close to the stall angle of the wing. Only shear power, and the fact that this is one hellava plane, saves me. I have absolutely no pitch control whatever. My knuckles are still hard against the forward fuel tank, and the plane is headed for heaven.

"I start cranking the landing gear up, and find for the first time that each turn of the crank bumps the control stick, causing the plane to roll abruptly each time. Also the air is slightly turbulent, causing the *Firecracker* to pitch up and down. But surprisingly, the plane is so heavy it feels sluggish in response to the rough air. I'm just barely flying—but I'm on my way."

The problem of communication

Communication between the pilot in the race and his crew on the ground was a real nightmare in the 1930s. Today, of course, we have miniaturized two-way, shortwave radios that weigh only a few pounds and can give clear, sure communication in any background conditions. In the thirties, it was something else. Radios were heavy, bulky, inefficient, and there wasn't even room for one in the smaller planes.

A typical communication problem for those early pylon racers was rigging some method of keeping track of the number of laps completed during the race. The race organizers didn't consider it their responsibility to provide any form of large number display of the lap count that could be seen by the pilots. The usual answer was to put small strips of masking tape across the instrument panel, one for each lap of the race. The pilot pulled off one strip each time he passed the start/finish line. Occasionally, in the heat of some tight racing maneuver, a pilot might forget to pull the strip off or might not remember later if he had pulled it off. This led to some interesting situations, both in the air and on the ground afterward.

Roscoe Turner got an idea from the Indianapolis auto racers, where the pit crews flashed cards to signal the drivers as they passed their pits. Don Young, Turner's crew chief, set up two large four-by-eight-foot sheets of plywood that could be seen from the air, with one to indicate the lap and one the pilots' position in the race. The crew changed the numbers on these sheets as the race progressed, and the two ground men varied the distance between the two sheets to indicate Turner's lead over the next place. With the three signals, Turner knew where he was in the race.

As for radio communication, Earl Ortman fitted his Rider R-3 with a small radio for ground crew contact in the late thirties, which never worked very well. The Seversky racers, which were converted pursuit planes, had much better military radios in 1937–1939.

This lack of effective communication between the race pilots and ground crews was a major factor in the outcome of several Thompson races. In the 1939 race, Tony LeVier failed to notice Roscoe Turner's early pylon cut and thought he was being lapped when Turner caught up and passed him a few laps later. This discouraged LeVier from really pushing in the last half of the race, when he thought Turner was so much faster. There was no effective ground communication to tell him he was in second place and might catch him.

When we look back at the whole situation, it seems incredible that those early Thompson teams didn't work out some practical way to facilitate this plane-to-ground communication during the race. It could have made such a difference in so many races. Roscoe Turner deserves double credit for even the crude system he worked out.

Flying the pylons: theory

Even though pylon piloting is probably more art than science, a surprising amount of careful scientific research and testing through the years has tried to determine the best flying technique for getting around a pylon with minimum loss of time and speed.

First, we need to understand that the lap length of a pylon race course was measured from pylon to pylon, not on the path followed by the planes. A plane would have to travel considerably farther than the stated lap length because of distance added in swinging around the pylons, especially with the long turns on a triangular or rectangular course. And of course, a plane loses considerable speed when it banks up for a tight turn, due to the extra wing lift required to counteract centrifugal force.

To put it very simply, the purpose in all this research and testing of pylon turns was to find the best compromise between the extra distance traveled in a loose turn and the amount of speed lost in a very tight turn.

Some interesting government tests

The first documented testing to determine optimum pylon technique was done by US military pilots in preparation for the 1925 Schneider Trophy seaplane race at Baltimore. Apparently this research was instigated by Lt. Jimmy Doolittle, who was flying the Army's Curtiss R3C-2 biplane in the race. The testing at that time, using those 600 hp planes with top speeds around 250 mph, indicated that a centrifugal loading in the neighborhood of 4.0 gs gave the best compromise between extra distance traveled and speed loss. In other words, from classic motion equations, this would imply a turn radius of around 1,000 ft and a bank angle of 76 degrees. Further, the testers found that a small amount of time could be saved if the pilot gained 50 to 100 ft of altitude on the ten-mile straightaways (50 km total course length) and then dived slightly going through the turn, to allow gravity to help overcome the centrifugal force.

Doolittle wrote a detailed NACA Technical Report, No. 203, following this research, in which everything was documented, and precise mathematical calculations made to prove these optimum curve paths and bank angles. His estimate then was that the average speed around a 50 km triangular course, allowing for turn losses, should be about one percent below the peak straightaway speed. My observation from actual straightaway speeds versus average lap speeds would put this figure closer to a 4–5

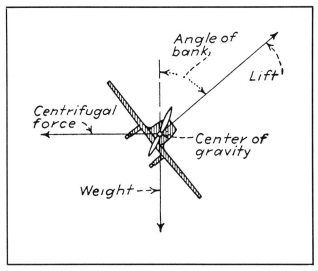

Forces acting on an aircraft in a banked turn. The angle of bank depends on centrifugal force in relation to weight. If both are equal—a one g turn—the angle is 45 degrees.

percent difference for a 50 km course (about thirty miles).

In the next few years after the Doolittle work, the British RAF people did considerable testing for pylon turns in the course of developing their Schneider seaplane racers, with over 2,000 hp and

Army Lt. Jimmy Doolittle did extensive testing on optimum pylon turns and straightaway flying in preparation for the

1925 Schneider seaplane race, using this Curtiss biplane. His findings were completely documented. Curtiss Aeroplane

top speeds up to 375 mph. Interestingly enough, their general findings agreed with the earlier Doolittle work, that is, optimum cornering loads around 4.0 gs. Of course, at these speeds the turn radii were up to 2,500 ft, but the difference between lap average and peak straightaway speed on the 50 km course stayed the same, at 4–5 percent. The British didn't try to use dive energy on their turns.

The next documented research was by the French Caudron pilots when training for the Deutsch 2,000 km races in the mid 1930s, using planes with around 300 hp and top speeds near 270 mph. They found that a wider turn and more dive was better for average speed on a long 100 km (62.1 miles) triangular course. They recommended climbing 300 ft on the twenty-mile straights, and easing through the turns at 2.5 to 3.5 gs, while dropping the 300 ft of extra altitude. Their average lap speeds were 2–3 percent below peak straight speed.

The Washington-based Civil Aeronautics Authority (CAA) in the mid-thirties, wondered if there should be some federal standards on race plane structures, with an eye to protecting spectators and pilots from unnecessary crashes at air shows. (This was shortly after the Roosevelt administration took office in 1933, and responsibility for air safety was taken from the Department of Commerce and put under a separate administrative office.) The CAA decided to have the National Advisory Committee for Aeronautics (NACA) run some tests on several typical pylon racers of large and small size, with the idea of checking actual g-loads reached in pylon turns. NACA engineers visited the Miami International Races in 1934 and 1935 and instrumented four or five planes with precision accelerometers mounted in the cockpits, which recorded instantaneous g-loads during racing maneuvers, using an oscillating pen on rolling graph paper.

Commercial aircraft manufacturers like the TravelAir company had top shop facilities and plenty of skilled help. One of the series R racers was under construction in 1930. Weaver Collection

To make a long story short, NACA came up with peak readings generally between 3.5 and 6.2 gs. From these findings, it was decided the loadings weren't high enough to warrant special standards or tests, since military fighter planes at that time were stressed for 10 or 12 gs. The investigation was dropped. (These tests were reported in NACA Technical Note Number 537.)

The implication is obvious: The Thompson race pilots, with no special knowledge or training on optimum pylon turns, were in fact, turning at just about the right g loads and bank angles. They were flying strictly by the seat of their pants, but the feeling and response of their planes were telling them what seemed to be optimum turning loads.

On a shorter ten-mile triangular or rectangular course, the difference between average lap speed and peak straightaway speed would be greater. My research suggests about ten percent. A lap average of 240 mph on a ten-mile course would suggest a peak straight speed of 240/.9 = 267 mph.

In an interesting footnote to all this prewar cornering work Gordon Israel, a prewar racer who worked for Grumman Aircraft during the war, said that some Grumman engineers got together and tried to calculate the optimum cornering g for tight pylon turns. They came up with 2.0 gs, not the 4.0 gs that most prewar experimental testing had revealed. Further, Israel was able to borrow several g meters from Grumman for the first postwar Thompson races and mount them in selected fighter/racers for the pilots to check during practice.

Israel claimed that those pilots who seriously tested at the 2.0 g cornering level found that their lap times were better than the usual postwar turns at 4.0 to 6.0 gs. Admittedly, these results fly in the face of all the other data, but they are interesting enough to report.

Flying the pylons: reality

It's easy to talk about optimum turning g-loads and bank angles. But it's something else to put theory into practice on a crowded race course.

Theoretically, going through a pylon turn at some particular g-loading or bank angle is merely a matter of banking into the corner, then playing the controls to hold some constant g-force—as monitored by a g-meter or the seat of your pants. (Some planes had g-force gauges on their instrument panels, but trying to monitor it in the heat of a race was really out of the question.) The elevators were played to hold the right turn radius, and the ailerons and rudder were played to hold the right bank angle. Since the g-load and bank angle are inherently related by the curvilinear motion equation, if the bank angle doesn't match the g-load, the plane will just slide inward or outward on the turn radius. Some pilots refer to this as mushing. It required experience, and plenty of it, to get through pylon turns fast and smoothly, with minimum mushing.

This is why the NACA report on the g-load tests at Miami in 1934 and 1935 was of such great interest. Here were the best pilots in the racing game in that day. But the accelerometer graphs of the changing g loads going through the turn were surprisingly erratic. They showed dramatically how very difficult it was to hold a really smooth, high-g pylon turn with those little planes.

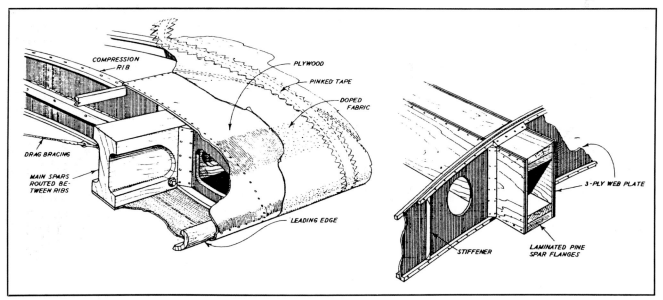

Typical wing construction techniques in the 1920s and 1930s, used both solid and boxed spars with plywood ribs, and plywood or fabric covering. Rolfe

75

Early Thompson pilots, when their planes were tested with instruments in pylon turns, proved to be flying close to the theoretical optimum by just the feel of the plane. Weaver collection

For example, one of the planes instrumented was the 260 hp Rider R-1, flown by Roger Don Rae. Here are instantaneous g-loads at one second intervals in a typical 180 degree turn that took roughly ten seconds:

1	2	3	4	5	6	7	8	9
5.2	3.5	5.2	6.2	3.9	–0.3	4.3	–0.4	3.0

Obviously Rae's manuever was by no means a steady turn as recorded on the g meter. Yet from the ground it looked like a beautiful, tight high-banked turn around the pylon that would be hard to improve on. The negative-g numbers indicate when the pilot released backward pull on the stick momentarily to prevent tightening up the turn too much. In these split second intervals, the plane actually stopped turning —and in fact, was turning outward, away from the pylon, as indicated by the negative g-value. These negative g numbers could be found on all the pilots' graph sheets, showing where they were playing the elevators to prevent the turn from tightening up into a stall.

Also realize that the plane was continually losing speed in the turn, due to the high induced drag needed to overcome centrifugal force. And as the speed gradually fell off, the turn radius required to maintain a constant g-load needed to tighten up. For example, going into a 5.0 g turn at 250 mph, a speed drop of 40 mph reduced the theoretical radius from roughly 840 ft to 600 ft. This effect alone certainly demanded some elevator action in the turn.

All in all, cornering was a highly complex maneuver to do smoothly. And to do it with other planes buzzing all around within a few feet took utmost concentration, guts and skill. And it's just as true that pilots who didn't have the skill, experience and reactions to turn on that ragged edge of a high-speed stall . . . well, they just didn't last long.

76

High-speed stalls at pylon turns were the major cause of fatalities in the Thompson races.

Was there really a best way?

After all the testing and theorizing that was done to determine optimum pylon turning techniques in the twenties, Jimmy Doolittle pretty much upset the whole science when he won the 1932 Thompson using a technique that no one had even thought of before.

The way it happened: Due to the terrible reputation of the stubby Gee Bee R-1 for erratic handling and unexpected tricks, Doolittle decided to don a parachute and take the racer up to 10,000 ft—where there was plenty of room to recover from stalls and spins—and put it through some maneuvers to try to sort out the cornering and stability characteristics that could be expected in the race. After that flight he decided there was only one reasonably sane way to fly the ten-mile rectangular Thompson course with the Gee Bee: With very wide, easy turns, at g-loads under 1.5—while staying 300–500 ft outside the pylons, out of the tight traffic of smaller ships. Doolittle knew this would add considerably to the distance traveled each lap, but he felt his speed advantage of 10 to 20 mph over the fastest of his opponents would offset this.

And that was exactly the way it turned out. In fact, it can be proved using trigonometry. If we assume a peak straightaway speed of 290 mph, turn radius of 4,500 ft and swinging 500 ft outside the pylons, it can be calculated that Doolittle traveled about .80 to .90 miles farther on each lap than if he had made tight 4.0 g turns 100 ft from the pylons. But with the wide turns the additional induced drag from centrifugal force would slow down the Gee Bee only 1 or 2 mph. Where with the tight turns the speed would be pulled down 20 to 25 mph. If we use these speeds with the calculated distances we come up with the very same lap speed average for both types of turns—around 265 mph. Which was just about equal to Doolittle's best timed lap of 266.6 mph in the 1932 Thompson.

The most logical conclusion from all this is that perhaps the *design* of a racing plane has a primary influence on optimum cornering technique. That is, a plane with a wide wing span and low wing loading—meaning low induced drag—might be faster by making tight, high-g turns. Where a plane with stubby wings, which would slow down radically in the turns, might be better off making wide turns. It's really never been proved one way or the other.

Don't cut a pylon

One more important point on cutting the corners concerned the distance of the flight path outside the pylon. Any study of air racing history will show that many races were lost when a leading plane cut a pylon—and either had to turn back and recircle it or was disqualified or penalized after the race if the pilot was not aware of the cut.

Cutting a pylon means to cut inside it on the turn. An official posted in the base of the pylon tower, with two or more sight rings above him at different levels in the tower, checked the planes. By sighting up through the rings the official had an exact vertical reference line extending up into the air. If a plane cut inside that imaginary sight line, or if any part of the plane even touched it, the official would signal the cut pylon. The racer then had to recircle and come around the pylon again immediately, or the official would make a note of the cut, and the pilot would be penalized one lap at the end of the race.

What if a pilot wasn't sure that he had cut it? With the lack of ground-to-air communications, he went around and was safe—better to lose a position or two than lose out on all the prize money.

On the other hand, a pilot would obviously help his lap time by cutting as close to the pylons as he dared. That is, if he was turning on a 1,000 ft radius, he didn't try to stay 1,000 ft outside the pylon. He started his turn several hundred feet before reaching the pylon and cut in within 50 to 100 ft of it—so that the center of his turning circle was well inside the course line. This 50 to 100 ft pylon clearance seemed to be a popular figure, according to writings of and interviews with previous Thompson pilots. This gave the minimum practical flight distance around the course.

Modern courses for pylon racing are laid out with multiple pylons, positioned in such a way that the planes are forced to turn in large radius arcs at relatively low g-loads, to help prevent high-speed stalls. On a typical 2.5 mile Formula I course, the pylons are positioned to force a turning radius of about 1,450 ft. At a speed of 240 mph, this would generate only 2.6 gs, and the planes' speed would drop only 10 mph or so in the turn. This is why lap speed averages are only a few miles per hour below top speeds in some modern air racing classes. Perhaps the Thompson races would have been safer with such "scientific" course layouts.

Flying the straightaways

It might seem as if there was no particular technique to flying the straightaways in a pylon race. Just fly a straight line to the next pylon—or actually a little to the right of it—and start your turn at the correct point. But here again, Jimmy Doolittle's NACA paper gave tips that might add a little speed, like flying at a bit higher altitude—up to 300 ft—on the downwind legs of the course, then running at

100 ft on the upwind legs. Reason: possible wind gradient effects. Due to surface friction and obstructions along the ground, the wind at very low levels has a bit less velocity than at higher levels, away from the ground effects. Doolittle said it was common to find 6 to 8 mph difference in wind velocity in the first 300 ft of altitude above the ground. He said the trick could add as much as 2 or 3 mph to lap average on a 50 km course.

Prop wash was another tricky problem on both turns and straightaways. This is the swirling air turbulence that trails up to 300 ft or more behind a speeding plane, due to the propeller whipping the air. It can upset precise steering or pitch control of another plane trailing close behind. One of Steve Wittman's tricks was to purposely try to keep a trail-

ing plane in his wash. If there was a crosswind from the right of the straight, he would fly farther to the right of the course line. This would let the crosswind blow his prop wash and wing turbulence toward trailing planes flying on the course line.

Prop wash could be especially vicious in the turns, when banking up steeply near wing stall. Most planes shuddered and gave the pilot some warning before a full stallout. In tight, high-g turns, the pilots had to be alert and responsive to these warnings. The tragedies occurred when prop wash and wing turbulence from planes ahead masked the usual stall warnings. They say this is what took Rudy Kling at Miami in 1938. He didn't have the years of pylon experience in smaller, slower ships to interpret the stall signals of his hot 300 mph Folkerts.

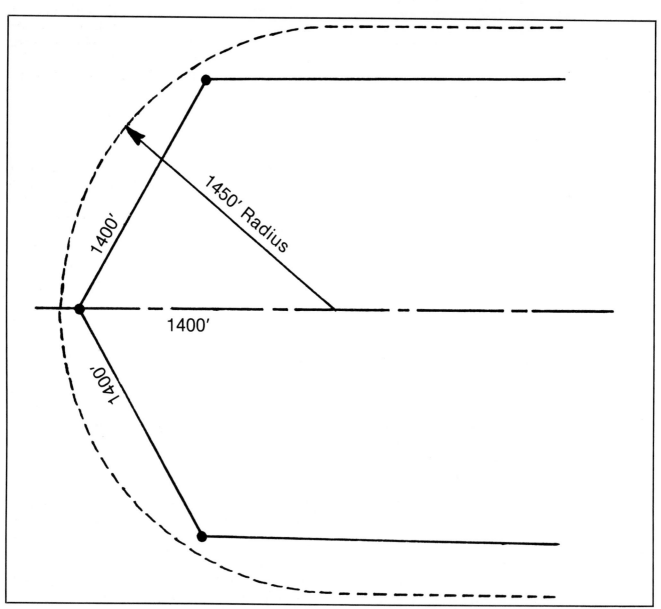

Modern race courses use extra pylons to force planes to corner on wide radius arcs, to reduce g-loads and high-speed stalls. This typical Formula I turn requires a 1,450 foot turn radius, which generates only about 2.6 gs on a plane flying 240 mph.

Pilots had to keep out of other trouble in the straightaway. This was where all the pilots were jockeying for position and trying to pass, while setting up for the next turn. Each man had to try to know where everybody else was. Steve Wittman tells of once feeling a heavy, sluggishness in his controls on a straightaway. He looked up and saw the landing gear wheel of a plane above him resting firmly against his cockpit canopy!

One final concern in straightaway flying was the seemingly simple matter of locating the next pylon turn. This required more attention on the part of the pilot than it might seem, especially in the postwar races, where distances between pylons were four miles or more and ground speeds could exceed 400 mph. Because of the long distances between pylons, race officials supplied schematic maps of the course, which could be studied ahead of time. These maps showed readily visible landmarks like a factory with a black roof, a red and white water tower or railroad tracks, and the pilots said it was surprising how much you didn't see on the ground even at 200 or 300 mph.

To go for it or to slow for it

Perhaps the most critical in-flight problem facing the Thompson racers was whether to push their engines to try to win the race or to hold back a little and settle for second place—or third place, or even fourth place. It was never, never a matter of just taking off and going flat out all the way, to finish as best you could. Every pilot knew pretty well ahead of time which planes he could likely beat and which ones he couldn't hope to beat—and which were close enough to him in speed potential that he would have to really race them, tooth and nail.

But this isn't to say that the Thompson races were just parades of different types of planes with widely varying speed potential, each pilot knowing pretty much where he was going to end up. Most teams made every effort to conceal their true speed potential, so that the other teams wouldn't know what to plan. Qualification runs could rarely be depended on to reveal any secrets. Some ran hard and some didn't. Most all-out speed testing was done in secret, at airports back home. Each racer wanted to psych the other racers as much as possible. No one could ever be really sure how fast the other guy was.

The question of where a pilot might try to position himself in the race field was always a tough choice, especially in the later Thompson races, in which they paid prize money down to tenth place. Then it was a question of how hard to run for which place prize: whether to settle for fifth and win $1,000, or push harder for the $2,000 fourth place

money—and maybe blow your engine and not win anything. And always pilots prayed that the leading plane would try to save his engine and set as slow a pace as possible.

In 1937, race officials tried an idea to promote closer wing-to-wing racing by offering $100 to the leading plane in every odd numbered lap. In this way, they figured that the boys would put on a little more power to pick up those $100 checks. A leader for most of the race's twenty laps could conceivably win a good amount even if he dropped out on the last lap.

Well, it didn't work. In that 1937 Thompson, Steve Wittman led seventeen of the twenty laps, cruising at speeds up to 20 mph below his potential, and nobody seemed to want to push his engine enough to try to pass him. They were still playing for the big finishing money, rather than the $100 lap prizes. Then Steve had engine problems and had to drop back on lap eighteen. But whether someone would have come up to challenge him in the last few miles will never be known. The question of whether to go for it or to slow for it was the real meat of racing on a shoestring in the thirties.

Racing just for money

One less obvious attraction of Menasco power for a 1930s racing plane was the dozens of secondary races at the Nationals and in other air shows around the country each year for planes with small displacement engines. The prize money for these lesser races was nowhere near what it was for the Thompson, of course. But if a racer could win or place well in three or four of them, he could go home with some much needed cash for his season's racing program.

The most famous of these small-engine class races was the series of Louis Greve Trophy races, sponsored by the Cleveland Pneumatic Tool Company, that was limited to planes under 550 ci, running annually at the Nationals from 1934 through 1939. Total purses ran up to $25,000, and all the serious Menasco engine racers, both four- and six-cylinder sizes, went all out for this one.

Harold Neumann raced Benny Howard's B6S powered *Mike* racer at the 1934 Nationals. He could only manage fourth place in the Thompson, for a prize of $1,000. But he won an additional $1,715 by placing in the necessary three heat races to take the first Greve Trophy on points. He won more in the Greve than in the Thompson.

An even more remarkable performance was that of Lee Miles and the Miles & Atwood Special in the 1934 season. Since Miles had the smaller four-cylinder Menasco, he was eligible for the 375 ci races as well as the 550 cube events. Miles entered every race that he could, pushing his plane no harder than it took to beat any other planes that he felt he could beat. Result: Miles placed out of the money in the Thompson, but won an astonishing $4,835 in nine other events at the Nationals and around the country that year. This performance won him the NAA pylon racing points championship for 1934. A lot of the big boys with their 800 hp Pratt & Whitneys wished they were running a little Menasco that year.

Lee Miles won more than $4,800 in the 1934 season, by concentrating on small displacement class racing with his tiny four-cylinder Menasco racer. Weaver Collection

Chapter 7

Prewar racers: the small engine school

Rider R-1, License R51Y

Keith Rider was a master builder and prolific idea man in 1930s grassroots pylon racing. But unlike most of his contemporaries, he had no stomach for the risks of the sport, so he never had any desire to fly the planes he built. He was strictly a creator in Thompson Trophy history.

His first pure racing plane—built in an abandoned casket factory in Santa Monica, California—was never entered in a Thompson race. It was an unusual all-wood monoplane with a stock four-cylinder Menasco engine of 125 hp. In its first race, an 800 ci event at the 1930 National Air Races, an aileron came off, and the plane crashed to destruc-

Keith Rider's first Thompson racer, the Model R-1, with its first pilot, Ray Moore, featured an all-aluminum fuselage and the first use of a supercharged Menasco. Weaver Collection

tion. Pilot Maj. James Macready was fortunate to escape with minor injuries when the plane came down in a soft, marshy area. The experience gave Rider an early respect for structural strength.

The Rider Model R-1 was started a few weeks later to compete in the coming 1931 Nationals at Cleveland. It was one of a pair of similar ships, a small four-cylinder and this larger six-cylinder R-1, both financed by a group of San Francisco businessmen headed by Robert Clampett. The larger one was known as the *San Franciscan*. Ray Moore was engaged as pilot for the 1931 races.

The R-1 was unusual in having an all-aluminum fuselage. Keith Rider wanted to experiment with metal construction, to check its strength in relation to weight, as compared with the all-wood construction of his first racer in 1930. The fuselage had aluminum formers, stringers, and sheet covering. Everything was bolted or riveted together because of the lack of reliable inert-gas welding techniques in the early thirties.

As it turned out, the aluminum construction proved to be quite light. Rider used wood construction with plywood covering for the wings, so the plane was part wood and part aluminum. Yet the airframe without engine weighed only a little over 450 lb; this was with a wing span of 19 ft 4 in, length of 17 ft, and wing area of about 65 sq. ft. With engine, the empty weight was 942 lb, as registered at the 1931 Nationals. And gross weight, with 30 gal of fuel and 5 gal of oil, was about 1,300 lb. The R-1 was definitely a lightweight.

Rider tried hard to reduce air drag, too. The landing gear was designed to unlock and swing up and back into openings in the wings (by cranking) so that only the lower half of the wheels were exposed. Low-pressure donut-like Goodyear air wheels were used to absorb bumps and impacts, eliminating the need for and extra weight of landing gear springs of any kind. This was the simplest and lightest retractable gear that Rider could come up with, and it had the added advantage of the partially exposed wheels that allowed a belly landing with minimum damage in case the gear locked in the up position.

Unfortunately, any reduction in air drag afforded by the retractable landing gear was offset by the high fuselage skin friction caused by the hundreds of exposed rivet heads. Calculations show that the R-1 had a parasite area figure of about 1.6 sq. ft., more than that of some small racing planes with fixed landing gears. From this standpoint, aluminum construction was a mixed blessing. (Note, however, that Howard Hughes's state-of-the-art racing monoplane of 1935 introduced flush riveting, which took care of the problem of the extra drag of rivet heads.)

The engine used in the R-1 was Al Menasco's first supercharged six-cylinder creation, the model C6S, with 544 ci and developing a maximum of about 270 hp at 2800 rpm. But it never delivered anywhere near this kind of power in the early years. From correspondence with some of the people involved with the plane, I learned that the engine seemed to be plagued with severe detonation on available 87 octane pump fuel, as supercharge pressure built up above 2500 rpm or so—possibly caused by a too high compression ratio or possibly by uneven cooling of the cylinders. The plane owners were always fiddling with the cowl scoops and vents, hoping.

The R-1's early racing record was hardly indicative of its true potential. Ray Moore won or placed well in several small displacement class races in the 1931–1933 period. Then Rudy Kling bought the plane in late 1933, and put Roger Don Rae in the cockpit. He took third in the 1934 Thompson, at an average speed of 213.94 mph. But all this time, the pilots of the R-1 could not hit straightaway speeds above 240 mph at 2400 rpm or so and 35 in. manifold pressure. One time, the vibration from the detonation actually split a welded seam in the fuel tank.

Finally, Rudy Kling decided to completely rebuild the plane and engine for the 1936 season, to see if he couldn't get more of its potential performance on the newly available 95 octane commercial pump gas. Changes included new engine cowling, adjustable pitch prop, prop spinner, closed and streamlined cockpit canopy, an engine rebuild— and even a new light blue paint job and new name, *Suzy*.

The R-1 did go considerably faster after Kling's rebuild on the improved fuel. In July, at the Mile High Air Show at Denver, he set a new world 100 km. closed course speed record for Class B lightplanes at 228 mph. Then at the Nationals at Los Angeles in September, he was able to hit straightaway speeds of 260–265 mph during qualifying trials. Rudy throttled back in the Greve race because he knew there was no hope of catching Detroyat's Caudron. But he planned to go all out for the best possible placing in the lucrative Thompson. Then it all ended. Kling had to swerve to miss another plane when landing after the Greve, and the R-1 crashed and was demolished. Fortunately Kling came out with only scratches. But poor R-1 never really did show its true potential in any race at any time.

Miles & Atwood *Special*, License NR225Y

This plane did not have much impact on Thompson history—it started only one Thompson

The Miles & Atwood Special *was a tiny racer with a four-cylinder Menasco, designed for small displacement class racing* *and was not competitive in the unlimited Thompson.* Repla-Tech

race, in 1934, and didn't even finish that one. But the *Special* was a good example of a small class plane, designed for racing in the 375 ci and 550 ci class races, and worth our consideration.

Lee Miles and Leon Atwood were close friends and air race enthusiasts from youth, learning to fly in their teens. In early 1933, they had an opportunity to buy a small steel tube fuselage framework, plus a supply of extra steel tubing, wood stringers, fabric and dope, from a pair of Navy mechanics who had started to build a half-scale replica of a Boeing P-36 military pursuit. Miles and Atwood could buy the whole shebang for $500. The idea immediately occurred to them that it might form the base for a tiny pylon plane for 375 ci class racing, with a four-cylinder Menasco engine.

They were able to make a deal with Lawrence Brown, a custom plane builder in Los Angeles, to finish the design, stress testing and construction. And Al Menasco offered to sell them a prototype supercharged version of his C4 engine for a pretty decent price. The whole bill added up to about $7,500, so it was all systems go for a debut at the 1933 National Air Races coming up in July at Los Angeles.

The Miles & Atwood *Special* was a tiny thing: 16 ft. 8 inch wing span, 50 sq. ft. wing area, 20 gal fuel capacity, and 3 gal oil capacity, with an empty weight of only 742 lb. All involved were determined that

this should be one of the smallest and lightest full-size racing planes in the nation. They did it by eliminating as much steel fuselage framework as possible and by using wood wing structure with fabric covering all over except for the engine cowl. Brown even omitted landing gear fairings to save weight.

However, that last decision wasn't such a good idea as a study of the performance evolution of the plane will show. The original 1933 version, without landing gear fairing, was propped to deliver about 150 hp at 2300 rpm at full throttle, and the Shell Dash average that year was a mild 210.64 mph. Average pylon speeds were around 180 mph, which won some prize money—but the boys knew there was a lot more in the supercharged Menasco.

In 1934, the Miles & Atwood *Special* showed up at the Nationals with beautifully cowled landing gear, a prop spinner and the prop blades reset to give an all-out top speed of 240 mph at 2950 rpm, with the engine delivering somewhere between 180 and 200 hp. But the important thing was that the pylon averages were pushed up in the 200–210 mph range, making the plane competitive in the 550 ci class as well as in the 375 ci races. Lee Miles won an amazing total of $3,935 in prize money at the Nationals that year by entering all the races he could. He was the NAA points champion in 1934

83

Benny Howard's famouse Mike *racer used a small super-charged six-cylinder Menasco, won a lot of prize money, but was barely competitive in the fast Thompson races.* Weaver Collection

and was allowed to wear the "No. 1" on his plane the following year.

Nineteen thirty-four was the big year for the little Miles & Atwood *Special*. Competition was getting tougher all the time, and the little four-cylinder Menascos were rarely able to win a 550 ci event after 1934.

In 1936, Miles decided to invest in a new production C4S Menasco, with the forged steel connecting rods and hotter camshaft. This upped his output to 220–230 hp at 3400 rpm, and flight performance picked up proportionally. Miles qualified for the 1936 Nationals class events at 223 mph on a five-mile course. But it quickly became evident to him that he couldn't stay with the upgraded Neumann Folkerts and Chester *Jeep* in the 375 ci events. So he didn't press his engine and settled for third place in several events.

Incidentally, the highest straightaway speed recorded for the re-engined *Special* was 263.63 mph on a measured course at a 1937 air show. That represented an impressive 53 mph gain over the performance of the original 1933 design, still using the same basic 363 ci supercharged engine. The *Special* exemplified both aerodynamic and engine

refinement on a typical small class racing plane in the 1930s.

Unfortunately, pilot Lee Miles was fatally injured in a crash when qualifying for the 1937 Cleveland Nationals. Apparently a wing bracing wire snapped in a high-g turn, and both wings peeled away from the fuselage in a split second. The plane was demolished.

Howard DGA-4 *Mike,* License NR55Y

Benny Howard built two nearly identical light monoplane racers in 1932, *Ike* and *Mike,* with standard Menasco B6 engines rated for racing at 180 hp at 2500 rpm. His reasoning was simple: He felt that he could build two identical planes for 50 percent more cost in money and time than one. Also, two planes could earn twice as much prize money as one, and that second plane could be a backup in case of breakdown so that Howard wouldn't miss out altogether on prize money in the very limited number of air race dates available in the 1930s.

As it turned out, Howard decided to invest several hundred dollars more in a supercharger for *Mike* in early 1933, boosting its usable horsepower to 230–240 hp. After that, *Mike* became the prime choice for all the more lucrative races, with *Ike* being used for lesser races and stunting demonstrations—Benny even leased *Ike* for use in traveling air shows. Though *Ike* may have had a more colorful career, it was *Mike*, No. 38, that ran in all the Greve and Thompson races, contrary to what some of the history books say.

Furthermore, since Howard was a pilot for United Air Lines during this period, his contracts forbad him from flying in pylon races, so it was necessary to engage various pilots to fly both ships in most events. Harold Neumann was the usual choice for *Mike*, though there were others. But this is why you rarely see Benny Howard's name on a race entry list.

In size, *Mike* wasn't a midget like the Miles & Atwood plane. But the light Menasco B6 engine permitted empty weight to be held to 830 lb, with 20 ft. 1 in. of wing span, 69 sq. ft. of area and the usual 30 gal of fuel tankage. Construction was the customary welded steel tube framework for the fuselage and spruce spars with plywood ribs and wire bracing for the wings. Fabric covering was used all over except for the aluminum engine cowling. There was much external wire bracing, with rather simple metal cowling of the landing gear struts and wheels.

So we wouldn't expect *Mike* to be any whiz from an aerodynamic standpoint. Its equivalent parasite flat plate area was about 1.9 sq. ft., suggesting that Roy Minor's Shell Dash straightaway speed of 241.61 mph in 1933 represented just about all there was available with the original supercharged B6 engine. But this was enough to win plenty of prize money in the lower displacement classes, since so many of the other planes couldn't use the horsepower they had, for one reason or another. (For instance, *Mike* had no trouble beating the Rider R-1, although the latter had a retractable landing gear and 55 ci more displacement.)

In 1936 *Mike*'s top speed was jumped to 260 mph when Benny Howard rebuilt the Menasco with the new beef-up parts and the late long-duration camshaft, which upped the power to 280 hp or so on 95 octane. By this time, though, the whole design was obsolete, compared with the new Riders and Folkerts with retractable gears. Benny sold the plane after the 1936 season, and it was not raced again in the Nationals.

Brown B-2, License NR255Y

The beautiful Brown Model B-2 low wing monoplane of 1934 was a joint venture between San Francisco plane builder Lawrence Brown and engine builder Al Menasco. Brown had hopes of using the B-2 as a demonstration prototype for a light, inexpensive military pursuit plane, with a

The beautiful Lawrence Brown B-2 was the hit of the 1934 Nationals. Not as fast as it looked, the B-2 was one of the best-known American pylon racers of its day. Repla-Tech

small amount of armament, that could use a small air cooled engine like the Menasco to get a top speed over 220 mph. And Menasco wanted to enhance his image as an engine supplier with a refined version of the 544 ci C6S engine that he had first sold for racing in 1931. His 1934 version was lightened over 60 lbs with magnesium castings, and a higher supercharger gear ratio boosted the horse-power over 300. The result was a really neat racer.

Brown concentrated strongly on light weight. With a wing span of 19 ft. 3 in. and 60 sq. ft. of wing area, the airframe weight was held to just under 460 lb by use of welded steel tube fuselage construction and all-wood wing framework, with fabric covering all over. The engine cowl was light aluminum sheet, and double ribs instead of the usual plywood, reinforced the wing leading edges. With the extensive lightening of the engine, the total empty weight of 882 lb gave one of the better power-to-weight ratios at the time. Gross weight was about 1,300 lb with 30 gal of gas and 4 gal of oil.

The performance promise of the B-2 was exciting, to say the least. With some 310 hp on tap and an estimated parasite area of about 1.8 sq. ft., the top speed figured to be near 270 mph. According to Menasco factory charts on the original engine and prop combination, the 6.5 ft. Story metal propeller was pitched for a conservative engine speed of 2500–2600 rpm at full throttle, well below the power peak at 2800 rpm. Owner Lawrence Brown's published descriptions of the plane indicated that he intended to eventually experiment with lower pitched props that allowed engine speeds up to 2900 rpm on the straights—apparently to give better acceleration off the turns.

As it turned out, though, the new lightweight C6S Menasco engine had so many bugs that the B-2 racer never did show its true performance potential: detonation on the available 87 octane gas, uneven cylinder cooling, weakness of the aluminum connecting rods, problems with the engine's front thrust bearing—you name it. Pilot Roy Minor clocked a best two-way average of 243.15 mph in the 1934 Shell Speed Dash, which would have required only about seventy-five percent of the available power. He then went on to place second in the Thompson, hitting straightaway speeds of around 240 mph. With other lesser events, however, Minor had a good year and won a total of over $4,000 at the 1934 Nationals. The B-2 was hailed as one of the great new Thompson planes.

However, 1934 was its only year of glory. The Menasco engine didn't get any healthier with age, and there is evidence that serious fabric warpage at the wing leading edges hurt the plane's flight performance in later years. Winnings were way off in

1935 and the plane was sold to Marion McKeen. He pushed the speed as high as 255–260 mph in 1936 with 95 octane gas in winning fifth in the Thompson that year. The next year was a downer, though, with no major wins and little prize money.

Then came the 1938 season, and the B-2 showed up at Cleveland with extensive modifications that had the brotherhood really scratching their heads. McKeen had converted to a much larger, thicker cantilever wing—21 ft. span and 75 sq. ft. area—with a new retractable landing gear designed to fold up into the wing. But these changes added 450 lb to the weight, and fellow designers at the Nationals couldn't see how they would increase pylon speed much. They were also a little surprised that McKeen had managed to scrape up over $2,000 for a new Menasco B6S engine for such an old plane.

Then the truth came out: The changes were financed by a Hollywood film studio that needed footage of an exciting wheels-up belly landing of a typical racing plane for the movie *Tailspin* that was being made at the time. The word is that owner Marion McKeen built the cantilever wing especially heavy and stout to take the force of this stunt without major damage to the plane. And sure enough, as he came in from a test hop at Cleveland that year, the camera crew was waiting in an unmarked truck near the runway. As McKeen bellied in, the truck appeared out of nowhere and sped alongside the skidding plane, cameras rolling. When a tow truck arrived to carry the helpless B-2 back to a hanger, McKeen calmly dropped the landing gear and the plane was towed in on its wheels!

This little episode ended 1938's racing activities for this plane. For 1939 McKeen returned the venerable old B-2 to its original braced wing and external landing gear, and put Lee Williams in the cockpit. This time the end came only too suddenly: The new pilot, who apparently lacked experience, was fatally injured in a high-speed stall at the scattering pylon, just starting the 1939 Greve race. The plane was demolished.

Caudron C-460, Serial No. 6909

The famous French Caudron C-460 that ran away with the 1936 Greve and Thompson races at Los Angeles was certainly one of the most interesting and controversial planes that ever polished the pylons in American air racing. Not only did the plane make US race designs of the day seem like toys by comparison, but it set new standards for aerodynamic efficiency and engine performance that looked good for years after.

This plane was one of a series of eight or nine racers built by the Caudron company for the famous

The French Caudron C-460 was the most highly advanced lightplane in the world in the mid-1930s. It held many world *speed records and won the 1936 Thompson with ease.* Whittington

Deutsch de la Meurthe long distance air races for eight-liter engines (488 ci), which were run in France in the 1933–1936 period. Because these Deutsch planes had to compete in heats of 1,000 km, or 621 miles, using 300 hp or more, they were designed with fuel tankage for upwards of 100 gal; they weren't midgets by any means. The C-460 model had a 22.1 ft. span, 23.1 ft. length and 75 sq. ft. gross wing area, and weighed 1,280 lb empty. (The gross weight in Thompson trim was less than 1,700 lb as it carried only 30 gal of gas for the 150 miles.)

One of the more interesting features of the C-460 was the all-wood construction. Most fuselage and wing framework was boxed or solid wood pieces and the outer skin was plywood that was stressed to carry part of the loading, in modern monocoque fashion. Full cantilever construction was used and eliminated any external bracing. Liberal fillets, used at junctions of wings and fuselage, reduced interference drag and turbulence. Extensive wind tunnel tests were made to refine the aerodynamics as much as possible. In fact the plane's parasite drag area was only 1.3 sq. ft.—and the C_d factor, when figured on a basis of wing area, was an unprecedented 0.016.

The Caudron C-460 embodied several other specially innovative features. One, the oil cooler was constructed like a coarse cellular screen on the left and underside of the engine cowling so that air could circulate freely without causing any appreciable drag. Also there was a long diverging scoop under the engine to ram air into the updraft car-

buretor behind the supercharger, similar to some of the late Schneider seaplanes. This feature could have been worth easily 20–30 hp with wide open throttle at 300 mph.

Clever internal power systems operated the Ratier switch pitch propeller, engine starter and retractable landing gear by compressed air. An internal storage tank was charged by an external tank to around 100 psi to operate landing gear, and a small rubber bladder in the propeller hub was inflated by a hand pump to set the blades in low pitch. The starter was operated from the external tank. These operations were necessary before each flight, which made the systems a little impractical for a commercial aircraft. But for racing, they gave maximum reliability with minimum weight.

The controversy that surrounded the Caudron fifty years ago in Los Angeles and that has boiled among air race historians ever since involved two issues: Was the plane financed on a cost-no-object basis by the French government? and Was the 486 ci Renault engine used to win the 550 ci Greve class trophy replaced by a more powerful 9.5 liter (580 ci) version for the unlimited Thompson race?

My best research has revealed the following. Was the French government funding involved? Definitely *no*. The Caudron company was successfully engaged in building fast sport and military planes for a variety of buyers, and the Deutsch racers were considered good public relations and useful research tools. Keep in mind also that Avions Caudron was not a small one-building operation but was owned in the thirties by the huge Renault conglomerate. This meant solid financial backing. Further, the Caudron people won the equivalent of some $400,000 in prize money in the four Deutsch races, which would have defrayed some of the cost of the planes.

In regard to the proverbial 9.5 liter engine for the Thompson, it's known that the team brought two of the highly refined inverted six-cylinder engines to Los Angeles. But Caudron officials, their mechanics and Detroyat himself have always maintained that both engines were the 486 ci Deutsch size and that the original Greve engine was never changed.

Where the rub comes is that Detroyat's second lap in the Thompson race was timed at 301.0 mph. Allowing for time lost in the turns, this would have required a peak straightaway speed near 330 mph. And according to published wind tunnel coefficients on the C-460, its power requirement at that speed was at least 400 hp. It was no secret that the world 3 km speed record of 314 mph, set with a similar plane in 1934, was done with a 580 ci engine rated at 380 hp.

Does this mean that the big engine was used in the Thompson and that the French team was blowing smoke? Not necessarily. What most historians don't allow for is the extensive development of the original eight-liter Deutsch engine after its introduction in 1934 at 320 hp. Improvements included a vaned supercharger diffuser, compression ratios as high as 8.0:1 and blower gear ratios ranging from 7.6:1 to 9.3:1. Furthermore, the Caudron people gave Army Air Corps representatives a sample of their special Shell fuel at Los Angeles, and according to an Air Force technical report released later, it tested to an octane rating of about 110! This would certainly support the theory that the French were using a very high compression ratio and manifold pressures of perhaps well over 50 in. with the stiffer blower gears, especially considering the bother they took to handle this special fuel rather than just pump commercial 95 octane out of airport tanks.

Put it all together, add another 20–30 hp for ram boost from the special air scoop at 300+ mph and that "mild" 486 ci engine in No. 100 Caudron at Los Angeles could have easily kicked out as much as 400 or 410 hp at Detroyat's stated maximum race revs of 3250 rpm.

Admittedly, it would have made a lot of sense to use the larger 580 ci job in the unlimited Thompson race. With technical refinements, the larger engine could have delivered over 400 hp without exceeding 3000 rpm, which would have been a much more reliable situation in such an important race. But all I'm saying is that Detroyat could have hit the Thompson speeds with the small engine. We'll never really know now.

Folkerts SK-3, License R14899

Clayton Folkerts had impeccable credentials as a designer of high performance aircraft when he decided to get into the racing game in the mid-thirties. He was responsible for the famous series of Monocoupe sport cabin planes of the early 1930s that gave such excellent performance in relation to the horsepower of their small radial engines. Folkerts knew how to cut weight and air drag to the bone.

His racing model SK-3 was essentially a scale-up of an earlier SK-2 that had been completely stress-analyzed by a Douglas Aircraft engineer, Fred Knack. The smaller SK-2 carried a four-cylinder Menasco C4S engine of 230 hp. Folkerts merely scaled up these dimensions and sections to take the heavier, more powerful six-cylinder C6S-4 Menasco of 400 hp, so he felt there was no need to repeat the analysis for this plane. The SK-3 was commissioned by Rudy Kling, the operator of a large and successful automotive garage in Lemont, Illinois. Folkerts went right to Kling's garage, and the two of them built the plane in the summer of 1937. The main components were trucked to an airport in St. Louis, Missouri, for final assembly.

The SK-3 was basically a midwing cantilever monoplane with a very tiny narrow track landing gear that folded up, through the leverage of a simple swing arm mechanism operated by the pilot, into the lower part of the fuselage. It used the usual welded steel tube fuselage construction, with fabric covering, and wings with all-wood framework and plywood covering. Engine cowling, of course, was aluminum. There was considerably more fuel and oil tankage than in earlier race designs because of the additional engine power and the extended 200–300 mile distance of the later Thompson races: 61 gal of fuel and 11 gal of oil.

What was especially noteworthy about the SK-3 was its super light weight. With the big Menasco, it was said to weigh only 841 lb empty, which meant that the airframe alone weighed only about 300 pounds. Some historians have questioned this weight figure, but it was quoted by Folkerts himself. And the plane was a tiny thing: 16 ft. 5 in. wing span, 51 sq. ft. area, and 21 ft. 7 in. overall length. Obviously, designers Fred Knack and Clayton Folkerts made every pound of structure do a maximum amount of work; for example, using three main longerons instead of the usual four, using very thin wood stringers and making the fuel and oil tanks of thinner gauge aluminum. Strength was marginal—fuel tank leaks were frequent, and severe wing flutter was encountered on several of Folkerts's designs—

but nobody else could touch him on power-to-weight ratio.

The small size paid off in good performance, too. The parasite drag area of the SK-3 was about 1.3 sq. ft., equal to that of the clean Caudron C-460, so the SK-3 could make a top speed of 310 mph on only 350 hp. The special prototype Menasco engine supplied to Kling was cammed to produce a maximum of 400 hp at 3300 rpm on 70 in. manifold pressure, which would have propelled the plane to 325 mph. But factory charts show the special wood prop used in 1937 was pitched to peak at 310 mph at 2600 rpm and 55 in. pressure. Menasco preferred the more conservative power setting, wanting to make the best possible first impression on the aviation industry with his new C6S-4 design. Kling rarely exceeded 2200 rpm and 35 in. pressure on the pylons that first year. He was hoping to use the full 400 hp and get 15 mph more speed in the 1938 season.

Unfortunately, 1938 never came for the SK-3. Owner Rudy Kling was a relatively new pilot, with only 250 solo hours when he took over the plane. His experience on the pylons was very limited, and this was a hot ship that would tax the skill of any expert. Kling hired Roger Don Rae to do the first flight testing. When the handling seemed acceptable, Kling took over for the first time at the St. Louis races in May 1937, where he won the fifty-mile feature. Then he entered the Cleveland Nationals in September and swept both the Greve and Thompson races. He was gaining more confidence with every turn of a pylon—maybe too much. In the plane's third outing, at Miami in December, Kling pulled a high-speed stall in a pylon turn and crashed fatally. Historians have always speculated about the cause of the crash: Was it the old curse of the mid-wing layout, with its delicate handling in pylon turns?—or possibly structural failure?—or maybe pilot error?

Chester *Goon*, License NX93Y

Art Chester was another grassroots American pylon racer who believed that a small, light plane designed tightly around the late six-cylinder Menasco C6S-4 engine could beat the big radial engine planes. He had gone to work for Al Menasco in 1936 and was involved in much of the development of that engine. Chester knew it inside and out. And he knew its potential. His famous midwing *Goon* racer, introduced in 1938, was his concept of the ideal Menasco powered pylon racer.

Construction was the usual welded steel tube fuselage with wood formers and fabric and aluminum covering. Wings were spruce ribs and spars with plywood covering. The landing gear was retracted by a hydraulic accumulator charged by a hand-cranked pump, and the gear was designed to allow one wheel to partially deploy under centrifugal force in a turn, thus giving air turbulence under the plane which tended to protect against the

The Folkerts SK-3 that won the 1937 Thompson was a new breed of US race plane, built around the powerful six-cylinder

Menasco C6S-4 engine. The SK-3 was very light and capable of well over 300 mph. Weaver Collection

dreaded high-speed stall. That was the theory anyway. Another interesting feature was a one piece bolt-in wing that could be slipped in and out of the fuselage for transporting the plane on a trailer.

Vital statistics were: wing span, 18 ft. 6 in.; length, 21 ft. 4 in.; wing area, 76 sq. ft.; weight, 1,210 lb empty weight; and tankage, 82 gal for gas and 10 gal for oil.

The headaches that Chester had trying to adapt the French Ratier switch pitch propeller to his racer are well-known. He assumed that the French prop would be designed for European clockwise rotation when he ordered it, so he reversed the rotation of the engine while waiting for delivery. When the prop arrived, it was set for our counterclockwise rotation, and Chester had to thrash to switch the camshafts and blower gearing and timing back in time for the Nationals in September 1938. He never had a chance to flight test the plane before his arrival at Cleveland.

How these rotation changes were made has been a source of much speculation among race historians, for documentation is lacking. There are various ways engine rotation can be reversed, but the C6S-4 was a special case because it had separate intake and exhaust camshafts and the respective ports on each side of the heads were identical. However, the rotation changes were accomplished, and the engine ended up with the supercharger outlet piped around behind the engine through an S-shaped tube to a long induction pipe on the left side (just the opposite from the standard induction on the right). Chester's engine always had the fans scratching their heads because the exhaust ports were on the wrong side!

There's more to the story of this engine than reversing the rotation. Art made other radical changes to the original factory configuration. As chief development engineer for the Menasco company, with access to all kinds of machining and fabricating equipment, he was in an ideal position to do this sort of creative hot rodding.

For instance, Art used special pistons with thin automotive type rings to reduce friction to a minimum. To further reduce friction, he came up with a fully counterweighted crankshaft for the engine, by attaching calculated weights to a stock Menasco crank. Vibration is a factor in engine friction, and this must have been the smoothest running Menasco in captivity! Art gave a lot of thought to cooling also. Sodium cooled Pratt & Whitney valves, custom cylinder baffling and some special machining of cylinder

Art Chester's Goon *racer of 1938–1939 was an attempt to use all the latest small engine technology and was built around a modified Menasco C6S-4.*

The famous Schoenfeldt Firecracker *was one of the few Menasco engine racers with the potential to win the Thompson* *against the big radials. It could top 350 mph with a modified 500 hp engine.* Kemp

head fins were included in his modifications, according to an article in a contemporary aviation magazine.

But judging from the plane's performance, the bizarre conversion didn't gain all that much power for Art. The thin piston rings were apparently a constant source of oil loss, due to blow-by of combustion gases into the crankcase and subsequent loss through the breather vents. Some sources say that the front main bearing oil seal was also a problem. Throughout its career, the *Goon* was always streaked with oil, and Art could barely make 200 miles in any race on his 10 gal supply. In 1939, he tried to correct the problem by putting five (count 'em) breather vents on the crankcase to relieve the internal pressure. This helped some, but there was doubt if the engine could sustain even 75–80 percent power for more than a few minutes.

Result: Chester ran out of oil in the 1938 Greve and Thompson races and reportedly in the 1939 Thompson. But he did win the 1939 Greve at a healthy 263 mph average, after LeVier dropped out with magneto trouble and Art could throttle back a little.

What was the true performance potential of this beautiful plane? From Chester's fastest timed lap of 278.3 mph on a ten-mile course, we can estimate the max straightaway speed at about 310 mph, with the engine delivering probably 350 hp at 2600 rpm (the rated output in standard form with the hot camshafts). That would figure to a parasite area of 1.3 sq. ft., or a performance almost exactly equal to Kling's Folkerts SK-3.

Rider R-4, License NR261Y

Keith Rider, noted as an innovator in the field of race plane design, explored some special idea in building each of his planes. The R-4, built in the spring and summer of 1936, featured a combination of steel tubing and wood for the fuselage framework, and a combination of fabric and aluminum was used for the covering. The cantilever wing was all-wood, with plywood covering.

Rider was also more careful about aerodynamics on the R-4 than on some earlier designs. He used a new retractable landing gear arrangement where the wheels had a wide stance and folded inward to be entirely buried in the wing, rather than swinging back and being partially exposed. It's also noteworthy that the R-4 had elaborate contoured sheet aluminum wing fillets to reduce interference drag, unlike some of Rider's earlier planes. The overall

91

result was a calculated parasite drag area figure of 1.4 sq. ft., indicating above average aerodynamic refinement for a plane with an 18 ft. wing span and 68 sq. ft. area.

Weightwise, the R-4 was around 500 lb without the original Menasco B6S engine, which included 55 gal of fuel tankage and a 10 gal tank for oil, plus the crankup gear retracting mechanism. With engine, the empty weight was about 920 lb, and this was with substantial internal structure that could handle up to 10 or 12 cornering gs if necessary.

Rider built the R-4 on speculation—on a very tight budget—and he had to borrow the engine for its first demonstration outing at the 1936 Nationals at Los Angeles. Roger Don Rae was collared on a prize-splitting deal to do the flying. With some 280 hp available from the stock B6S, top speed was about 285 mph, and Don Rae was able to win the Shell Trophy race for 550 cube planes and place third in the Thompson. His total winnings of $4,275 were quite impressive for a new and unproven plane.

Wealthy Los Angeles sportsman Bill Schoenfeldt was attracted enough by the new R-4 to buy it a few weeks later without an engine. His idea was to install a larger and more powerful C6S-4 Menasco that was just being tested for introduction in Rudy Kling's new Folkerts. At that time, the new engine was pretty much untried, and Al Menasco was giving all his attention to the Kling installation, wanting to make a good first impression on the industry. But Al was willing to sell a similar prototype build-up to Schoenfeldt for the R-4. Bill, on the other hand, wanted to immediately modify his C6S-4 for an output way over the stock potential of 400 hp. His famous *Firecracker* racer went through many trials and tribulations in the next three years, but things finally came together fairly well in 1939.

The modifications were carried out largely by Ed Winfield, the Los Angeles race engine builder who was famous from Indianapolis to the powerboat circuits. He wasn't particularly sharp on aircraft engines, but he figured basic hop-up principles should apply to anything with cylinders, spark plugs and pistons. His changes to the Menasco were classic hot rod practice: reground camshafts with more valve lift and timing duration, special high-dome pistons with 6.3:1 compression ratio, a larger Stromberg carburetor with automatic boost enrichment and a set of Pratt & Whitney sodium cooled valves machined to fit the Menasco heads. Also, various fuel blends of methyl alcohol and toluene were tried to get some internal cooling effect with high knock resistance and decent volatility.

As it turned out, these super fuels conjured up by Schoenfeldt's racing friends were of questionable worth in extra power. For instance, due to the low BTU content of methanol, it's necessary to open up carburetor jetting radically. But somehow this simple principle seemed to get scrambled during initial experiments in 1938. When it wasn't done, the lean fuel-air mixtures caused cylinder temperatures to shoot up and limited the engine to under seventy-five percent power. In 1939, the race crew caught onto the need for richer jetting, and the engine performed better. But then the richer fuel-air mixtures greatly increased fuel consumption and required another 35 gal of fuel capacity in the tiny *Firecracker,* which opened up another can of worms.

Think about it a second. Think of the screwed-up weight balance of the R-4 resulting from the various modifications made after Schoenfeldt bought it. Replacing the original B6S engine with the C6S-4 added 130 lb in the nose. Originally, the race crew balanced this with 22 lb of lead in the tail. An entirely new wing was constructed after damage during landing after the 1938 Greve race. They used the NACA 23012 airfoil section, which had a better stability moment curve than had the original wing. But when the alcohol blend fuel required an additional 35 gal of tankage for the 1939 season, the only place there was room for this was behind the cockpit. The lead was removed, but the center of gravity was still out of whack. Furthermore the gross weight at takeoff had by then grown by some 450 lb to 1,950 lb, which meant a wing loading of 30 lb per sq. ft. with the original 68 sq. ft. of wing area. Pilot Tony LeVier must have had his hands full getting this beast off a wet, grassy field for the 1939 Thompson!

Admittedly, that Winfield modified Menasco did crank out some healthy horses. It was never test on a *dyno,* but pilot LeVier opened the throttle wide on one secret test flight and hit a corrected straightaway maximum of between 350 and 355 mph at 3500 rpm and 72 in. manifold pressure. This would have required well over 500 hp with the known parasite area of 1.4 sq. ft.

But there is no record that LeVier ever used all this power for even a few seconds on the pylons. To the contrary, he quoted his usual race cruising speed as 320 mph at 3200 rpm and 55 in. manifold pressure. And for that matter, he couldn't sustain this power level reliably until late in the plane's career, after the race crew rebuilt the magnetos and provided special air vents to cool them. The overheated magnetos had been causing misfiring on and off for two years, unknown to the crew. The *Firecracker* had just one race, the 1939 Thompson, when all the bugs were worked out and everything was clicking right. Then she was one fantastic race plane and very likely the fastest of all the prewar Menasco powered Thompson racers.

Chapter 8

Prewar racers: the big engine school

Laird LC-DW-300 *Solution*, **License NR 10538, and** *Super Solution*, **License NR 12048**

Matty Laird was another well-known builder of commercial high-performance sport planes who was attracted by the healthy Thompson purse in the initial 1930 race near his home factory in Chicago. The LC–DW–300 was his *Solution* to that particular performance problem. Unlike most of his contemporaries, Laird felt that a biplane was the answer for tight pylon turns. He built two nearly identical biplanes in 1930 and 1931: the *Solution* and the *Super Solution*. The *Solution* won the 1930 Thompson race with comparative ease, but by 1931, both planes were barely competitive, even in upgraded form. Nevertheless, both are of interest.

Construction was very typical for the day: welded steel tube fuselage framework and wood wing structure, with all-fabric covering except for

The Laird Solution *was the last biplane designed for the Thompson Trophy race. This 1931 modification used a Wright engine, new front cowling and heavily cowled landing gear.* Weaver Collection

engine cowling, cockpit area and so on. Both planes had 21 ft. upper wing span, 17 ft. 8 in. length, with 112 sq. ft. total wing area. And both used Pratt & Whitney Wasp Junior engines, though in different states of tune.

The major differences between the two planes was that the *Super Solution* of 1931 had a fully streamlined landing gear and cleaner engine cowling and cockpit shielding, plus extra fuel tankage and instrumentation to race in the cross country Bendix. The *Solution* had an empty weight of 1380 lb with 50 gal of fuel tankage; the *Super Solution* weighed about 200 lb more with the extra equipment.

The Wasp Junior engines were basically the same, but the one in the *Super Solution* had a higher compression ratio and blower gear ratio to get 535 hp at 2400 rpm, versus 470 hp at 2300 rpm for the *Solution* in 1930. Jimmy Doolittle experimented with a geared Wasp Junior engine in the 1931 *Super Solution*, hoping to get better propeller efficiency at lower blade tip speeds. But the geared down propeller generated proportionally more torque reaction on the tiny plane, and control became a problem during takeoff and certain flight maneuvers. Doolittle opted to go back to a direct drive engine rather than hassle the torque effects in tight wing-to-wing racing. (Jimmy was always a neat combination of prudence and daredeviltry!)

In performance, of course, the *Super Solution* was faster. Doolittle's Shell Dash average was 255.34 mph on 535 hp in 1931; the earlier *Solution* could hit about 240 mph on 470 hp. However, the original *Solution* was radically upgraded in 1931, with a 525 hp Wright Whirlwind engine, a cleaner engine cowling, landing gear cowling and better cockpit closure. The two planes were probably pretty close in performance and aerodynamic efficiency that year. I would estimate the parasite area of the original *Solution* at 3.9 sq. ft., with both planes probably close to 3.7 sq. ft. in 1931.

Laird's racers were the last biplanes seriously considered for the Thompson race. They were good in pylon turns, but their straightaway aerodynamics were just not competitive with those of the monoplanes.

Gee Bee Model Z, License NR77V

The Granville brothers of Springfield, Massachusetts, had been building fast one-and two-place sport planes for several years when they decided to build a special racer specifically to win the $7,500 first prize in the 1931 Thompson. They were confident enough of their design to form a corporation and sell shares to the townspeople to finance the venture. The Pratt & Whitney people were impressed enough with early plans to loan them the Wasp Junior engine out of the 1930 Thompson winner (with refinements) to help the project along.

The Model Z Gee Bee was essentially a first step in the Granvilles' evolving theory of the ideal fuselage shape as a teardrop. The Z was stubby, but nothing like the later Gee Bees. Wing span was 23 ft. 6 in., length 15 ft. 1 in., with a wing area of 75 sq. ft. The construction was typical of the day and featured welded steel tube fuselage framework, wood wing structure, with fabric and aluminum sheet covering. Rather elaborate wing fillets and landing gear fairings were hand-hammered out of thin sheet aluminum. And a minimum of external bracing wires was used, giving a fairly clean plane from an aerodynamic standpoint.

The weight of the plane was reasonable: 1,400 lb empty, with 103 gal of fuel tankage and 11 gal for oil.

The Model Z Gee Bee also included coil springs and shock absorbers to allow six inches of landing gear travel, which was not a bad idea with the 100 mph landing speed. There was also an interesting screw-and-jack mechanism to pretrim the elevators for possible stability problems. This was not needed, however.

With the Wasp Junior engine upgraded to 535 hp at 2400 rpm in 1931, the top speed of the new Model Z proved to be near 270 mph. It had a parasite drag area of 3.2 sq. ft. And the new plane didn't disappoint at the 1931 Nationals at Cleveland. Pilot Lowell Bayles won the Thompson with comparative ease, after Doolittle dropped out with a broken piston. And by entering the Z in several lesser events for planes under 1,000 ci, the Granvilles went home with total prize winnings of more than $10,000. They were able to pay their stockholders a 100 percent dividend!

Flushed with this kind of success, the Granvilles dreamed of even greater feats for the Model Z. Since the plane had proved capable of nearly 270 mph with a 535 hp Wasp Junior engine, it seemed reasonable to think about the possibility of fitting a larger Wasp of 650–700 hp and attacking the world land-plane speed record, which at that time was held by France at 278.4 mph. The Pratt & Whitney people, who had been so cooperative in supplying engines, were just as enthusiastic about the speed record project. They could see strong worldwide publicity for both companies, as well as a much needed dose of national pride in the aviation world. They even took the plane right to their factory in East Hartford, Connecticut, where they installed the Wasp engine with stronger mounts, plus the required larger cowling ring and a proper propeller. Everybody was gung-ho.

The speed flights were scheduled for early December 1931 over a 3 km course near Detroit, with official timing by the FAI. One thing the Granvilles hadn't planned on at first, though; FAI rules required existing world records to be exceeded by at least 8 kph, which meant that Bayles needed to turn a four-way average of at least 283.4 mph to establish a new record. This made the whole project a bit more marginal right from the start. On the first set of runs, one of the timing cameras malfunctioned, and the average couldn't be certified. The next four best runs averaged 281.75 mph, acceptable as the US national speed record, but not as the world record because of the 8 kph rule.

A few days later, after Pratt & Whitney technicians did some tuning of the engine, Bayles went up again for a last try. Entering the speed trap at what appeared to be over 300 mph, the plane suddenly went out of control, snap-rolled, shed a wing and crashed, fatally injuring Bayles. Reconstructing the accident, it appeared that the automotive type gas cap ahead of the cockpit came loose, crashed through the celluloid canopy and knocked Bayles unconscious. The plane was totally demolished—and the grim saga of Gee Bee devastation had begun.

Gee Bee Model R-1, License NR 2100

The Gee Bee R-1 of 1932 was probably the most famous racing plane of all time, if for no other reason than its unique bumblebee shape. It was the ultimate expression of the favorite Granville design theme of the teardrop-shaped fuselage. But at the same time, its short length and the large projected side area near the center of gravity of the plane—without very large tail surface areas to compensate—inevitably meant marginal longitudinal, directional and torque stability. It's a great credit to the intrepid race pilots of that day that anyone could actually take off, fly and land that R-1 without incident. It didn't happen very many times.

The Gee Bee was a very soundly constructed ship. The structure was stress-analyzed by a degreed engineer, Howell Miller. At the Granvilles' insistence, he stressed the entire plane for 12 gs positive, which was the standard for military pursuit type aircraft in that day. They didn't want the embarrassing wing flutter or structural failure that was seen on so many low-budget experimental planes in the racing sport. (However, it's unlikely that the R-1 ever reached even half these loadings in any kind of maneuver, considering its erratic handling characteristics.)

Construction was similar to that of the earlier Model Z, except the R-1 wing was plywood covered, rather than fabric, to eliminate any stretching or warping that might reduce the lifting efficiency. It's also interesting that the landing wheels were fitted

The Gee Bee Model Z of 1931 was the first example of the Granvilles' teardrop streamlining. It was much more stable and airworthy than later designs. Weaver Collection

The famous Gee Bee R-1 and R-2 designs represented the ultimate expression of the Granville teardrop theory. However, the *short length and small projected side area behind the center of gravity made them extremely unstable.* Weaver Collection

with a new style oleo-pneumatic strut that combined air cushioning with oil damping and had nearly six inches of travel. They were made by the Cleveland Pneumatic Tool Company, the company that was to later sponsor the famous Greve Trophy races. The plane also had a complete set of instruments in case of later long distance races. (A twin plane, the R-2, was built with a smaller engine and increased fuel tankage, specifically to compete in the Bendix.)

The R-1 was considerably larger than the earlier Z: wing span, 25 ft.; length, 17 ft. 9 in.; wing area, 100 sq. ft., empty weight, 1,840 lb; with 160 gal of fuel tankage and 11 gal for oil. The Wasp engine was again loaned by Pratt & Whitney, and this one was hopped up with 12:1 supercharger gears to develop 770 hp at 2350 rpm with full throttle. (Special fuel with added lead and rich carburetion were needed to control detonation.)

The R-1 was a fairly clean plane from an aerodynamic standpoint. Its parasite drag area figure appeared to be very near that of the Model Z, 3.2 sq. ft., despite the much larger frontal area. The teardrop fuselage theory was at least sound from an aerodynamic standpoint, if not from a practical one.

We don't need to belabor the issue of the unstable flying characteristics of the R-1. It didn't do anything right, and a lesser pilot than Jimmy Doolittle himself might not have been able to win a pylon race with the thing. Only the plane's superior speed, and the fact that Doolittle could fly wide, flat, easy pylon turns, made winning possible. The plane did seem to be reasonably stable on top speed straightaway runs. Doolittle averaged 296.29 mph on his Shell Dashes and said that he had left a bit of power for owner Russell Boardman to put the record above 300 mph later on. As it turned out, Boardman had the R-1 fitted with a larger 850 hp Pratt & Whitney Hornet engine in 1933, along with additional fuel tankage, to contest the Bendix race, which was being run from New York to Los Angeles that year. His idea was to test plane and engine in the Bendix race, then try for the world record with the more powerful Hornet. His average speed from New York to the first fuel stop in Indianapolis was a record 275 mph.

But disaster struck on the takeoff from Indianapolis with a full fuel load and almost 4,000 lb gross weight. Boardman apparently pulled the plane into the air before sufficient speed was built up for crisp response to the control surfaces, and the huge torque reaction of the big Hornet engine just flipped the plane over. Boardman died later of his injuries, and the plane was badly damaged.

To complete the story, the remains of the R-1 were combined with the remains of the R-2, after a landing crash. The hybrid R-1/R-2 then crashed on its first takeoff in 1935, killing pilot Cecil Allen.

Wedell-Williams Model 44, License NR278V, NR536V, NR 61Y

With the long-term backing of Louisiana millionaire Harry Williams, Jim Wedell undoubtedly had access to the best brains, manual skills and physical facilities of anyone in the prewar US racing sport. And yet he was said to lay out his designs with chalk marks on a hangar floor. He was the epitome of the seat-of-the-pants designer, engineer and builder. Blueprints were usually made after a plane was completed!

His model 44—"hot as a .44 and twice as fast"— was one of a series of three nearly identical planes built in the 1930–1932 period to race in the big US pylon and long distance events. He referred to them all as Model 44s, in keeping with his deep interest in handguns. And there were indeed only minor differences in cowling, bracing, instrumentation and

so on. The second plane, No. 92, NR536V, was retained by the Wedell-Williams Corporation and flown by various pilots in the next few years. The third plane was built for Roscoe Turner and funded by the Gilmore Oil Company.

Some confusion about this last ship should be cleared up for the record. The first version of this model 44 series for Turner, license NR54Y, came apart in the air on an early test flight, due to violent wing flutter, forcing Wedell to bail out and abandon the ship to destruction. The blueprints were then modified by Dr. Howard Barlow to beef up the design, and Jim Wedell built Turner another racer to these specifications, license NR61Y, that was delivered in the summer of 1932. It was the only one of the three ships that could be considered professionally engineered.

There is no reliable record of what these beef-up changes cost in extra weight. The empty weight usually quoted for the original Wedell model 44s was 1,510 lbs with Pratt & Whitney Wasp Junior engines. This was with conventional steel tube fuselage construction with fabric and aluminum covering, and wood wing structure with plywood covering plus doped fabric coating. Each plane had approximately 180 gal of fuel tankage, 14 gal for oil, a wing span of 26 ft. 2 in., length of 23 ft. 4 in. and total wing area of 108 sq. ft. The engine made up

Jimmy Wedell had no technical training, but his Model 44 was one of the most successful early radial engine pylon racers. Weaver Collection

nearly half the weight of the complete plane, so it's obvious that there was no material in those original 44s that wasn't definitely needed.

We might estimate that the Turner version, with the Barlow modifications, weighed perhaps 100 lb more, or 1,600 lbs empty. (And of course, it eventually weighed near 2,000 lb, with the big Hornet engine installed in 1934.)

It was interesting to compare the relative speed performance of the three ships, since they were so similar in external cowling, bracing, and so on. We might think that there would be little difference between them, given equal engines. But such did not seem to be the case. Compare the maximum Shell Dash speeds for each plane with Wasp Junior and Wasp engines:

Plane	Shell Dash speeds (mph)	
	Wasp Junior	Wasp
No. 44	278.92	306.21
No. 92	272.06	—
Wedell-Turner	266.67	289.90

The explanation for these considerable variations in speed with seemingly identical planes probably lay in the amount of engine horsepower used. Jim Wedell's edge in speed might have been because his engines had more special goodies: higher compression and high ratio blower gears—or maybe it was because he could tune his engines better, or maybe he just pushed them harder. But these discrepancies were a hard pill for Turner to swallow, as it was common knowledge that his failures to match Wedell's speeds with similar equipment were always a source of bitter frustration to him.

Turner's switch to the Pratt & Whitney Hornet engine in 1934 was a direct response to Jim Wedell's world record of 304.98 mph with a Wasp engine the year before. Turner expected to go well over 300 mph with the Hornet. But it didn't turn out that way at all. His Shell Dash average went up only 5 mph, from 289.90 mph to 295.44. The reason is obvious: The increased diameter of the Hornet engine (4 in.) required a much larger cowl, with more frontal area, and the increase in air drag just about offset the additional 100–150 hp. The ultimate exercise in aerodynamic futility. Roscoe was really chewing nails with his Wedell after that.

This information leads to another general conclusion about the aerodynamic efficiency of this Model 44 Wedell design: For some reason not clearly evident, the parasite drag area was unusually low for a design of this size and configuration. Using fairly certain horsepower values for the No. 44, these areas figure out to around 2.9 sq. ft. for the Wasp Junior installation, and maybe 3.1 sq. ft. for

the Wasp. This was cleaner than for either the Gee Bee Model Z or R-1 design.

The three planes met different fates. Jim Wedell was killed in June 1934 in a commercial flying accident, and No. 44 broke apart a few months later in a tight pylon turn in the 1934 Thompson, with Doug Davis piloting. No. 92 was eventually sold and was converted, unsuccessfully, to a Bendix racer in the late 1930s. Turner's plane survived and raced effectively the whole decade and is today being restored to its former glory.

Rider R-3, License NR 14215

Keith Rider's famous R-3 of 1934 was his attempt to combine small plane aerodynamics with the power of a large radial engine for a variety of racing applications. The original design was laid down primarily to contest the $75,000 MacRobertson London-to-Melbourne race, scheduled for the summer of 1934. Wealthy Edith Boydston Clark of Santa Monica financed the R-3, after Rider had convinced her that the project would be a prudent investment. When the plane, which had a huge fuel tankage for 225 gal, wasn't finished in time, it seemed like a natural to run the Bendix cross country races and to try for various city-to-city records, as well as to compete in major pylon events with less fuel load. The R-3 eventually became one of the most familiar US speed planes of the decade.

Like other Keith Rider racers, the R-3 featured an unusual scrambling of construction methods. This time the fuselage was all-aluminum, aluminum stringers and formers, with sheet aluminum covering riveted on. It was Rider's first attempt to integrate the outer skin as part of the structure, in true monocoque fashion. The wings, however, were the usual spruce spars with plywood ribs and covering, plus an outer coating of fabric for smoothness. The retractable landing gear was the early Rider arrangement, with wheels swinging back up into the wing.

The ship had a wing span of 26 ft. 3 in., length of 23 ft. 4 in., and wing area of 122 sq. ft. The original empty weight with a Pratt & Whitney Wasp Junior engine was around 1,800 lb, which was about average for a plane of this size and configuration. Apparently, the attempted monocoque construction didn't save any appreciable weight.

The really serious racing life of the R-3 started in 1936, when Hal Marcoux and Douglas Aircraft engineer Jack Bromberg bought the plane from Rider and did a complete rebuild: partial reskinning, additional beefing, moving the oil tank back for better balance, fuel tank repair and modifying the wing leading edge for better stall characteristics. The engine had already been upgraded to a Pratt & Whitney Wasp by that time, with a very tight cowl that had individual humps for each cylinder rocker cover, to minimize any increase in frontal area from the larger engine diameter.

We can judge the aerodynamic efficiency of this 1936 configuration from pilot Earl Ortman's report of a top speed of 312 mph at an engine speed of 2425 rpm and manifold pressure of 49 in. For that particular type SD Wasp engine, this rpm and pressure should have given about 850 hp and a parasite drag area at about 3.4 sq. ft., which would be only average in aerodynamic efficiency for a plane of this size.

A major upgrade to the plane came in 1937 when Pratt & Whitney leased the Marcoux-Bromberg team a prototype fourteen-cylinder Twin Wasp Junior R-1535 engine, with its one-hour power rating boosted to 1,000 hp at 2675 rpm on 95 octane fuel. The extra power required fuel tankage to be increased to 240 gal for competitive cross country racing, and empty weight increased to 2,240 lbs. The smaller diameter of the Junior engine, though, permitted a complete redesign of the cowling, which improved the aerodynamics of the R-3 by 10–15 percent. Engineer Jack Bromberg calculated the potential top speed with the new engine at 360 mph. (Actual race performance, though, would put it closer to 340 mph.)

The racing record of Ortman and the R-3 and the new twin row engine was spotty, to say the least. He won only one major race in three seasons; that was a split second victory over Roscoe Turner's *Meteor* in a 150 mile race at Oakland, California, in May 1938. Ortman won a number of seconds and thirds in Bendix and Thompson races, but victories eluded him. He was not an aggressive race pilot, preferring to baby his engine and finish high in the prize money rather than to push all out to win. He did this time and again. The Rider R-3 in the hands of another pilot might have had an entirely different race record.

Howard DGA-6 *Mr. Mulligan*, License NR273Y

Benny Howard's *Mulligan* racer was a complete departure from any large radial engine design that had been tried. Essentially it was a Monocoupe design scaled up to take a Pratt & Whitney Wasp engine, with four seats and a humongous 300 gallon fuel capacity. Howard had long been impressed with the performance of Clayton Folkerts's high-wing cabin monoplane, and he figured that a similar design with much more power and minimum possible weight might be competitive in both the Bendix cross country and Thompson pylon races.

His idea was a cabin plane that would permit a team of pilots, using bottled oxygen, to fly the Bendix at very high altitudes, where the plane would be above the weather and could streak along in the thin air at high speed with minimum fuel consumption. His plan was to fly the 2,043 miles from Bur-

Keith Rider's Model R-3 was originally designed for the MacRobertson race to Australia, but ended up in long distance and pylon racing in United States. Weaver Collection

bank to Cleveland nonstop at over 250 mph on 300 gal of fuel, and still have at least 275 mph available at low level when stripped down for the Thompson.

Mulligan was built on a shoestring and a used fifty-dollar Wasp engine in a shutdown aircaft plant in Kansas City, which was a convenient layover point for Howard on his United Airlines flights. He was able to hire engineer Gordon Israel and builder Eddie Fisher for the design and construction, and Howard was able to spend many evenings and weekends on the project at the central Kansas City location. The job went forward quickly, especially because the construction was very conventional welded steel tube for the fuselage framework, with fabric and aluminum covering, and all-wood wings with plywood covering. The fairing for external wing braces and the landing gear were hand-hammered aluminum sheet, done by specialists in Ohio.

Everything was built as small and light as feasible for a cabin plane with 300 gal of fuel tankage. The final design had a wing span of 31 ft. 8 in., length of 25 ft. 1 in., gross wing area of 151 sq. ft. and empty weight with Wasp engine of about 2,600 lb. *Mulligan* was, indeed, a grown-up Monocoupe.

When the Pratt & Whitney people got wind of the radical new high-altitude racer, they offered to loan a fresh Wasp engine with special 13.85:1 super-charger gears, which gave a solid 500 hp at 2200 rpm up to 11,000 ft. altitude on 87 octane. This was the maximum recommended sustained rpm for cross country racing. The speed of the plane under these conditions was calculated to be 283 mph, using reported wind tunnel drag figures, with a range of about 1,750 miles, allowing for takeoff and landing. By cutting the engine to seventy-five percent power, the range could be extended to 2,550 miles at around 255 mph.

Howard's whole program made *Mulligan* look very promising for the Bendix, figuring a nonstop flight from Burbank to Cleveland at 260–270 mph. But Howard's calculations were badly flawed in regard to pylon racing near sea level. For one thing, he figured on using 100 octane fuel. This was still in the laboratory stage when *Mulligan* was designed in 1933, and where Howard got the idea that the magic juice would be available to him commercially by 1934 or 1935 has eluded my best research. It didn't become generally available for another five years. Benny also overestimated engine power capacity at sea level with the stiff 13.85:1 blower gears, which were very inefficient at low levels. He was planning on over 800 hp from the Wasp engine at sea level on 100 octane; he ended up with Pratt & Whitney engineers recommending a maximum of 500 hp at 2200

Benny Howard's Mr. Mulligan *was an attempt to combine high-altitude long-distance racing with competitive low-level pylon performance.* Fraites Collection

100

rpm on 34 in. manifold pressure on the available 87 octane.

Imagine what this rude awakening did to Howard's expectations for pylon performance. Instead of producing a projected top speed over 280 mph, *Mulligan* was actually safe to about 250 mph at low levels on commercial avgas, though Benny never commented on this in later published accounts of the plane's development.

How did theory work in practice? For the 1935 Bendix race, Howard got a rare release from his commercial airline employers to fly *Mr. Mulligan*, with Gordon Israel as copilot. They decided to go up to 26,000 ft, above bad weather, and fly on reduced power at 260 mph or so. When word came on the radio of fog at Cleveland, they decided at the last minute to stop for fuel at Kansas City, in case they couldn't land at the finish line. Going on, they did finish at Cleveland, with a winning average of 238.7 mph. But the fuel stop almost beat them. Roscoe Turner was only 23 seconds behind in his Hornet engine Wedell. One contributing factor was that they inadvertently left the flaps down after the takeoff from Kansas City, and did not realize it until the approach to Cleveland. This had to reduce the average speed some on that last leg.

Harold Neumann was called on to fly *Mulligan* in the 1935 Thompson. He used his qualifying laps to experiment to see how much power he could pull on a doped 87 octane fuel. He ran up to 40–45 in. manifold pressure and burned a piston as he was completing the run. It was an all-night thrash to get the Wasp ready to race the next day. Cutting back to 480 hp for the race, Neumann could only hope that Turner would burn up his Hornet, which was far in the lead. He did just that, and Neumann won at a lazy 220.19 mph.

So Benny Howard's concept of a big Monocoupe that could double for both long distance and pylon racing worked for him, but whether it was really a sound theory is questionable. The idea of a cabin plane for a team of pilots to race long distances nonstop at high altitude was certainly a good one. But trying to race a big cabin plane on the pylons at low levels . . . well, his 1935 Thompson win was just sheer luck.

The following year Benny, with his wife as copilot, ran the East-to-West Bendix. Somewhere over New Mexico, a propeller blade flew off. Benny had to make a forced landing in the desert. He and his wife were injured, and the plane was pretty much demolished.

Laird-Turner LTR-14 *Meteor*, License R263Y

Roscoe Turner's famous silver *Meteor* No. 29 definitely had the last word in prewar American pylon air racing: That much horsepower could beat aerodynamic refinement if given half a chance!

And yes, the general layout of the plane—midwing cantilever monoplane, fixed cantilever landing gear, fourteen-cylinder Twin Wasp engine—was all Turner's idea. He had been so frustrated by the mediocre performance of his "1,000 hp" Hornet engine Wedell that he was willing to throw all his resources into a last ditch effort to put up the most powerful US racing plane of all time. The Pratt & Whitney Twin Wasp was the strongest aircraft engine available in early 1936, when the plane was conceived. Roscoe thought that he could wangle one out of the company, though it would require a special release from military development contracts. He knew the rest would cost at least $50,000, even allowing for some free help. He was ready and willing to mortgage everything he had to make it fly. Which he did. And it flew—and won.

Turner got the services of practically the whole Department of Aeronautics at the University of Minnesota to prepare the design and blueprints for his plane. The thing was well engineered if nothing else. And the Pratt & Whitney people did loan him the engine. But from there on, the tribulations Roscoe went through in getting that plane built and ready to fly read almost like a comic opera.

First, the plans went to builder Lawrence Brown in Los Angeles, with instructions to go full speed ahead. When Turner's crew chief, Don Young, visited the Brown shops a few weeks later, he found to his horror that Brown had beefed up the fuselage structure on his own, feeling that the blueprints didn't look right for a 1,200 hp engine—meanwhile adding some 800 lb to the projected weight.

It didn't take Young long to haul the half-built hulk out of the Brown shops and across town to the diggings of Keith Rider, who was sure that he could take care of the remainder of the build-up. A few more weeks passed. Then Young found much the same thing again: Rider was conferring with engineer friends at Douglas Aircraft about how they might make the *Meteor* better and stronger and faster. All the while, nothing very constructive had been done on the airframe.

This time, Young stuffed the whole bundle of parts and assemblies into a railroad boxcar and shipped them to Turner's last hope, good old Matty Laird in Chicago. This time the job did get done. Laird stuck with the original plans as much as possible, though by now they had to increase the wing span by three feet to get enough wing to lift the extra weight. But some weight was taken out by using cable type controls rather than aluminum tubes and rods, fabric covering on the rear of the fuselage, all-wood wing construction and so on. The fixed landing gear also saved considerable weight, but it cost in aerodynamics. The final empty weight came in at 3,300 lb, with 25 ft. 4 in. of wing span, 95 sq. ft. of area, and 215 gal of fuel tankage. The modest fuel tankage for a 1,200 hp engine reflected Turner's plans not to race the *Meteor* cross country in the Bendix; he only needed fuel for 300 miles.)

The Pratt & Whitney people supplied Turner with a military protype engine for the *Meteor*, a Model B R-1830 Twin Wasp, with one-hour rating on 95 octane of 1,200 hp at 2650 rpm and 47 in. manifold pressure. There is no evidence that he used all this power until 100 octane gas became available in 1938. This would account for some of the plane's improved performance in the later races.

Keep in mind also that the *Meteor*'s aerodynamics were improved perhaps ten percent between the 1937 and 1938 seasons. Don Young replaced the large 10 in. oil cooler under the fuselage with two smaller cores inside the fuselage on the right side, fed by two small air scoops. Also they called on aluminum man John Hill, of Cincinnati, for the beautiful set of wheel pants seen on the late version of the *Meteor*. I estimate the parasite area of the plane in this final form at about 3.6 sq. ft.

The net effect of the improvement in aerodynamics and power was to increase the plane's apparent top speed from about 310 mph in 1937 to somewhere around 350 mph in 1938–1939. Turner always claimed a top speed of 380 mph for the *Meteor*. But his fastest timed lap of 299 mph on a ten-mile course would require a peak straightaway speed of less than 340 mph. Perhaps the truth was somewhere between the documented performance and the proud claims. Anyway, *Meteor* was certainly the fastest of the prewar Thompson racers.

Roscoe Turner's famous Laird Meteor *was the most powerful of the prewar Thompson designs.* Weaver Collection

Chapter 9

Prewar Thompson Trophy races

The 1930 Thompson Trophy race

The first Thompson Trophy race in September 1930 was part of the National Air Race program at the Curtiss-Reynolds Airport, just south of Chicago. It was the only Thompson race in which the planes were flagged off at intervals, as had been customary in most of the world's great air races. It was also the only Thompson in which the competing planes were not required to fly a qualifying flight to prove performance before the race. It was a free-for-all contest open to any plane approved by the NAA contest committee and with DOC licensing.

Those seven starters in the first Thompson race included the much publicized Curtiss XF6C-6 Hawk fighter that had been modified by Marine Capt. Arthur Page and Navy technicians into a pure

Speed Holman won first Thompson Trophy race in 1930 with a clean Laird Solution *biplane, the last biplane design aimed at the Thompson.* Weaver Collection

racing plane. The plane had a top speed near 250 mph and was expected to just run away from the other ships.

Speed Holman entered at the last minute in the hastily prepared Laird *Solution* biplane; he left the factory in Chicago only forty minutes before race time, pulling up to the starting line as the others were taking their places. Two nearly identical Travel-Air R racers were entered, powered by 400 hp Wright engines—one belonging to Shell Oil, flown by Jim Haizlip, and the other representing Texaco, with Frank Hawks at the controls. Errett Williams was entered in an early version of the Wedell-Williams Model 44 racer, with an uncowled 300 hp Wright engine. Benny Howard flew his little 90 hp Gypsy engine *Pete* for what prize money he could pick up, and Paul Adams tried a commercial Travel-Air Speedwing sport biplane.

As everyone expected, Capt. Page in the Curtiss racer ran away from the field, starting to lap slower planes from his third lap on. The best race was between Holman in the Laird biplane and Haizlip in the Shell R. Frank Hawks's Texaco TravelAir R, which might have been in this battle, began dropping back almost from the start with a faltering engine—caused by what later proved to be a restriction in the fuel supply circuit. He dropped out on his third lap. Williams dropped out on his eighth lap with fouled spark plugs. Meanwhile Holman and

Haizlip continued to battle it out wing-to-wing as the race went on, both with lap speeds very close to 200 mph—but both miles behind the speeding Curtiss racer of Page.

Then tragedy struck as Capt. Page rounded the home pylon finishing his seventeenth lap. The plane just suddenly rolled over and crashed into the ground, throwing up a cloud of dust 50 ft high. Later investigation indicated that Page was overcome by carbon monoxide fumes in the tight cockpit and lost consciousness. From then on, it was strictly a race between Holman and Haizlip. Holman had a small margin in straightaway speed and won at an average of 201.9 mph, compared with 199.8 mph for Haizlip. Howard was fourth and Adams fifth.

Recalling that first Thompson race many years later, Jim Haizlip noted that his TravelAir R might have given Holman's Laird a tougher battle but for his fuel. Holman used an early blend of leaded gasoline supplied by Standard Oil, who also happened to co-own the Ethyl Corporation that made the patented lead additive. The Shell people, who owned Haizlip's plane, didn't want to use their competitor's ethyl, so they loaded his tank with a mixture of straight run gasoline and slow burning toluol, which had a smiliar octane rating. But all it did for Haizlip was to lose him some 100 rpm and 10 mph of speed on the straightaways. He always felt that the toluol cost him the race, that he could have stayed

A highly modified Curtiss Hawk fighter was the fastest plane in the 1930 Thompson, but the pilot, overcome by carbon monoxide fumes, crashed fatally. Weaver Collection

with Holman with leaded gas. We know today that just a 10–15 degree advance in the spark timing would have gained him back the lost rpm. But that's modern combustion technology. They knew nothing about such things in 1930.

From the standpoint of the spectators, though, that first Thompson race was disappointingly unexciting. With a course length of five miles, with ten-second intervals between starts and with seven planes starting, the first starter was almost in sight around the course before the last one took off. So the spectators were thoroughly confused as to which plane was ahead, which planes were racing for second and third and so on. It was mostly just a parade of fast planes making a lot of noise. These conditions were accepted in the more formal, military dominated Pulitzer and Schneider races of the twenties. But the savvy Thompson promoters quickly saw there was no future for this new form of amateur pylon racing unless the spectators could identify closely with individual planes and pilots and follow their progress in a race.

The infamous racehorse start and the wild scramble around the first pylon were the gimmick that took care of all this in later years. It was a bold new idea in the early thirties credited to NAR promoter Cliff Henderson, and was inaugurated at the 1931 races in Cleveland. It literally saved the sport.

The 1931 Thompson Trophy race

This was the first of the Thompson Trophy series at the new Cleveland airport. They set up a ten-mile diamond shaped course, and the race ran for ten laps from a racehorse start, with planes lined up on the ground. This proved to be the feature that really made these races exciting for the spectator. The race clock was started when the first plane crossed the starting line in flight, after rounding the scattering pylon—not when they were flagged off on the ground.

Prerace qualifying runs were exciting straightaway speed dashes in front of the main grandstand, with a minimum two-way average of 175 mph required. But since the sponsoring Shell Oil Company posted no prize money for these dashes and since there was so much ballyhoo in the press and on the public-address system about some planes beating the existing world landplane speed record of 278 mph, some pilots chose to prove their speed from previous closed course races or even from ATC certified top speeds for the commercial planes. It was this, or subject themselves to a lot of public embarrassment by running 50 or 75 mph under the world record. As a result, the Shell Dashes drew relatively little activity in 1931.

The early timed speeds indicated that the tightest competition would be between Lowell Bayles in the stubby Gee Bee Z and Jimmy Doolittle flying a new Laird *Super Solution* biplane, both using nearly identical modified Pratt & Whitney Wasp Junior engines. This latter plane was owned by a group of Cleveland businessmen, and they hired Doolittle to tune it up and get the bugs out prior to the Thompson. (Doolittle had left the Army in 1930 and was

Two nearly identical TravelAir R racers were entered in the 1930 Thompson. Frank Hawks's No. 13 was forced down because of a restricted fuel supply. Weaver Collection

Lowell Bayles won the 1931 Thompson with ease in a stubby Gee Bee Model Z. It could hit 270 mph with its 535 hp Wasp Junior. Paramount

Jimmy Doolittle averaged 228 mph in a new Laird Super Solution *biplane in the 1931 Thompson, until a burned piston forced him out.* Weaver Collection

working for Shell Oil at the time.) Dale Jackson was entered in last year's winning Laird *Solution*, now with a stronger 525 hp Wright engine and some extra streamlining, and Robert Hall was flying a Gee Bee Model Y commercial sport plane with 450 hp Wasp Junior. Jim Wedell was entered in his first Thompson, flying his famous No. 44 with stock 450 hp Wasp Junior. Benny Howard was back in his little 90 hp *Pete* and Ira Eaker and William Ong flew fast commercial planes.

At the starter's flag, Doolittle was away and into the air first, pulling out as much as two miles ahead of Bayles on the first lap. But his engine began trailing smoke almost immediately, from what later proved to be a disintegrating piston. His speed dropped off some, and Bayles passed him on the third lap. But Doolittle held on doggedly, hoping to finish the race. Meanwhile, what looked like a tight race between Wedell and Dale Jackson ended early when Jackson clipped a tree top and bent a propeller blade. The vibration forced him to throttle back. About lap six Jim Wedell nosed the No. 44 past Doolittle into second place, and shortly after Doolittle had to drop out, after averaging 228 mph. So Bayles came home an easy winner at 236.2 mph,

with several laps over 240 mph, and Wedell placed second at 227.9 mph. Jackson was fortunate to finish a distant third at 211.2 mph. Robert Hall, Ira Eaker, Benny Howard and William Ong rounded out the field in that order.

That 1931 Thompson definitely put an end to experiments with biplanes for racing in America. It was plain to see that the Gee Bee Z was at least 10 mph faster than the Laird *Super Solution* with an identical engine. And Jackson's streamlined *Solution* was still not quite as fast as the Wedell No. 44, even with 50–75 more horsepower. It was fruitless.

The 1932 Thompson Trophy race

Eight planes started the 1932 Thompson. The race was flown over the same ten-mile course at Cleveland, and again for ten laps or 100 miles. The Shell qualifying speed dashes were spiced up a lot that year by posting substantial prize money for several classes of planes and by using a surveyed 3 km course with FAI timing, so that any possible speed record could be certified. And as it turned out, Jimmy Doolittle did set a new world landplane record at 294.38 mph with the new Wasp engine Gee Bee R-1.

Designer Robert Hall flew his own Gee Bee Model Y commercial sport single-seater in the 1931 Thompson. It wasn't fast enough, even with 450 hp. Yeager

Benny Howard flew his 90 hp Gypsy engined Pete *in several early Thompson races for what prize money could be won with its modest top speed of 180 mph.* Weaver Collection

Jimmy Doolittle flew an erratic Gee Bee R-1 to victory in the 1932 Thompson by flying very wide, flat, low-g turns. Its speed of over 290 mph made up for extra distance. Weaver Collection

Lee Gehlbach flew the Gee Bee R-2, a twin to the winning R-1, in the 1932 Thompson. However, it still had the smaller engine and larger fuel tanks used for the Bendix race and wasn't as fast as the R-1. Mandrake

The Guggenheim family financed Robert Hall's famous Bulldog *design for the 1932 Thompson. A restricted air inlet kept the racer from showing its true potential.* Strasser

This performance made him the hands-down favorite to win the race, being over 15 mph faster than any of the other qualifiers. It might also be mentioned that Jimmy downplayed the erratic handling characteristics of the Gee Bee in prerace press interviews, probably in deference to the Granville brothers who hired him. But he had done extensive high-altitude maneuverability testing with the R-1, and there was never any doubt that he was well prepared for practically any weird trick the plane might display.

Doolittle's competition in 1932 was capable, if not quite as fast. Jim Wedell was back with a hopped-up 535 hp Wasp Junior in his No. 44, and Roscoe Turner and Jim Haizlip were flying nearly identical Wasp Junior powered Wedells. Lee Gehlbach was in the Gee Bee R-2, twin to Doolittle's plane, but with a smaller Wasp Junior engine. Ray Moore was entered in the first Thompson for Keith Rider's R-1, and Benny Howard hired William Ong to fly his new DGA-5 *Ike* racer, with a 180 hp Menasco engine. Finally, there was Robert Hall in his beautiful new gullwing Wasp powered *Bulldog*, financed by the wealthy Guggenheim family.

With the drop of the starter's flag, Gehlbach and Hall were first into the air and around the scattering pylon with their Smith controllable pitch propellers. Doolittle had a Smith prop, too, but he deliberately took off at half throttle to avoid torque problems on initial liftoff (the problem that killed Boardman in the same plane a year later). But the R-1's 770 hp Wasp pulled it into the lead in the next two miles. Doolittle continued to open up that lead, sweeping around the pylons in wide, flat turns to prevent any unusual loads on the Gee Bee. He actually flew nearly eleven miles on each ten-mile lap. The rest of the field lined up behind him pretty much in the order of their speed potentials: Wedell, Turner, Haizlip and so on.

The tightest competition was between Roscoe Turner and Jim Haizlip in the two nearly identical Wedells, with nearly identical qualifying speeds. They passed and repassed each other several times in the course of the race; Turner eventually outflew Haizlip and finished third behind Jim Wedell's faster No. 44. Doolittle came home about half a lap ahead of Wedell at 252.7 mph for the 100 miles. Gehlbach finished fifth behind Haizlip, followed by the Hall *Bulldog* and William Ong in the Howard *Ike*. Ray Moore dropped out of the race on his second lap with unspecified engine trouble.

Many of the fans were surprised that Hall's new *Bulldog* didn't show more speed with the 600 hp Wasp engine. The problem was later traced to a

The aluminum Rider R-1 was first entered in the 1932 Thompson. Pilot Ray Moore dropped out with engine trouble after qualifying at 238 mph. Albanese

The entries lined up before the 1933 Thompson at Los Angeles. Jim Wedell won it in his No. 44 (foreground), which qualified at an impressive 279 mph with a Wasp Junior. Whittington

restricted air inlet to the carburetor, so as much as 100 to 150 hp was being literally choked off. The carefully designed and highly financed plane never was perfected, though, as the Guggenheims lost interest after the poor showing in the 1932 Thompson; it never raced again.

The 1933 Thompson Trophy race

The 1933 National Air Races were moved to Los Angeles on the fourth of July weekend, to avoid conflict with the big International Air Race program on Labor Day at the Chicago World's Fair. And the events were limited to racing aircraft, in place of the

Lee Gehlbach took second in the 1933 Thompson with the Wedell No. 92, very similar to No. 44. Wedell-Williams Air Service owned the plane and hired various pilots. Weaver Collection

Roscoe Turner was leading the 1933 Thompson in a Wasp engine Wedell, but cut a pylon, recircled it on the next lap and was disqualified—a bitter pill for the Colonel. Weaver Collection

usual ten-day affair for racing, commercial and military craft. It made a more exciting, faster moving show.

Six planes lined up for the feature Thompson race. Roscoe Turner, who had replaced the Wasp Junior engine in his Wedell with a 650 hp Wasp, had an apparent 10–12 mph speed advantage over Jim Wedell's No. 44 and was favored to win. Lee Gehlbach flew the No. 92 Wedell that year, and the elder Granville brother, Z. D., flew the company's Wasp Jr. engine Model Y. Benny Howard had added a supercharger and some 50 hp to his Menasco engine *Mike* racer and gave the controls to Roy Minor for the Thompson. George Hague rounded out the field in the little four-cylinder Rider R-2 *Bumblebee*, recently purchased by wealthy George McGrew.

At the drop of the starter's flag, Turner and Wedell were first off, battling nose-to-tail into the first lap. Turner continued to trail Wedell into the second lap, when suddenly he wheeled around to recircle a pylon. It later came out that Turner thought he had cut that pylon on the first lap, but waited until the second lap to recircle it due to excessive traffic around the pylon at the time of the cut. Meanwhile, Wedell had inherited a lead of several miles, with Gehlbach in second and Turner starting to move up after the recircle. Turner passed Gehlbach on the fourth lap and gobbled up Wedell shortly after the start of the fifth lap. From that point on, the six planes strung out in the order of their speed potentials. Turner finished first at an average of 241.0 mph to Wedell's 237.9 mph in second place.

That's when the fun started. The race officials summarily disqualified Turner, as the rules clearly stated a pilot had to recircle a cut pylon immediately, not on a later lap. Turner argued that the dense cluster of planes around the pylon on that first lap would have made such a maneuver extremely dangerous. But the officials had no choice but to go by the rules. Turner ended up out of the money, and Jim Wedell was declared the winner. It's noteworthy that Roscoe was practically paranoid about cut pylons in later Thompson races!

The 1934 Thompson Trophy race

The 1934 Thompson was back in Cleveland, but this time the course was shortened to an $8\frac{1}{3}$ mile triangular shape, to make the planes visible to the grandstand spectators for more of the lap distance.

Benny Howard's Menasco engine Mike *racer, No. 38, appeared in several early Thompsons, with various pilots. Harold Neu-* *mann won the first Greve Trophy race in 1934 with* Mike. Weaver Collection

Roscoe Turner was sponsored by Heinz 57 Varieties when he won the 1934 Thompson. His Wedell racer was painted up to let the world know it. Sunyak.

It then of course required twelve laps to make up the 100 miles.

Most of the planes contesting that 1934 Thompson had raced here before. But some had bigger, more powerful engines, so the press and fans speculated much about possible sandbagging in the qualifying trials. Jim Wedell had been killed in a flying accident in June of 1934, and his No. 44 was being flown by Doug Davis. The Wasp Junior had been replaced by a 770 hp Wasp after the 1933 Thompson, the same engine that had powered Doolittle's Gee Bee in the 1932 Thompson. With it, Davis averaged a sizzling 306 mph for qualifying in the Shell Dash. But Roscoe Turner was the puzzler. He now had a huge "1,000 hp" Pratt & Whitney Hornet in his Wedell, yet hit only 295 mph in the Shell Dashes. Was he sandbagging? Betting was hot and heavy.

Then there was Roy Minor in the beautiful new Brown B-2 with a new model 300 hp Menasco engine, said to be capable of 270 mph. John Worthen flew the venerable Wedell No. 92 that year, and newcomer Harold Neumann was in Benny Howard's *Mike* racer. The field of eight planes was filled out by Roger Don Rae in the Rider R-1 and with little 185 hp four-cylinder Menascos in Art Chester's Special and Lee Miles's Miles & Atwood Special.

As expected, Turner and Davis were away first at the starter's flag, flying wing-to-wing around the scattering pylon and into the first lap. But what looked like a nip-and-tuck race between them quickly changed to a parade. Turner made no attempt to keep up with Davis. He settled back into second place, flying wide around the pylons to avoid a cut, while Davis pulled away to a lead of three or four miles, with the other six planes trailing out in order of their speeds. It seemed obvious Turner was expecting Davis to burn up his engine.

But it was tragedy that struck on the leader's eighth lap. Just what happened to Doug Davis at that south pylon has always been the subject of much controversy. It appeared that he cut the pylon and wheeled around to recircle it. At the apex of this high-g turn, the No. 44 Wedell spiraled into the ground. Some who saw the event said it was a high-speed stall. Others said there was structural failure, that a wing collapsed. Some said the whole tail assembly broke away from the fuselage. It was hardly possible to reconstruct the events from the remains of the plane, as it was literally rolled up in a ball. Davis died instantly.

From this point on, Roscoe Turner cruised home the winner at an average speed of 248.1 mph. Roy Minor in the Brown B-2 was miles behind at

Doug Davis crashed fatally in a high-g turn as he led the 1934 Thompson by a wide margin in the Wasp engined Wedell No. 44. He qualified at a record 306 mph. Weaver Collection

Roy Minor piloted a sleek new Brown B-2 racer to second in the 1934 Thompson with a new 300 hp Menasco and reported a top speed of 270 mph. Weaver Collection

Lee Miles entered his tiny four-cylinder Menasco engine special in the 1934 Thompson for prize money, but dropped out with engine trouble. Weaver Collection

Harold Neumann was the surprise winner of the 1935 Thompson in the Howard Mr. Mulligan *cabin plane. Neumann's* *victory was unexpected because he could use only limited power on the available 87 octane gas.* Weaver Collection

214.9 mph, and John Worthen was third in the Wedell No. 92, nursing a rough engine. In retrospect, there seems little question that Davis would have won, but for the crash: His average speed up to that point was 253 mph, and he had a long lead over Turner.

The 1935 Thompson Trophy race

Feeling that the shorter 8⅓ mile triangular course and tighter turns of the 1934 Thompson might have contributed to the Davis crash, race officials went in the opposite direction and decided to lengthen the 1935 course to a fifteen mile rectangle and to extend the race length to 150 miles, or ten laps. They decided that a longer race on longer laps might be a safer race. The Shell people discontinued their support of the straightaway qualifying dashes after the 1934 Nationals, and qualifying after that used average lap speeds around the race course.

Seven planes faced the starter's flag at Cleveland that year. Roscoe Turner was back in his Hornet engine Wedell, as was Roger Don Rae in the Rider R-1. The Brown B-2 had a new owner and pilot, Marion McKeen, and the venerable Howard *Mike* was flown by Joe Jacobson that year. Lee Miles and Art Chester wanted to enter their tiny four-cylinder Menasco powered racers for whatever prize money might be available, but tests showed

they didn't have sufficient fuel tankage for the 150 mile distance at reasonable race speeds. Miles didn't give up. He talked Alexander deSeversky into letting him fly his new Model SEV-3 twin float high-speed amphibian, which he was displaying at Cleveland. What better way to showcase it than in the Thompson race?

An important introduction in 1935 was Steve Wittman's unusual new homebuilt *Bonzo* racer, an attempt to get maximum performance on a low budget by using an old used liquid cooled Curtiss D-12 in an airframe of minimum size and weight. But certainly the most interesting entry was Benny Howard's radical Wasp powered *Mr. Mulligan* four-seat cabin monoplane, which had just won the Bendix cross country race. Howard had designed the structure for the rigors of pylon racing, but he knew the odds were against him from a standpoint of weight and aerodynamic drag. His airline pilot contract prevented him from flying the pylons, so Harold Neumann was chosen to fly *Mulligan* in the Thompson. It was an unlikely plane in an unfamiliar role.

Despite the raft of new planes, pilots and owners, it appeared early on that Roscoe Turner had the race sewed up. His practice and qualifying speeds were well above those of everybody else, and the promising challenge from *Mr. Mulligan* went up in smoke when pilot Neumann burned a piston

Roscoe Turner led the 1935 Thompson by big margin, but burned a piston on the last lap. Note a more compact dimpled cowling for the big Hornet engine. Wigton

Steve Wittman's homely D-12 powered Bonzo, *first seen in the 1935 Thompson, took second place after serious cooling problems.* Albanese

Lee Miles talked deSeversky into letting him fly a new twin float amphibian in the 1935 Thompson and won fifth place money.

This plane later set a world speed record for amphibians at 230.4 mph. Weaver Collection

while qualifying the day before the race. It required an all-night thrash just to get the engine repaired and running again, and it was plain that Neumann wouldn't dare press Turner too hard in the race without special fuel to compensate for the less efficient low-level operation of the high-altitude supercharger designed for the Bendix.

And that's just the way the race went. Turner jumped out into a long lead on the first lap, with Wittman second and McKeen third. Neumann had the added handicap of having his Wasp engine load up on the ground and was late getting away. (Pratt & Whitney engineers had richened the carburetion a lot to help cooling and control detonation.) Turner's lead built up to over three miles on the third lap, so he throttled back to an easy cruise at lap speeds of 230–235 mph. Wittman was running in second, but his engine was overheating due to an undersize radiator, so he was literally flying by his temperature gauge. On the fourth lap, Neumann crept by McKeen into third place, but always with an eye on his cylinder head temperature gauge, watching for any sign of detonation. It was a perfect example of the importance of engine instruments in early pylon racing. On lap six, Neumann passed Wittman into second, but by then they were both nearly half a lap behind Turner, who was still just cruising along at an average of 233 mph.

It would have ended that way . . . but fate stepped in again. On his ninth lap, only twenty miles from the finish, Turner burned a piston in the big Hornet and had to dead-stick in near the south end of the grandstand. It was the worst of luck, too, because he was only loafing the engine. In fact,

Harold Neumann didn't even realize that he had won the race until officials rushed up to his plane after he landed. His average speed was an unexciting 220.2 mph, with Wittman second at 218.7 mph. Roger Don Rae finished third at 213.9 mph.

The 1935 Thompson illustrated the old racing adage: You have to finish to win. If Neumann had tried to keep up with Turner, he would undoubtedly have blown the engine again; instead Neumann flew conservatively and that, with Turner's misfortune, took him to first place.

The 1936 Thompson Trophy race

The 1936 National Air Races were moved to Mines Field in Los Angeles, with five- and ten-mile courses laid out in rather narrow rectangles, which had relatively long straightaways and short end crossovers. Most class races and qualifying heats were run on the five-mile course, for better spectator viewing.

The hands-down sensation of the meet was the magnificent Caudron Model C-460 that had been sent over from France with pilot Michel Detroyat. The story goes that Louis Greve, founder of the US series of Greve Trophy races for planes under 550 ci, had spoken to Detroyat in 1935, when he was at an international aviation meeting in Cleveland representing the French Morane-Saulnier company. Greve felt that one of the 486 ci Caudrons, designed for the Deutsch small engine races in France and holder of many world lightplane speed records, might add some spice to his series. He challenged Detroyat to try to work out a deal with friends in the Caudron company to bring over a 460 model the following year, mentioning the lucrative prize money in both the Greve and Thompson races. Detroyat's parting words were, "See you next year with a Caudron."

As things turned out, most American grassroots racers wished that Greve had kept his mouth shut. Detroyat and the Caudron absolutely dominated all the US planes, big and small engines alike. And this included some promising new designs from our people. A new Wasp engine Rider R-3 was flown by Earl Ortman, with top speed well over 300 mph. Roger Don Rae was in a new Rider R-4 with a 280 hp Menasco B6S. Harold Neumann had his new Folkerts SK-2 with a supercharged Menasco C4S, and Harry Crosby entered his handbuilt CR-3 with C6S Menasco. Marion McKeen was also on hand with the Brown B-2, and Lee Miles was hired to fly the Granvilles' QED racer, which had been built for the London-to-Melbourne race.

At the drop of the starter's flag, Detroyat—with his unique switch pitch Ratier propeller—was off and away ahead of everybody. And his lead just started to build up from there. His average speed for the first lap was down because of the time lost on the takeoff, but he clocked 301 mph the second time around, flying wide open to build up a good lead. His third circuit averaged 293 mph as he throttled back a little, and eventually he dropped down to lap speeds in the 250 mph bracket. At the finish, Detroyat had lapped all the planes except Ortman, averaging 264.3 mph for the 150 miles, with Ortman miles behind at 248.0 mph. It could hardly be called a race. It was more like a massacre. Ortman could have gone considerably faster, but felt that he couldn't beat Detroyat and that it was foolish to risk a blown engine in a futile chase. Don Rae and Neuman finished third and fourth with impressive averages of 236.6 and 233.1 mph with their smaller engines. McKeen was fifth, and Crosby was held back by a balky landing gear that wouldn't retract. Lee Miles dropped out with engine trouble in the Granville QED.

The gorgeous French Caudron C–460 racer won the 1936 Thompson going away. Its top speed of nearly 330 mph was turned with a small six-cylinder engine of only 400 hp. Whittington

119

Roger Don Rae took third in the 1936 Thompson in a new Rider R-4 with a small six-cylinder Menasco. The performance attracted a buyer for the plane on the spot. Repla-Tech

Harold Neumann took fourth place in the 1936 Thompson with a new midget Folkerts SK-2. It could hit 270 mph with only 230 hp from a four-cylinder Menasco. Weaver Collection

Rudy Kling completely rebuilt the old aluminum Rider R-1 for the 1936 season, with added streamlining and top speed *increased to 260 mph on 95 octane fuel. He wrecked the plane on landing just before the Thompson race.* Repla-Tech

The American pylon brotherhood turned out to be rather poor losers. Following the race, controversy exploded in the press and among our racers about amateur low-budget backyard builders struggling against government financed racers—which was really not true. The Caudron racer was developed entirely by the private French company. Admittedly, that company had more resources than

Benny Howard's Mike racer was another Menasco that gained 20 mph on the new 95 octane fuel in 1936. Pilot Joe Jacobson flipped it over on landing just before the Thompson. Mandrake

121

The Granville brothers entered their R6H racer in the 1936 Thompson; it was originally designed for the MacRobertson race to Australia. Pilot Miles dropped out with engine trouble. Weaver Collection

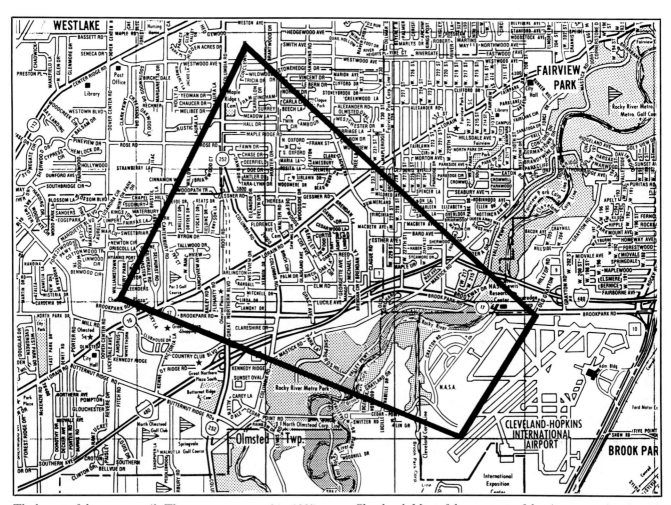

The layout of the new ten-mile Thompson course used in 1937, 1938 and 1939 is superimposed on a modern street map of Cleveland. Most of the area west of the airport was farmland in late 1930s. G. Pickard

Rudy Kling won the 1937 Thompson by a split second in a beautiful new Folkerts SK-3, using a 350 hp Menasco that gave a top speed well over 300 mph. Worster

did American backyard builders, especially as Caudron was part of the vast Renault conglomerate. But it was not a government program with unlimited financing. Then Roscoe Turner, who watched the race from the sidelines after his racer was damaged, made some unfortunate remarks over the public-address system when interviewed after the race. He complained bitterly about budget-built private racers having to compete against "million-dollar, government-sponsored" planes, and that the prize

Steve Wittman led the 1937 Thompson for seventeen laps in his D-12 powered Bonzo, *averaging over 260 mph. Then an oil leak cut him to fifth place.* Kemp

Roscoe Turner's famous Laird Meteor *was first seen in the 1937 Thompson. With an uncowled oil cooler and landing gear, it was 20 to 30 mph slower than later versions.* Repla-Tech

money and trophies should be returned. All in all, the 1936 Thompson wasn't one of American racing's finer hours. Detroyat and the Caudron crew left the States vowing never to come back. The unfortunate incident made headlines across the world.

The 1937 Thompson Trophy race

The 1937 Thompson race at Cleveland continued the trend toward longer race distances, with the contest set up for twenty laps of a ten-mile course, or 200 miles. Officials hoped that longer races would encourage the development of more practical aircraft with more reliable engines. A new rectangular course was set up mostly over farmland northwest of the airport, with one short 1.2 mile straight and two pylons in front of the main grandstand. The former course area east of the airport was becoming quite populated.

An unexpected bonanza of interesting new planes entered that year. Two civilian versions of the new Seversky P-35 pursuit planes with 1,000 hp Pratt and Whitney Twin Wasp engines were flown by Frank Sinclair and Ray Moore. Millionaire Frank Fuller had worked out a deal with the US War Department to release this basic military design for conversion to civilian use, with a limited number offered for sale. Roscoe Turner had his new Twin Wasp powered Laird-Turner *Meteor*, said to be capa-

ble of near 380 mph, and Rudy Kling was entered in the Folkerts SK-3, powered by a new Menasco C6S-4 engine of 350 hp. Bill Schoenfeldt had purchased the Rider R-4 after its good showing in the 1936 race and replaced the Menasco B6S with a C6S-4, putting Gus Gotch in the cockpit. Earl Ortman was back with the Rider R-3, but now with a stronger Pratt & Whitney Twin Wasp Junior engine of 1,000 hp. Steve Wittman had an improved cooling system in his D-12 engine *Bonzo*. The field was filled out by Marion McKeen in his Brown B-2 and Joe Mackey flying Roscoe Turner's old Hornet engine Wedell.

Prerace speculation and betting was hot and heavy in 1937 because of the unique five-lap qualifying heats, where the entered planes actually raced against each other for cash prizes before the feature Thompson. Steve Wittman, with the highest lap speed of 275.6 mph during these heats, was established as one of the favorites to win the race. But everybody was wondering how much speed Turner and the Seversky P-35 pilots were holding back on their qualifying runs. For the first time, race officials posted $100 prizes for the leading plane at the end of each odd-numbered lap to encourage the pilots of the faster planes to race more aggressively over the full 200 miles.

That 1937 Thompson didn't go the way anybody expected it to. The $100 lap prizes didn't seem to light a fire under the racers. As expected, Steve

Wittman jumped out into the lead right at the start and set a fairly brisk pace at 260 mph or so. Steve was known for pushing his engines a little harder than most, so this was no surprise. But race promoter Cliff Henderson was a little disappointed that none of the other pilots seemed willing to up the ante above that 260 mph level to try to pass Wittman. Steve won every lap prize through lap seventeen, with Turner, Ortman, Kling and Sinclair strung out two or three miles behind him. It seemed obvious that these pilots with the hotter planes were saving their engines for a final dash to the checkered flag on the last two laps.

Then, just after Wittman started into his eighteenth lap, he suddenly pulled up with a burst oil line, forcing him to throttle back. Whitman said later that he clipped a bird and bent a prop blade and that the resulting engine vibration broke the oil line. Very quickly he was passed by Turner, Ortman, Kling and Sinclair in that order. Going into the last lap, Turner was still ahead by a quarter-mile or so and looked like the sure winner. But fate stepped in again on the veteran racer. Blinded by the late afternoon sun on the westward leg of the course, Turner missed the Number two pylon and had to wheel around to recircle it. This allowed Ortman and Kling to streak by, though Sinclair was far enough back so that Turner was able to hang onto third place.

But it was what happened up front in the next few seconds that has generated so much contro-versy among historians. Kling was flying some 200 ft above and 500 feet behind Ortman as they approached the finish line. Just at the right moment, Kling dove toward the finish line, letting gravity build up his speed, so that he crossed it barely 200 ft ahead of Ortman. Their official race speeds were listed as 256.910 versus 256.858 mph.

Now talk about controversy! Earl Ortman said he was sure that he had lapped Kling during the race, so that was why he didn't speed up when Turner had to recircle the pylon. He claimed that Kling only completed nineteen laps. Apparently there was confusion among race officials, too, as no checkered flag was displayed when Kling and Ortman finished their twentieth laps. Yet the timers had it all on the timing strip and credited Kling with the fastest lap average of the whole race: 279 mph for his twentieth lap. The tape showed him gaining on Ortman through that lap and winning by 0.57 second total race time.

So take your pick. Surely this treatise will do nothing to settle this fifty-year-old controversy!

The 1938 Thompson Trophy race

The 1938 Thompson race was characterized by a complete shake-up of the rules, with most changes aimed at curbing a possible takeover by advanced military planes like the modified Seversky P-35s that had done so well in both the Bendix and Thompson races the year before. In view of the $35,000 cost of these planes (and possibly higher prices in the

Two civilian versions of Seversky P-35 fighter plane were entered in the 1937 Bendix and Thompson races, tough competition for the low-budget grassroots guys. Frank Fuller in No. 23 won the Bendix and placed fourth in the Thompson. Weaver Collection

125

Roscoe Turner won the 1938 Thompson in the refined Laird Meteor, with a fast lap at 293 mph. The Twin Row Pratt & Whitney could pull 1,200 hp on 95 octane fuel. Sunyak

future), the Thompson people felt that they had to act immediately to keep their series alive for low-budget grassroots American racers with homebuilt planes.

Accordingly, the new 1938 rules stipulated a maximum engine size of 1,860 ci, to ban any huge future military engines. Qualifying was changed to two laps of the race course, with a minimum average

Earl Ortman finished a distant second to Turner in the 1938 Thompson in a revamped Marcoux-Bromberg Rider R-3. An oil leak slowed him down, and he landed with an empty tank. Yeager

Art Chester's sleek new Menasco powered Goon was the crowd favorite at the 1938 Nationals, hitting speeds over 300 mph. It ran out of oil in the Thompson race. Bradd

of 225 mph and with no more than fifteen planes starting. The race was lengthened to 300 miles to encourage more practical planes with reliable engines, and the purse was nearly doubled to $45,000. And a key rule change was that no plane could compete in both the Bendix and Thompson races, though this did not apply to pilots. It was felt that this would give the big military planes a shot at one title but would prevent any domination of both series.

The new rules successfully gave the race back to the little guys. No military planes were entered. The eight-plane entry list in 1938 was an interesting

Frank Hawks's old Time Flies speed record plane was rebuilt as a military prototype and entered in the 1938 Thompson. Pilot Leigh Wade took fourth place. Weaver Collection

gathering of the best products of American grass-roots and amateur aviation technology of the day—boosted by the first general availability of 100 octane commercial avgas.

Roscoe Turner had made several improvements on his *Meteor,* which upped its speed 20–30 mph—but so had the Marcoux-Bromberg team on Earl Ortman's Rider R-3, which they felt was now safe at 1,000 hp on 100 octane. The two planes looked pretty even that year. Steve Wittman had made some more cooling system changes on *Bonzo* and had it running the best ever. The Granvilles had bought back Frank Hawks's *Time Flies* and rebuilt it as a two-seat military prototype, the HM-1 model, which was entered with Leigh Wade piloting, for whatever prize money might be available. Joe Mackey was back again in the ageless Wedell-Turner, and Harry Crosby had spiced up his racer with a stronger Menasco C6S-4 engine.

The most interesting new plane was Art Chester's tiny *Goon,* with a highly modified C6S-4 engine and French Ratier two-pitch prop. Before the Thompson, Bill Schoenfeldt had put young Tony LeVier in the cockpit of his Rider R-4 *Firecracker* racer, with some additional modifications to the powerful Menasco. These two planes seemed quite even in the preliminary Greve Trophy race for 550 ci engines before Chester ran out of oil. But that competition evaporated from the Thompson when LeVier damaged the Rider on a rough landing after the Greve. Keith Rider did enter his latest all plywood R-6 design, with Joe Jacobson flying, to demonstrate for prospective buyers.

The race started with Ortman, Wittman and Chester leading into the first lap in that order. Turner, confident of his superior speed, purposely took off easy and was very careful around the scattering pylon, applying more power down the long west straightaway. He caught up with the front-runners on the second lap, then eased back, letting Ortman set the pace in the 270 mph bracket. On lap six Ortman cut a pylon, and Turner took the lead when he turned back to recircle it. The order was then Turner, Ortman, Wittman and Chester.

But Wittman and Chester were both in trouble: Wittman losing coolant and Chester blowing oil out his engine breather vents. Then on the thirteenth lap, Ortman began trailing smoke. By the sixteenth lap, Chester had slipped back to sixth place. But Ortman and Wittman held on doggedly to second and third, even though they fell back gradually behind Turner, who was lapping easily in the 280 mph bracket. Finally on the twentieth lap, Chester had to come down—out of oil. Shortly after, Ortman

Roscoe Turner entered his old Hornet powered Wedell-Williams in most Thompsons of late 1930s, hiring various pilots. Joe Mackey brought it in fifth in the 1938 race. Sunyak

Keith Rider's plywood Model R-6, with a 350 hp Menasco, was entered in the 1938 Thompson, flown by Joe Jacobson, but the engine didn't run well. Weaver Collection

was lapped by Turner, and finally, on Ortman's twenty-seventh lap, an oil line ruptured and his pressure went to zero, spraying oil all over the fuselage and canopy. Still Ortman hung on, hoping against hope to finish the thirty laps before his oil supply was gone entirely. He just made it, finishing second at 269.7 mph to Turner's winning 283.4 mph. Ortman's oil tank was empty when he landed. Wittman hung on, too, despite a dwindling coolant supply, and was fortunate to finish third at 259.2 mph. Leigh Wade passed Mackey on the last lap to take fourth place, and Jacobson was flagged down

Harry Crosby's refined CR-4 racer showed lots of promise with its new 350 hp Menasco, but gas fumes in the cockpit forced him out of the 1938 Thompson. Kemp

on his twenty-seventh lap in the Rider R-6, far behind the pace. Luckless Harry Crosby was overcome by gas fumes and landed on his tenth lap.

If that 1938 Thompson proved anything, it was that a big high-power radial engine in a big plane was more than a match for a little hard-working Menasco in a tiny lightweight plane.

The 1939 Thompson Trophy race

The 1939 Thompson, again for 300 miles, promised to be the fastest and most competitive of any to date. Roscoe Turner had turned a lap at 299 mph in qualifying, and said that *Meteor* still had something left. Again the Marcoux-Bromberg team had made several refinements on the Rider R-3, and word leaked out that pilot Earl Ortman had turned a hand-timed practice lap at 307 mph by overspeeding the Twin Wasp Junior to 2800 rpm, using a new three blade Hamilton constant speed propeller. He told friends that he thought he could stay with Turner.

Then there was the team of Tony LeVier piloting Bill Schoenfeldt's Rider R-4 *Firecracker,* with the Menasco C6S-4 now hopped up to an estimated 500+ hp, and said to be capable of 350 mph on an alcohol base fuel. Harry Crosby had his CR-4 racer running the best ever, and Steve Wittman was back once again with more cooling improvements on *Bonzo.* Art Chester had made numerous refinements on his Menasco engine *Goon,* and there was much speculation that he might place high in the Thompson, after a nip-and-tuck battle with LeVier in the earlier Greve race. Finally Joe Mackey appeared once again in the old 1932 Wedell-Turner, believe it or not. By 1939 it was too slow to win, so Mackey was resigned to cruising the old rig for as much prize money as possible.

The 1939 Thompson race was a classic example of the inefficient pilot-to-crew communications that plagued the 1930s air racers. This problem may have profoundly affected the outcome of the race, in fact.

The race was postponed one day due to a torrential rain, and the planes were flagged off on a wet, soggy grass field the next day with a brisk wind blowing from the first pylon at the north end of the field—so no scattering pylon was required. But the soft ground lengthened takeoff runs to a scary degree for the planes without variable-pitch propellers. Turner again purposely held back at the flag, out of the traffic, planning to use his speed advantage to catch up later on. Art Chester and Steve Wittman, with their light weight and switch pitch props, were first off the ground and around the No. 1 pylon, with Earl Ortman right behind. LeVier was slow getting away because of his heavy fuel load, but he quickly picked up speed as the load eased. By the fifth lap he had pulled past Ortman, Wittman and Chester into the lead. Meanwhile Turner had cut a pylon on his first lap, and went around to recircle. This put him way behind the field right at the start, and forced him to use more power than he had planned. But he came up stead-

Roscoe Turner repeated as a Thompson Trophy winner, this time in 1939 with Meteor *sponsored by Champion Spark Plugs. He turned in a qualifying lap at 299 mph.* Yeager

The Schoenfeldt Firecracker *racer, with a modified 500 hp Menasco, was practically as fast as Turner's* Meteor *in the 1939 Thompson—but pilot Tony LeVier got mixed up on the lap count.* Yeager

ily through the pack, finally passing LeVier into the lead on the ninth lap.

But here's where the communications glitch occurred. LeVier never did see Turner at the beginning of the race, when he was slow getting away and when recircling the pylon on the first lap. LeVier had his hands full getting the grossly overloaded *Firecracker* off the ground and then cranking up the landing gear—and he just assumed Turner was long gone. So when Turner breezed past him on the ninth lap LeVier thought he was being lapped. With no ground communication to tell him different, LeVier figured if Turner could lap him in nine laps there was no way he could hope to catch Turner even with full power. So LeVier settled down to his usual "race cruise" setting—3200 rpm and 55 in. manifold pressure—and just kept on turning easy laps around 280 mph average, enough to stay well ahead of third place Art Chester. But all the while LeVier's plane was potentially capable of laps over 300 mph at 3500 rpm and 72 in.

And that's the way it ended. Turner won at 282.5 mph, with LeVier second at 272.5 mph—and Ortman four laps behind at 254.4 mph. Art Chester was running in third place for much of the race, at lap speeds around 265 mph. But as in prior races he was gradually blowing his oil out the breathers, and it was gone by the 18th lap. Ortman inherited third

place. Wittman finished in fourth place, ahead of Harry Crosby by the clock, averaging around 250 mph. But Wittman had unknowingly cut the first pylon at the start, and was penalized one lap after the race—which left him in fifth place at 241 mph average, behind Crosby. Joe Mackey brought up the rear in the old Wedell.

The Turner-LeVier skirmish in that last prewar Thompson might have turned out differently had communication been better. In fact LeVier admitted later that his plane owner, Bill Schoenfeldt, was more than a little ticked after the race because he had failed to detect the Turner pylon cut, and didn't race him all out on the late laps. But then, could that little Menasco have turned out 500+ horsepower at 3500 rpm for 150 or 200 miles? Turner might have run him right into the ground with his big 1,200 hp Twin Wasp. We'll never know.

As it turned out, the 1939 race was the last prewar Thompson. There were several reasons. Gathering war clouds in Europe. The Henderson brothers managing team resigned for other business interests in California. But most important, the Thompson prize money didn't attract the $75,000 or so it would require to build a plane that could beat Roscoe Turner's *Meteor*. The jolly Colonel had the last laugh after all.

Chapter 10

Making racers out of fighters

When the National Air Races and Thompson Trophy event were resumed at Cleveland in 1946, after World War II, the pylon sport was upset from top to bottom. Compared with the immediate pre-war scene, practically nothing was the same, not even the shape of the pylons.

The planes were no longer little homebuilt midgets with relatively small air cooled engines, which could be trailered around behind a car. They were highly sophisticated World War II fighter planes that cost Uncle Sam tens of thousands of dollars and incorporated the latest technology in aerodynamics, structures, stability and engine performance.

Furthermore, there was an entirely different racing brotherhood in the postwar years. Most of the pilots and mechanics were young bucks fresh out of the Air Force or Navy who had their training

It didn't cost much to race in postwar Thompsons. For $750 you could buy this surplus P-63 fighter, strip out weight, paint it up and go racing. Sunyak

entirely in military aviation. They were used to hard, fast, high-g flying in dangerous combat conditions. Flying a closed pylon course a few feet off the ground at 400 mph was brand new to them, but it was another type of precision flying and they were precision flyers.

This new pilot was in gross contrast to the typical prewar Thompson racer. The prewar guy likely taught himself to fly, or at best, had a minimum of professional instruction. He was accustomed to flying in and out of small, rough grass airfields that made every flight a challenge. And his early training plane was probably a rickety World War I surplus Jenny with performance and handling that in no way prepared him for later rigors of pylon racing.

Then there were the early racing planes themselves: Usually designed on a sketchpad by a man with no technical training, the planes were hand built in a garage or unused corner of a hangar and powered by a used or borrowed engine with questionable performance and reliability. And of course, the whole operation was usually on shoestring financing with dollars-and-cents compromises everywhere.

These widely different backgrounds for prewar and postwar pilots and planes inevitably spawned an entirely different type of racing in those early postwar years.

Racing gets cheaper

Looking back at those early postwar years now, it's hard to imagine the level of aircraft performance and state-of-the-art technology that a person could buy from the War Assets Administration for pennies-on-the-dollar prices. Consider the national situation at the time—a country suddenly at peace, sitting on literally thousands of new and slightly used fighting airplanes and accompanying replacement parts—and realize that the possibilities for the potential user of a high-performance plane were huge. He was like a kid loose in a candy store.

Washington sold hundreds of our World War II surplus aircraft to small countries in the Middle East and South America that wanted to build up small air forces. But these were only a drop in the bucket from that ocean of surplus hardware. And our own air forces couldn't use them. Congress was in a peace-making mood, and military budgets were being cut right and left.

Practically all the World War II planes were propeller driven, but the design trend in military aircraft was already headed unerringly toward the jet engine. Several advanced propeller planes were

World War II fighter planes made ideal pylon racers, having been developed for quick takeoffs and high-speed, high-g maneuvers. Bell

in the development stage at the end of the war, and it was planned to keep them in the military arsenal until the jets were fully developed. Also some of the best World War II fighters were held in reserve for two or three years for emergencies, while experimental jet models were perfected. Some of these fought in the Korean War in 1950.

It all added up to a lot of obsolete World War II planes and parts that were no more than junk in the eyes of the country's leaders. The only logical answer was to sell off as much of the stuff as the country (and the rest of the world) could swallow, at the highest prices the market would bear, and salvage out the rest. The law of supply and demand was

given free reign. Prices for individual planes and components were usually posted, but they were established as much as possible by demand. The War Assets people didn't give anything away if they thought there was a buck to be made.

For example, a garden variety Bell P-39 fighter, widely used and highly produced, sold for as little as $600. A more rare P-63 upgrade might go for $1,000. The average Lockheed P-38, with two engines and tons of parts, was around $1,200. But the most prized high-performance fighter of all, a P-51 Mustang with a two-stage, intercooled Rolls-Royce Merlin, would set a buyer back up to $3,500, depending on model and condition. (Rolls-Royce at one time tried

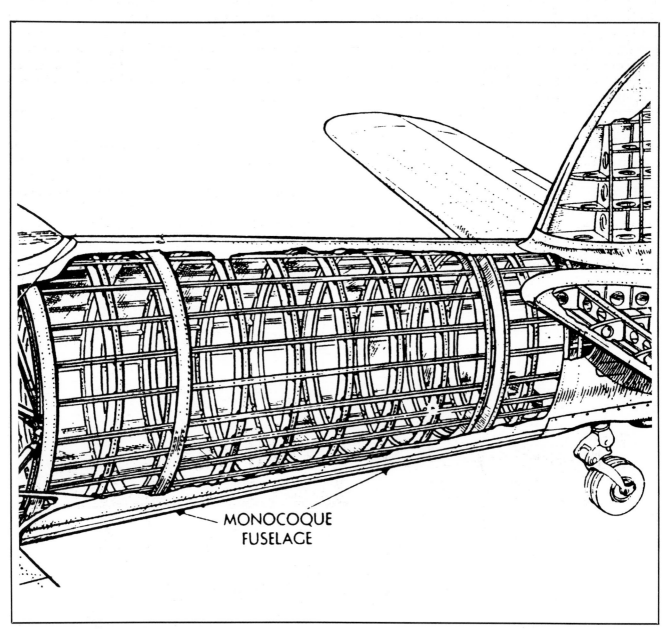

Modern all-metal monocoque construction of World War II planes gave better strength-to-weight ratio than did early framework construction. Millar

134

to stop the sale of surplus Mustangs because the company didn't want their prized Merlin engine in the hands of the public; their pleas were ignored).

The engines were another market entirely. The big air cooled radials pulled relatively high prices because they could be used by the commercial airlines. But the liquid cooled V-12 Allisons and Packard built Merlins were orphans with few welcoming homes. There weren't any commercial planes designed to use them at the time, and the cost of converting planes designed for radials couldn't be recovered in practical features such as reduced fuel consumption or longer life. They couldn't be economically modified for marine use. A few enterprising souls adapted them for stationary applications like irrigation pumps and large generators, often with the supercharger removed and the engine fitted with several automotive carburetors. But high fuel consumption limited their usefulness in such applications. The result was predictable: You could buy a brand-new Allison or Merlin in a crate after the war for anywhere from $75 to $300.

Fighter racing technique

Inevitably this bargain basement cost situation on aircraft and components had a profound influence on the way the equipment was used on the race course.

Picture the difference between the typical prewar and postwar racer. The typical prewar Thomp-son racer had his life savings in his airplane. He sweated blood to build it. He had probably dreamed about building his own plane since childhood. Further, the Thompson race wasn't his only bash for the season. Many prewar pylon racers competed in five or six other regional events around the country during the year, and depended on the prize money for much of their livelihood. Racing was their life. Their planes were their bread and butter. They loved them like a member of the family.

Contrast this with the typical postwar racer. He could buy his racing plane with a few weeks' wages. Repair parts were cheap and plentiful; many racers just bought an extra plane to cannibalize for parts. He was trained in the military at government expense. He was fifteen years younger than the prewar pilot. He probably never saw an air race in his life. This young hot dog's flying career was born and weaned on flying that was anything but conservative. All he knew was an all-out, life-and-death style of flying.

Imagine how these two diverse backgrounds influenced pilot behavior on the pylons. Where the typical prewar Thompson pilot might baby his plane to win as much prize money as possible and still have something left for that race coming up in Miami, the typical postwar ex-Air Force pilot might push his plane near the limit, just for the fun of it if nothing else. Those postwar racers flew a lot harder

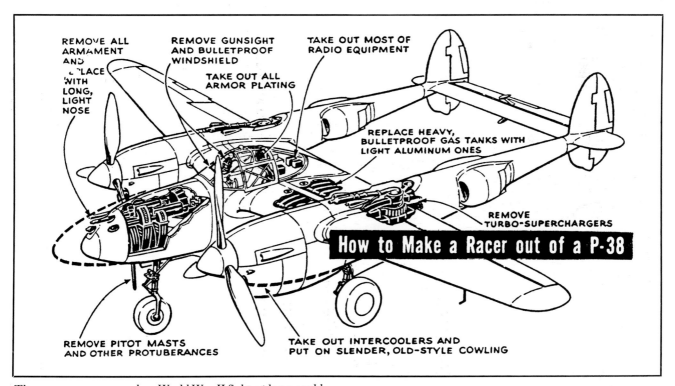

REMOVE ALL ARMAMENT AND REPLACE WITH LONG, LIGHT NOSE

REMOVE GUNSIGHT AND BULLETPROOF WINDSHIELD

TAKE OUT ALL ARMOR PLATING

TAKE OUT MOST OF RADIO EQUIPMENT

REPLACE HEAVY, BULLETPROOF GAS TANKS WITH LIGHT ALUMINUM ONES

REMOVE TURBO-SUPERCHARGERS

How to Make a Racer out of a P-38

REMOVE PITOT MASTS AND OTHER PROTUBERANCES

TAKE OUT INTERCOOLERS AND PUT ON SLENDER, OLD-STYLE COWLING

There were many areas where World War II fighter planes could be lightened and cleaned up for pylon racing. A racing team could strip over 2,000 pounds out of a P-38.

and more aggressively than the prewar racers. Admittedly, the smarter ones tried to conserve their engines to finish the race. But generally speaking, a greater percentage of planes dropped out of the postwar Thompson races from overstressed engines than in the prewar races.

What it really boiled down to was that the postwar Thompson planes were modified, designed and tuned for roughly forty-five minutes of all-out racing; the prewar planes were set up and flown for a season of racing. This made a big difference in the way they were flown on the pylons.

Why fighter planes were good racers

Certainly the price was right on surplus World War II fighter planes for the young postwar pilot who wanted to take a shot at pylon racing and the lucrative Thompson prize money. But did these planes really make efficient pylon racers? Consider some of their attractive points.
• Wartime airframes used state-of-the-art all-metal monocoque construction, which assured maximum structural strength with minimum weight.
• Their structure was design-stressed for twelve to fifteen positive gs for combat conditions, so there was no great danger of a plane's breaking up in a tight pylon turn, as a few prewar homebuilts had.
• Pilot visibility was excellent, a necessary design ingredient in any combat plane. Some prewar racers were horrible from this standpoint.

• World War II fighter planes provided reasonable cockpit comfort and ventilation for the pilot—at least in unmodified form.
• They were fully instrumented, for accurately monitoring engine operating parameters during the race.
• Modern constant speed propellers gave quick takeoffs, maximum acceleration off the turns and efficient top speed operation.
• Extensive engineering development of all flight characteristics assured planes that were stable, predictable and responsive to the controls. There were no erratic man-killing Gee Bees among those wartime fighter planes.
• Altitude supercharging of the engines offered a large reserve of horsepower capacity at low altitudes that was generally limited only by detonation with available fuels and water injection.

There were hardly any disadvantages with these World War II fighter planes as potential pylon racers. And if there were, they could be minimized with a few modifications that most amateur crews could perform with normal hangar equipment and tools.

Popular modifications
Reducing weight

Weight could be eliminated in a dozen places on a World War II fighter plane that was being modified specifically for pylon racing. Most obvious

Some World War II fighters, like big 3,500 hp Goodyear F2G Corsairs, were especially bulky and heavy and had to depend on brute horsepower for speed. Sunyak

would be removal of all guns, firing controls, ammunition racks, bomb racks, and any armor plate to protect the pilot or vital parts. The laminated puncture-resistant rubber fuel cells in wartime fighters were relatively heavy in relation to volume capacity; these were sometimes replaced with light aluminum tanks. It wasn't usually possible to reduce fuel capacity much, though, because a surprisingly great amount of fuel was needed for 45–50 minutes of all-out racing, in some cases more than 300 gallons!

Radio equipment was a question. Some teams wanted to keep the radio for pilot-to-crew communication during the race. Others tore it out to save weight and depended on the old 1930s tactics of pilot counting the number of laps or ground signals, which were risky at the 400 mph speeds involved. In the last Thompsons, radios were banned because they distracted the pilots too much.

Some planes had exhaust driven turbo-superchargers for flying at 40,000 ft altitudes. These were

useless at sea level, yet represented several hundred pounds of turbines, ducting, scoops and intercoolers. These whole systems had to go. Many smaller items could be removed to save weight: navigational instruments, gun sights, cockpit heaters, oxygen equipment and so on.

Add it all up, and it was common to remove over 1,500 lb from a plane's normal empty weight. That helped a lot in takeoff distance, pylon turning radius and acceleration off the turns.

Reducing parasite drag

Parasite drag is the aerodynamic drag of the entire plane at zero lift. Naturally, it should be as low as possible for a racing plane. It can be measured in terms of the area of an imaginary flat plate with the same drag as the plane. As an example, the wind tunnel and flight test parasite area of a standard P–51D Mustang was about 3.5 sq. ft.

It wasn't easy to effect substantial reductions in parasite drag on those World War II fighters. It normally required drastic modifications that were

Making big streamlining improvements on a World War II fighter plane was not easy. This effort added only 2 mph. Repla-Tech

The age-old practice of wing clipping was alive and well in postwar Thompsons. The excessive clip on this P-63 made the plane so that it could not hold altitude in a tight 180-degree turn! Carter

far beyond the facilities and know-how of the average owner and crew in those days. Oh, they could remove a little vent scoop here and there and the external radio antenna system, or maybe trim a pitot tube, or fill in a surface cutout or even reroute an air duct to an area of less critical ram air flow. Of course, there was the old trick of smoothing exterior surfaces; many teams spent hundreds of man-hours applying ten or twelve coats of paint and then polishing to a mirror finish.

But it appears from all the evidence we can find that these minor aerodynamic tricks reduced total parasite drag less than ten percent. In terms of top speed increase, these minor modifications might have added 5–10 mph—probably not enough to make a winner out of a loser.

However, a handful of better financed teams went the radical route on cutting parasite drag, for example, by completely removing the radiator tunnel on the bottom of a Mustang and by moving the coolers into wing scoops. The total drag saving with these deeper mods might have added 15 mph to top speed. Reducing parasite drag just wasn't as easy as it looked.

Wing clipping

Yes, the age-old idea of clipping a few inches or feet off the ends of a race plane's wings was definitely alive and well in the postwar years. The trick was to reduce wing surface area and thus reduce skin friction and profile drag. Wing clipping could be classed under reducing parasite drag but there were so many side effects involved in the process that it needs to be looked at separately.

The bad side of wing clipping was that the reduction in effective wing area and aspect ratio had the direct effect of increasing the induced drag generated by lift. This could have a devastating effect on the plane's cornering characteristics. Not only could it pull down the plane's speed in the turn an additional 15–20 mph, but the increased wing loading stretched out the turning radius. The plane tended to mush outward and lose altitude in a turn, not being able to turn with planes having more wing area and span. And possibly worst of all, clipped wings increased the chances for a high-speed stall in a very tight pylon turn.

Just as in prewar conditions, compromise was in order. But unfortunately the practice of wing clipping has had a hairy, macho image throughout the history of pylon racing. So just as in prewar years, there were cases where clipping the wings of those 400 mph World War II fighters appeared to actually have a negative effect on lap averages. We live, but never learn!

Picking the right fighter

Practically every US military fighter plane from World War II that was available in any quantity from surplus sources was tried at one time or another in the postwar National Air Races. Only four or five gained any degree of popularity in this unique application.

North American P-51 Mustang

This one didn't have a wild power-to-weight ratio for takeoff and acceleration off the turns. But it had the cleanest aerodynamics of any World War II fighter, so its potential top straightaway speed in relation to available horsepower was good. And that available horsepower was not too shabby with the highly refined Packard Merlin engine, with two-stage supercharging and intercooling.

By far the most plentiful and least expensive Mustang—and probably the one most practical for the Thompson—was the P-51D model, with the medium-altitude V-1650-7 Merlin engine. The only

negative was that the -7 Merlin engine was not fitted for water injection. This posed a problem to Mustang owners that was met with some ingenious solutions, as we'll see. Some Mustang racers chose an earlier B or C model, with the pilot's canopy flush with the dorsal hump of the fuselage. They felt that the parasite drag was a bit less.

Bell P-39 and P-63 Cobra series

This series of Bell fighters was unique in having the engine behind the pilot, with a long shaft going forward to drive the propeller in the nose. This configuration, with most of the mass concentrated near the center of the plane, made a very maneuverable, responsive plane, with very decent aerodynamics. They were also plentiful and cheap on the surplus market. The worst limitation of the early P-39 design was the garden variety Allison engine—not much horsepower potential.

The P-63 King Cobras were essentially upsized P-39s with more sophisticated two-stage supercharged Allisons. They were heavier and more cumbersome than the P-39s, but buyers felt that the extra horsepower potential more than offset the extra size and weight. The most popular model was the P-63C, which was not only the most plentiful and least expensive, but also had a built-in water injection system. It was fairly easy, incidentally, to swap a

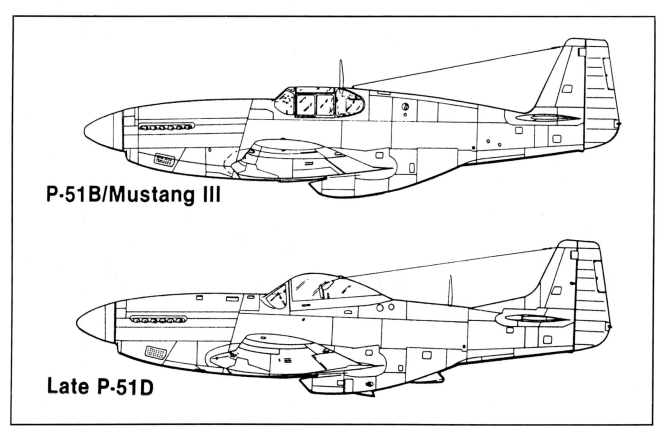

P-51B/Mustang III

Late P-51D

Some teams felt early Mustangs, with flush canopies, had less drag than later models with the bubble type. Squadron-Signal

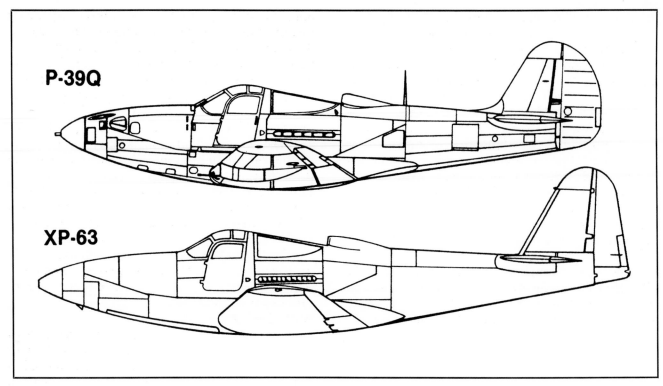

The Bell P-63 King Cobra was essentially an upsized and upgraded P-39, with more horsepower—but also more weight. Squadron-Signal

P-63 engine into a P-39 to get a better power-to-weight ratio and higher top speed with the smaller airframe.

Lockheed P-38 Lightning

This big plane, with separate engine pods and a center cockpit pod, was very heavy with lots of parasite drag. But some felt that the potential power-to-weight ratio with the two Allisons run full bore would give quick acceleration off the turns, offset-ting any lack of straightaway speed due to high parasite drag.

Vought Corsair series

This big, beefy Navy carrier fighter was heavy and needed a lot of horsepower to do its job. Early F4U versions usually were fitted with the big Pratt & Whitney R-2800 eighteen-cylinder radial, with up to 2,400 hp in standard form with two-stage supercharging and water injection. It was an iffy proposi-

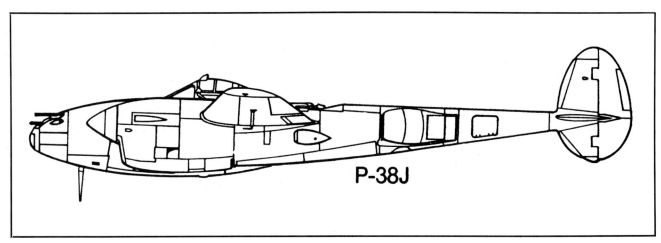

Some teams chose the Lockheed P-38 Lightning because the high power-to-weight ratio gave good acceleration off the turns. Squadron-Signal

140

tion for the Thompson, though, as the Corsair didn't have the power-per-square-foot of parasite area for a high top speed at sea level.

The Goodyear built F2G Super Corsairs were another matter. These were essentially standard Corsairs modified to take the huge twenty-eight cylinder Pratt & Whitney R–4360 engine of 3,000–3,500 hp. The original goal behind this design was a plane with an unheard-of power-to-weight ratio that could take off from a carrier deck and climb to moderate altitude in a matter of seconds (to defend against the Japanese suicide pilots that were cutting our Navy to pieces in the late stages of the Pacific war). The war ended before they could be perfected, though, and only eighteen planes were ever produced.

But you can imagine how effective a formula like this could be on the Thompson pylons. Mu-u-u-rder. Five of the existing planes were eventually bought for racing—and they certainly made their mark.

Digging for horsepower

After picking out the ideal surplus fighter plane for pylon racing and making some basic modifica-

tions, the big, big problem—as in every age of air racing—was in getting a horsepower advantage on the competition. This problem differed little in the postwar years from the prewar years. Just like commercial engines, the military engines still had to be designed for limited power settings to assure reliable operation and reasonably long life between overhauls. The same design principles applied for getting a little more power, that is, running the engine above recommended rpm and manifold pressure levels. The big difference in the postwar years was simply that rpm and manifold pressure numbers were much higher, due to undreamed-of advances in engine and fuel technology during the war. In these areas, it was a whole new world.

In the wartime years, developments were made in power technology that were perhaps little more than theories in the 1930s. Four had special significance in the racing scene.

Water injection

The idea of injecting water into the manifold of a highly supercharged engine, to cool the fuel-air mixture through heat absorbed by the evaporation of the water, went back to the 1920s. It was known even in those early days that combustion detonation

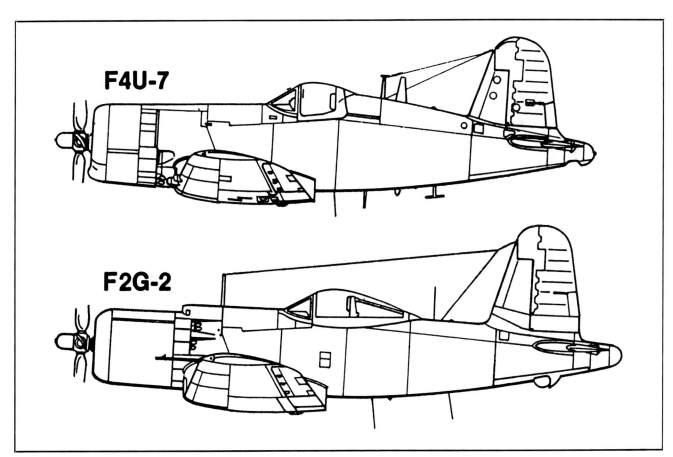

The F2G Corsair was essentially an F4U with nearly twice the horsepower. The F2G made a formidable Thompson competitor.
Squadron-Signal

or knock was heavily influenced by the temperature of the fuel mixture at the time of combustion. Since compressing the mixture with a supercharger increased its temperature radically, it was felt that if the fuel mixture could be cooled somehow before reaching the cylinders, an engine could stand more manifold pressure and develop more power on a given fuel octane.

But the idea of carrying a supply of water in a combat plane specifically for a temporary power boost was never seriously considered until the War Department gave the Wright Aeronautical Company a research and development contract in 1942 to come up with a generalized system that could be adapted to any Allied aircraft engine. The broad plan was some sort of system that would permit the engine to deliver short bursts of extra power for emergency combat situations, for maybe one to five minutes at a burst, with a total water supply for maybe ten to fifteen minutes of extra power per flight.

It proved to be a very practical idea. Wright's anti detonant injection (ADI) system used a 50–50 mixture of methanol and water, which proved optimum from a cooling and power standpoint, and the methanol prevented freezing at high altitude. Wright also engineered a hookup of tanks, feed pump, metering valve and a nozzle to spray the fluid into the inlet eye of the supercharger. The system was set to automatically inject the fluid when manifold pressure reached the war emergency level, and the metering valve was tied into the carburetor to inject ADI fluid at about forty percent of the fuel rate. This was found to be the best compromise between allowable power boost, which was 10–15 percent, and the weight and bulk of the fluid supply

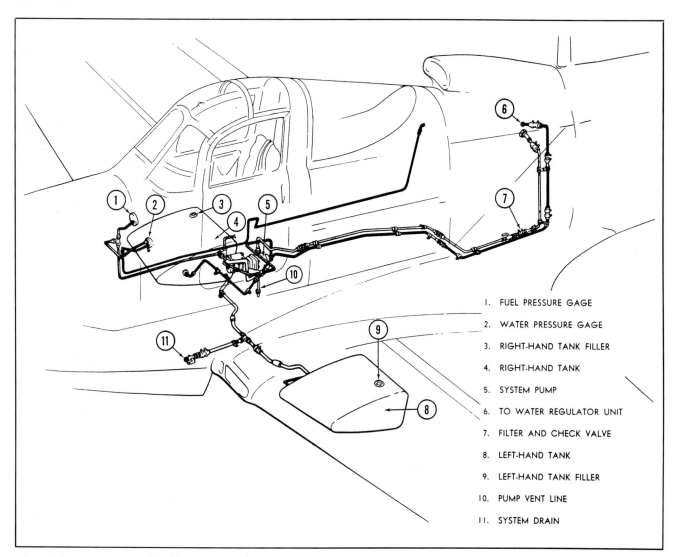

1. FUEL PRESSURE GAGE
2. WATER PRESSURE GAGE
3. RIGHT-HAND TANK FILLER
4. RIGHT-HAND TANK
5. SYSTEM PUMP
6. TO WATER REGULATOR UNIT
7. FILTER AND CHECK VALVE
8. LEFT-HAND TANK
9. LEFT-HAND TANK FILLER
10. PUMP VENT LINE
11. SYSTEM DRAIN

Water injection permitted 15 to 20 percent more horsepower on a given fuel octane, by cooling the fuel-air mixture going to the cylinders.

and tankage necessary for ten to fifteen minutes of injection per flight.

It should also be noted that increasing the water flow to sixty or seventy percent of the fuel rate would increase power a few more percent. This required careful remetering of the carburetor and injection control valve for optimum results, however, which was beyond the engineering know-how of most of the race teams. The record is uncertain as to which teams did or didn't try this remetering. Anyway, water injection was definitely one of America's great contributions to horsepower science during World War II.

Fuel octane quality

Developments in fuel profoundly influenced race performance in the 1930s. This factor was perhaps even more important in the early postwar years, as there had been tremendous "forced draft" progress in fuel technology during the war.

It's important to understand the new Performance Number (PN) method of rating fuel, which generally replaced the octane scale in World War II. The principle was that gasoline fuels would permit considerably higher manifold pressures and power outputs at rich fuel-air mixtures than at lean mixtures. This of course was because of the cooling effect of the extra fuel—the same principle as water injection. But the early octane rating method had not recognized this effect of fuel-air ratio and measured fuels only at lean mixtures. A new rating scale was set up by assigning a Performance Number of 100 to regular 100 octane fuel rated at a lean mixture. Then it was determined that this same fuel with a rich mixture would permit about thirty percent higher manifold pressure and power. The lean/rich PN rating of basic 100 octane fuel was thus designated 100/130.

This 100/130 was the standard combat fuel used in most Allied planes throughout the war. Toward the end of the war an improved 115/145 combat grade was developed that allowed about fifteen percent more power. But it was never used in any great quantity overseas. However, these two commercial avgas grades, 100/130 and 115/145, were the generally available fuels at the first postwar Thompson races in Cleveland. A fuel company usually gave a team 300–500 gal in return for displaying its decal on the plane.

The Shell and Sohio companies, and possibly others, also had technical representatives at all the races, and they would frequently offer to dope a racers fuel with some unspecified hydrocarbon additive to jazz it up for qualifying or racing. (These were probably compounds like toluene, xylene, aniline, cumene and triptane.) Many teams took advantage of this service, even though they didn't always understand what was going into their tanks.

Then in 1948, with a little fuel war heating up, Shell Oil surprised everybody by bringing one of these exotic additive compounds, triptane, to Cleveland in the form of a bulk fuel. It was said to have a PN rating of 200/300! They sold it to any interested team for $1.75 a gallon—which probably didn't begin to cover its cost—but with the proviso that pilots would report certain pertinent instrument readings after the race. About ten teams used the stuff that year, including Cook Cleland's two big F2G Corsairs. But the triptane proved to be their undoing. Due to a slower burning rate, spark timing was quite critical, and both of Cleland's 1948 entries were forced out from horrendous backfiring.

Needless to say, the word quickly got around that triptane was touchy stuff. This opened the door for Sohio to bring in a compromise fuel in 1949 with a PN rating of 130/170. Sohio offered to *give* 400 gal of the stuff to any team that would display its decal. Most of the teams went with Sohio that year.

But the important point is this: In the first two postwar races, engine outputs were limited by the anti-knock ability of standard wartime fuels and any

The oil companies made tremendous progress on aviation gas during World War II. Lab technicians here test various hydrocarbon compounds.

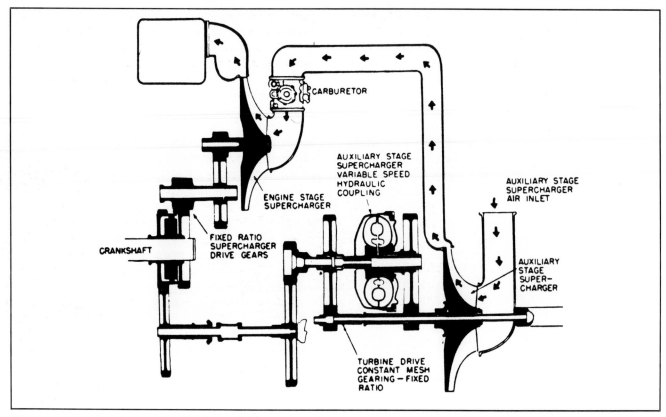

Two-stage supercharging permitted high manifold pressures of 80 to 100 in. at sea level for racing.

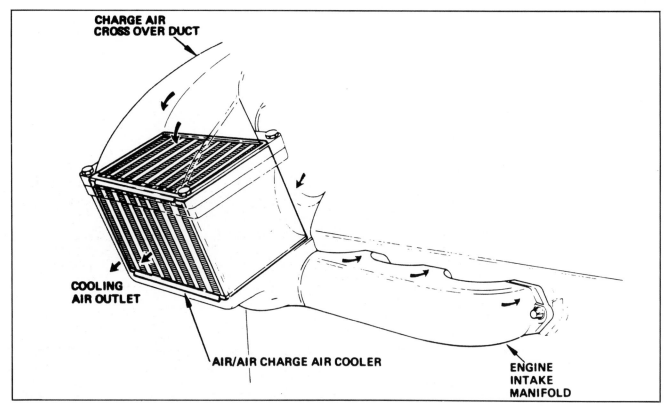

An intercooler radiator was effective in cooling the fuel-air mixture going to the cylinders, much like water injection. The two tricks together were dynamite!

contribution of octane additives and water injection. But in the 1948 and 1949 races, the availability of triptane and Sohio 130/170 grade—*plus* the help of water injection—left engine output limited more by the *mechanical strength* of the engine than by the anti-knock ability of the fuel. This is an important distinction to keep in mind.

Two-stage supercharging

Another important wartime power development for aircraft was two-stage supercharging. The principle was simple: One supercharger pumped its output into a second supercharger, so that the compression pressure of the first stage was multiplied by the second. In other words, if both stages gave seventy percent supercharge (or a compression ratio of 1.7:1), the final compression would be $1.7 \times 1.7 = 2.9:1$, or at sea level that would be a manifold pressure of around 84 in.

Most of the big wartime aircraft engines had certain models that featured two-stage supercharging. It was most practical for high altitudes. But the teams could pull some wild manifold pressures at low levels for racing with these two-stage engines—with the right fuel.

Supercharger intercooling

Compressing the fuel-air mixture with a supercharger radically increases its temperature. Not only does this bring on combustion detonation, but the expansion of the heated air means less weight of fuel-air mixture can be packed into the cylinders at a given manifold pressure.

Why not use some form of heat exchanger or radiator to cool down the hot mixture going from the supercharger to the cylinders? This principle is called intercooling and is very effective. One of the great features of the Rolls Merlin engine was a compact intercooler tucked into the supercharger outlet ducting that could drop the temperature of the fuel-air mixture 100 degrees Fahrenheit or more. It allowed several hundred more horsepower on a given fuel octane, much like a constant flow of water injection.

Engine designs used in the postwar Thompsons
In the Allison camp

General Motors bought out Allison Motors in 1935 and began serious development of their 1,710 ci liquid cooled V-12 for both military and commercial aircraft applications. The commercial market never opened up, but within a couple of years, several top military fighter planes were using the base design, which featured single overhead camshafts on each bank, four inclined valves per cylinder, one-piece head castings with fabricated cylinder barrels and water jackets, and a single-stage, single-speed supercharger on the back. A variety of blower

gear ratios, two-speed systems and provisions for hooking into an auxiliary exhaust turbo-charger gave the aircraft designer a huge choice of performance options at all altitudes up to 35,000 ft.

About midway through the war, a two-stage supercharging system was developed with a mechanical or fluid drive to a separate auxiliary stage behind the engine. This was used mostly in Bell P-63 fighters where there wasn't room for turbo-charging. Still later came the G series Allisons with crankshafts, rods and bearings upgraded to permit 3200 rpm for combat situations—plus improved two-stage supercharging and fuel injection. These engines were used in a few late P-63s, but mostly for North American P-82 Twin Mustangs used in the Korean war. They were still under development after World War II, and thus not readily available to the Thompson racers.

When picking an Allison for racing, it must be admitted that run-of-the-mill E and F series models, as used in P-38s, P-39s and P-40s, without exotica like intercoolers and such, were just not top performers. Manifold pressure with wide open throttle was pretty much determined by supercharger gear ratio, which varied from 7.5:1 to 9.6:1 on various models. But the actual prop shaft output wasn't always proportional to manifold pressure because the high blower speeds soaked up so much engine power at

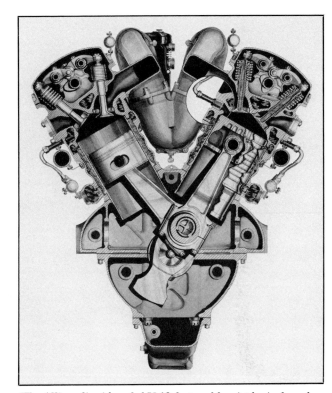

The Allison liquid-cooled V-12 featured hemispherical combustion chambers, elaborate split flow intake manifolds and huge forged steel connecting rods. Allison Motors

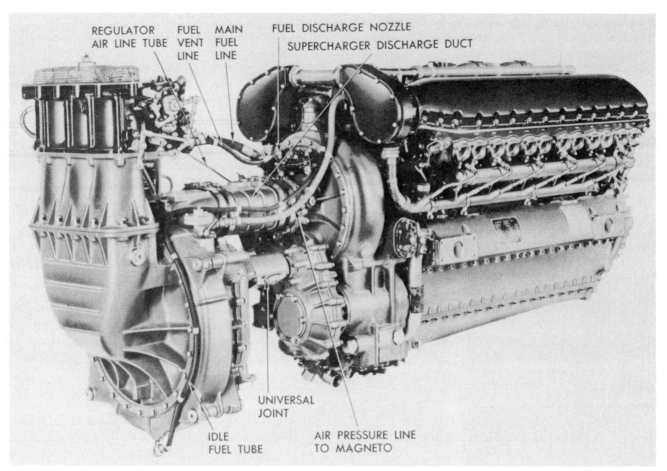

REGULATOR
AIR LINE TUBE

FUEL
VENT
LINE

MAIN
FUEL
LINE

FUEL DISCHARGE NOZZLE

SUPERCHARGER DISCHARGE DUCT

UNIVERSAL
JOINT

IDLE
FUEL TUBE

AIR PRESSURE LINE
TO MAGNETO

The popular Bell P-63C fighters used a two-stage Allison with a separate auxiliary supercharger behind the engine, and a large three-barrel Bendix carburetor with water injection. Allison Motors

The late Allison G6 two-stage fuel injection model was under development at the end of the war, and not for sale. Insiders got one for a 1948 Cobra II and broke Thompson lap record at 413 mph. Allison Motors

146

sea level. Overspeeding wasn't a potent trick with those early Allisons, either. About 3200 rpm was the limit for forty-five minutes of racing. At this speed, full throttle outputs ranged generally from 1600 to 1750 hp at 60 to 75 in. manifold pressure, depending on blower ratio. But durability was marginal, as BMEPs (combustion pressures) were on the ragged edge of severe detonation with 115/145 grade fuel.

Perhaps a better deal was to race a Bell P-63C with a two-stage Allison and water injection, or to get just the engine and swap it into a lighter P-39. Here a racer could run up to 85–90 in. manifold pressure with the injection and 115/145 fuel and get around 2,000 hp. Or with the super fuels available in 1948 and 1949, a pilot could open the throttle wide and pull over 2,200 hp at 3200 rpm on pressures over 100 in.

One specially effective hop-up trick for Allison engines (and Merlins) was to adapt a huge Bendix Model PR-58 water injection carburetor from a late Pratt & Whitney R-2800 or Wright R-3350 engine. This unique carb design had a rectangular air passage and throttle blades, with four small booster venturis to sense mass air flow. It was often mistakenly called a "four-barrel" carburetor for this reason. But the large air passage area practically eliminated any suction loss on the inlet side and could add as much as 200–300 hp over the standard two- and three-barrel Bendix carbs found on most Allison and Merlin engines. (This PR-58 carburetor was very popular in the 1950s and 1960s for hopping up Merlin engines in the Gold Cup hydroplanes.)

The magnificent Merlin

The roots of the wartime Rolls-Royce Merlin V-12 engine can be traced back to the famous R engines that the Rolls people developed for the Supermarine Schneider Trophy seaplanes in 1929 and 1931. It was a proud, productive heritage that no one can logically minimize. The Merlin was destined for great things from the late thirties on.

The US Packard built versions, familiar because they were used in the P-51 Mustangs, had 1,649 ci displacement, four vertical overhead valves per cylinder, cylinder block and head construction similar to the Allison and were boosted by a two-stage, two-speed supercharger and intercooler core built compactly into the back of the engine structure. All used large Bendix two-barrel carburetors, but the V-1650-9 models, used in late P-51H Mustangs, were fitted for water injection.

The Merlin's intercooling system was described earlier. But one point about its operation is frequently misunderstood. The intercooler used regular glycol type engine coolant to absorb heat from the fuel-air mixture going to the engine. Most impor-

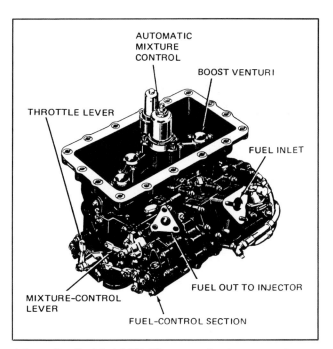

A huge Bendix Model PR-58 rectangular passage carburetor from big Pratt & Whitney or Wright radial could add 100–200 hp to an Allison or Merlin engine by reducing inlet suction loss to practically zero. Bendix

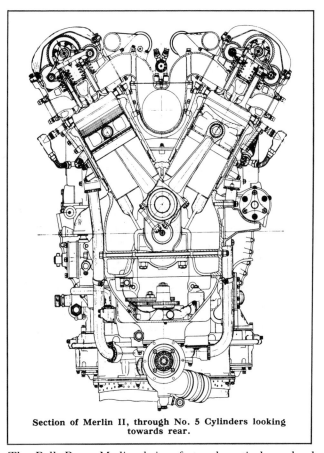

Section of Merlin II, through No. 5 Cylinders looking towards rear.

The Rolls-Royce Merlin design featured vertical overhead valves, four per cylinder, with flat combustion chambers and all accessory gear drives at the back of the engine. Rolls-Royce Heritage Archives

tant, it was an entirely separate cooling system, *not* tapped into the engine cooling system, as is often believed. The intercooler had its own little pump and radiator in the main ram air duct. This made it possible to take as much as 100–120 degrees of heat out of the fuel-air mixture. The intercooler would have been much less efficient if it had been plumbed into the hot engine cooling circuit. Some racers tried to save weight by plumbing the intercooler into the engine cooling circuit and getting rid of the extra pump and radiator. But they didn't realize that they were drastically reducing its effectiveness and actually cutting engine power by doing so.

The -7 Merlin in P-51D Mustangs could deliver roughly 2,000 hp at 3000 rpm on 80–85 in. manifold pressure with full throttle in low blower gear. But

detonation was a problem on straight 115/145 grade fuel, even with the intercooler. With water injection and more exotic fuels, a -7 engine could top 2,500 hp at 3200 rm on 100–105 in. in high blower gear. It made a very practical powerplant for the Thompson—more so than the -9 model, in some ways, because the lower blower gear ratios were more efficient and less strain on the engine at low altitudes. But a -9 Merlin with the right fuel and properly calibrated water injection was probably the ultimate: It was good for 2,800–3,000 hp at 3400 rpm on 120 in. when everything was right. But durability at these output levels was measured in minutes.

The big disadvantage with the -7 Merlin was that it wasn't fitted for water injection in the P-51D airframe. It may not sound like a big thing to rig up, but this was more than just a problem of swapping a

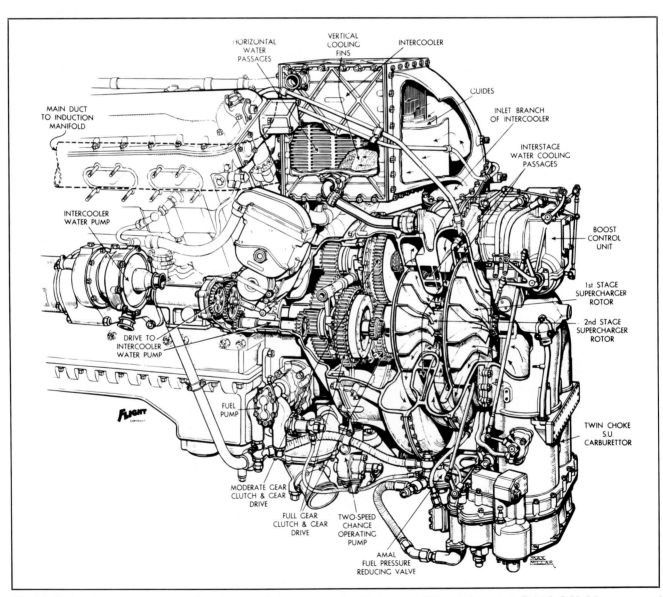

The Merlin's unique two-stage supercharger and built-in intercooler were worth an extra 400–500 hp over the conventional Allison setup. This carburetor is British S.U. Mustangs used Bendix carburetors. Quadrant-"FLIGHT"

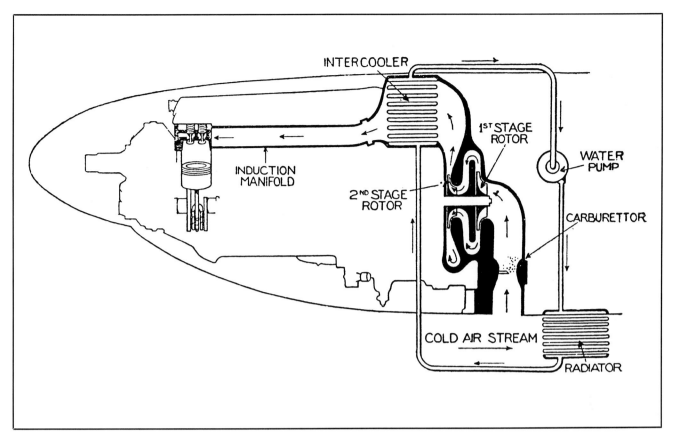

The intercooler on a Merlin engine had its own separate cooling system, with a radiator and small pump to circulate the coolant. It was not connected to the engine cooling system. "FLIGHT"

The left-side view of a Merlin engine shows the large two-stage supercharger, the intercooler and the intercooler coolant pump as well as the generator driven from a common gear takeoff.
Rolls-Royce Heritage Archives

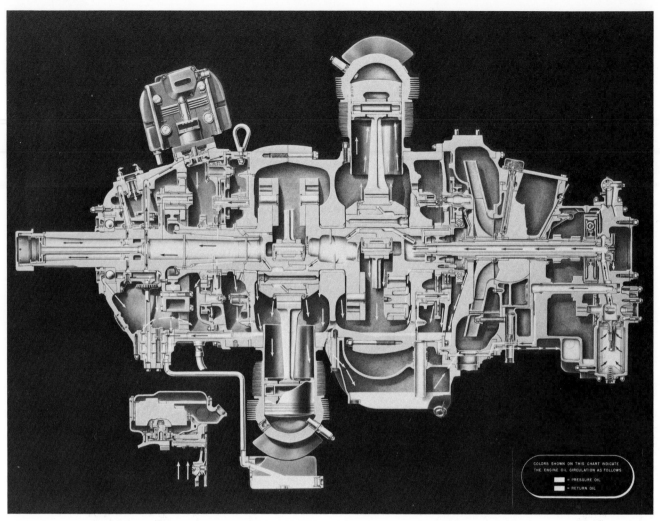

A sectional view shows the Pratt & Whitney 18-cylinder R-2800 single stage, used in Vought F4U Corsairs. This engine was capable of about 2,800 hp at 2800 rpm with water injection. United Technologies

carburetor. A water injection system included a lot of parts: tanks, pumps, filters, check valves, pressure regulators, all kinds of plumbing—*plus* a carburetor with the needed metering control. Ideally, a racing team could pirate a system from a P-51H plane with a -9 Merlin. But these aircraft were not declared surplus in the early postwar years, so the parts were hard to find.

There were a number of interesting solutions to this dilemma. The most common was to merely swap a complete system from one plane to another—from a P-47 or P-63C fighter to a P-51D Mustang—and then try to find a carburetor with the necessary jetting and controls. The race crew just about had to swap the carburetor, too because the systems were calibrated to de-rich the carb when the fluid was being injected, to prevent flooding the engine. The systems didn't work nearly as well if the fluid squirted in with the carburetor at full rich. As usual, it was a situation where raw ingenuity won the day.

Those big Pratt & Whitney Double Wasps

The R-2800 eighteen-cylinder twin-row engine didn't figure too prominently in the postwar Thompsons; it was used only in a P-47 Thunderbolt and two or three F4U Corsairs that were entered at various times. It never made much of a splash. The late versions of this engine had two-stage, two-speed superchargers and so could develop high manifold pressures for racing. But low altitudes were an inefficient range for the blowers because mixture temperatures were high.

With water injection, maximum usable performance on 115/145 fuel was about 2,800 hp at 2800 rpm on 75 in. manifold pressure. It sounds like a lot of punch, but the weight and size of the big fighters pretty much neutralized the power.

The huge R-4360 Wasp Major was the Pratt & Whitney that really made a splash in the postwar Thompson races. It was so big that it just overpowered everything else in sight. It was a twenty-eight cylinder, four-row radial developed primarily for

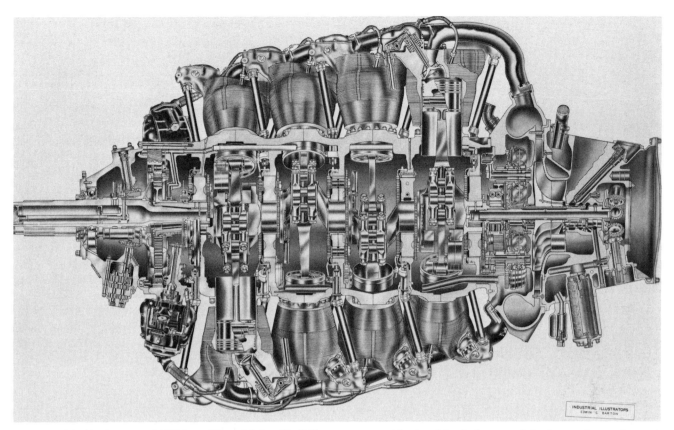

The huge 28-cylinder Pratt & Whitney Wasp Major, R-4360, used in F2G Corsairs, could develop 4,000 to 4,500 hp at 2800 rpm with the right fuel, water injection and an air scoop. United Technologies

the B–36 bomber. It was also used in the Goodyear F2G Corsairs as a defense against Japanese suicide planes late in the Pacific war. Only a handful were ever produced, but Cook Cleland, Ben McKillen and Ron Puckett were able to corner five planes, and they proved to be a tremendously potent combination for sea level pylon racing.

The R-4360s had a unique boost control system that was an important factor in their excellent sea level performance. It eliminated throttling suction losses on the inlet side at reduced power levels. Instead of using the usual throttle to control power, the supercharger (single-stage) was driven through a small fluid coupling that had a system to vary the amount of fluid in the torus, which changed the effective blower drive ratio by changing the amount of slip of the coupling (it operated much like a car's automatic transmission). The fluid coupling automatically maintained a preset manifold pressure. Or a pilot could override the automatic control with a hand lever and pull any manifold pressure up to maximum. This was known as slipping the blower.

As used in the F2G, the R-4360 had a war emergency rating of 3,500 hp at 2700 rpm on 60 in. manifold pressure, using water injection and 100/130 grade fuel. This sounds like a horrendous amount of power, but in fact that huge engine was

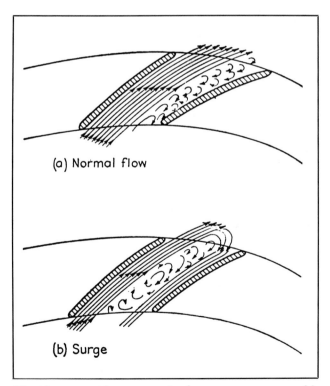

The phenomenon known as supercharger surge was caused by the stalling of diffuser vanes, usually triggered by restricted air inlet at high revs. Violent air oscillation could put the affected plane out of the race.

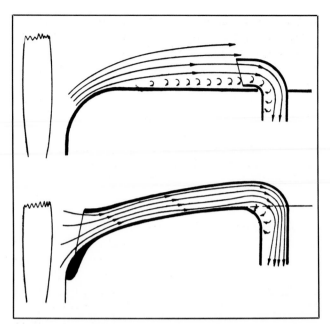

The location of the carburetor air scoop was critical on high-speed postwar fighters because unpredictable air turbulence could starve an engine of air and cost up to 1,000 hp. F2G Corsairs suffered from air starvation until they were modified by extending the air scoop shroud.

relatively lightly stressed at this power level, in terms of cylinder pressures and manifold temperatures. With improved racing fuels and water injection, the teams were able to pull up to 4,500 hp at 2800 rpm on 65–75 in.

Don't let the power leak away

Several special powerplant problems often reared their heads on fighter planes that were set up for pylon racing, problems that may have been entirely unfamiliar to pilots and mechanics exposed only to normal military combat flying.

Supercharger surge

This phenomenon was an uncontrolled low frequency oscillation of air in the induction system caused by stalling and backflow of air on the supercharger diffuser vanes, which caused excessive heat buildup, engine vibration and power loss in the blower. The plane would actually surge and jerk in flight. The condition was usually triggered by closing the throttle too quickly at high engine speed or sometimes by a restricted air inlet at high speed. Two-stage Merlin engines seemed especially susceptible to the problem.

Standard propellers were often modified to absorb added power at higher speeds. These experimental Hamilton blades on the Beguine *Mustang were very thin and cost $2,500 each! They were said to increase the plane's top speed 10–20 mph.* Aldrich Collection

Sometimes the pilot could stop the surge by opening the throttle wide and then closing it slowly. But this surge put more than one Mustang out of a race. And most teams didn't know what was happening.

Restricted air inlet

It's a basic premise that a piston engine is really nothing more than an air pump, and anything that would restrict the free flow of air into the carburetor is bound to choke off horsepower. Most of the World War II fighter planes had very efficient air scoops in standard form. But when the backyard racers began fussing with things to get better streamlining—especially without wind tunnels to test modifications—sometimes the air inlet would be exposed to turbulent conditions, and power would be lost. Maybe the odd air flow might come only at certain speeds. Anyway, carburetor air scoops were a critical factor in the performance of some of the postwar Thompson racers, and this was the very key to unlocking the tremendous performance of the F2G Corsairs in these races.

Propeller problems

Propellers were not a major performance limitation in the postwar Thompsons. All the planes had state-of-the-art hydraulic or electric constant speed props, three- or four-bladed, that would automatically maintain any engine rpm the pilot selected by varying the pitch or blade angle. This was one less thing the pilot had to do under the stress of wing-to-wing racing. He could preset the engine speed he wanted at the start of the race and then control the plane's speed by varying manifold pressure with the throttle.

But some problems arose when those neatly engineered combat propellers were subjected to the rigors of pylon racing. The props were originally designed to absorb a certain horsepower at a certain rpm, air speed and altitude—conditions that were probably very different from racing conditions. Operating under less than ideal conditions, of course, meant a loss of efficiency. An especially tight limiting factor was blade tip speed, which needed to be below sonic velocity for good efficiency, specifically 1,100 feet per second at sea level. At engine revs above 3000 rpm and air speeds over 400 rpm, this tip speed might be well over sonic, with resulting losses. More than one Thompson team clipped inches off their prop blades just like they clipped feet off their wings!

In the absence of funds to commission propeller manufacturers to produce custom racing props—some $50,000 even fifty years ago—about the best the boys could do was to pirate a four-bladed P-63 prop for a P-39, or a P-51H prop for a P-51D. And benefits were always uncertain.

But at least *somebody* thought of just about everything there was to think of to go faster in those postwar Thompson races.

Chapter 11

Great postwar racers

Cobra II: **The fastest P-39**

The Bell P-39 Airacobra fighters made pretty decent pylon racers because of good aerodynamics, light weight and quick control response because of the central engine location—which reduced the flywheel inertia about the center of gravity. Their worst feature was the early single-stage Allison engine with limited power potential.

One team was determined to squeeze the full potential from a pair of P-39s for the first postwar

Thompson in 1946. Three Bell test pilots—Alvin "Tex" Johnston, Jack Woolams and "Slick" Goodlin—formed a corporation, Slylanes Unlimited, to procure, prepare and race P-39s as a private venture, with no connection to Bell Aircraft. They were permitted to use Bell facilities, and they even bought two late P-39Q models from the Bell experimental department for a nominal dollar apiece. But legal considerations prevented Bell from directly sponsoring the effort.

The Bell P-39Q Cobra II *was one of the most famous postwar Thompson racers, under various owners, pilots, modifications and engine swaps.* Fraites Collection

154

Most important, this project enjoyed more than the usual amount of educated engineering input, skilled help from volunteer Bell workers and the best hangar and job shop facilities at the Bell plant. This was not any backyard operation like so many of the postwar racing programs were.

The two P-39Q models were modified in several areas. First, all unneeded weight was stripped out: guns, ammunition racks, armor plate, radio equipment, high-altitude equipment and so on. One big weight saving was replacing the original puncture resistant fuel tanks with light neoprene fuel cells from U.S. Rubber. This proved much more practical than trying to seal off portions of the wing structure, as some other teams were doing. In all, over 1,000 lb were removed, which brought the empty weight of the planes down around 4,500 lb.

Another important, but simple, modification was increasing battery voltage from twenty-four to thirty-six for the electric landing gear retracting mechanism, so that the gear could be completely retracted in five seconds. Great for the racehorse starts. Another significant modification, suggested by high-speed flight tests that showed some ballooning of the fabric covering on the ailerons, was to re-cover the control surfaces with sheet aluminum and fit fixed trim tabs, adjusted by flight tests. These modifications sound so simple and logical. But pinpointing problem areas on a given plane designed for 400 mph pylon racing could get pretty hairy. Spotting this particular one almost caused a fatal crash, when fabric tore off the ailerons at 400 mph.

Perhaps they key change on these P-39s was replacing the original early Allison engines with late G4 models, a type that was being tested in an upgraded Bell P-63F King Cobra at the end of the war. This particular Allison configuration had the late improved crankshaft and rods that could sustain 3200 rpm under military conditions, with an enlarged single-stage supercharger for medium altitudes. The Bell team felt that it would make a good sea level combination when fitted for water injection (with the fluid capacity increased from the usual 25 to 75 gal). In keeping with the added power, larger four-bladed P-63 propellers were fitted.

High-speed flight tests showed engine cooling to be adequate, using the original inboard wing radiators. But the high sustained engine speeds caused excessive oil heating and foaming. This was cured by increasing the system capacities from 8 to 13 gal and by mounting larger oil coolers in special air ducts in the bellies of the planes.

With these modifications, it was felt that the engine speed could be increased to 3400 rpm, which gave an estimated 2,200 hp at full throttle with manifold pressure of 80–85 in. and water injection. Indicated air speeds reached 430 mph in early flight tests. (A few inches of manifold pressure were due to air scoop ram effect.) Everybody was confident that this was ample performance to win the the 1946 Thompson on the large thirty-mile course.

Hopes were multiplied when pilot Woolams qualified *Cobra I* for two laps at 392.7 mph, and Tex Johnston scorched the pylons the next day in *Cobra II* at a record 409.1 mph! No other contestants were even close to the Johnston speed that year.

When Johnston's qualifying speed exceeded *Cobra I*'s by some 17 mph, Woolams felt his engine may have been damaged by detonation. He decided to make a quick trip back to the Bell plant at Niagara Falls, New York, to have one of the spare G4 engines installed—four of them had been purchased for the project. On his return flight, skimming along the shore of Lake Ontario at 400 mph, the plane suddenly flipped up sideways and plunged into the water, killing Woolams instantly. The exact cause of the crash was never pinpointed, but the accepted theory was that the plexiglass windshield, which had been installed to replace the heavy bullet-proof glass, shattered from high aerodynamic pressure, probably knocking Woolams unconscious. Johnston's plexiglass windshield in *Cobra II* was carefully reinforced with wire before the 1946 Thompson race. He won that race with ease, averaging 373.9 mph, well below the maximum capability of the plane.

After the Woolams crash, the Bell people became somewhat disenchanted with pylon racing. And Johnston was too occupied with Bell X-1 rocket testing to take time off for the 1947 Thompson. So shortly before that race, *Cobra II* was sold at a nice profit for $10,000 to Indianapolis car dealer Rollin Stewart, who was at the Bell plant buying a helicopter. He quickly made a deal with another Bell test pilot, Jay Demming, to fly the plane in the coming Thompson and to share any prize money. However, there wasn't time to make any significant mechanical changes from the 1946 setup.

Strange as it seems, the same problem that was thought to have caused the Woolams crash—shattering of the plexiglass windshield—almost clobbered Demming on his 1947 qualifying run. Despite special wire bracing, the plexiglass shattered again at 400+ mph, near the end of the run, and it was all Demming could do to keep control of the ship and finish the lap. His two-lap average thus dropped to a disappointing 393.9 mph, but it was the third fastest time behind the two Super Corsairs of Cleland and Becker.

After further beefing-up of the front cockpit windshield and bracing, Demming was confident that he had enough power to stay with the flying

Corsairs with their big twenty-eight cylinder Pratt & Whitneys. But they just had too much raw power. Demming finished a tight third behind Cleland and Becker, flying most of the race at 3200 rpm and 75 in. That was below maximum power, but it was all that he felt he could safely pull on the 115/145 gas for the 300 miles. His average speed was 389.8 mph, about 5 mph short.

At this point, owner Rollin Stewart could see his *Cobra II* was going to need a healthy transfusion of horsepower to handle the big Corsairs in the 1948 Thompson. Fortunately, he had influential friends in the Allison Engine Division in his home town of Indianapolis, and it didn't take much arm twisting to get their chief test pilot Chuck Brown and engineer Don Nolan interested in a serious effort to win the coming race. It was an ideal hookup, too, because not only did Brown and Nolan know Allison engines inside and out, but they had the connections to get the loan of a prototype G6 model that had all the latest goodies and was not available to the public.

The "stock" G6 engine had two-stage supercharging with a new Bendix interstage fuel injection system and boasted a War Emergency rating of 2,250 hp at 3,200 rpm on 100 in. manifold pressure, with water injection and 115/145 grade fuel. To prepare for racing, engineer Don Nolan decided to remove the auxiliary supercharger stage—it didn't help much at sea level—and then to compensate by raising the engine blower gear rato to 8.8:1. He also replaced the restrictive fuel injection air meter with a big Bendix PR-58 carburetor from a late R-2800 Pratt & Whitney.

Obviously, they had a mighty potent power package here. Nolan even experimented with exotic fuels to get the last ounce of power. He tried a blend of methanol, benzol and acetone, similar to an old Rolls-Royce Schneider formula from 1931! But when he found that Shell was going to provide triptane fuel at the 1948 race—with that impressive 200/300 Performance Number rating—all thoughts of hassling with the problems of alcohol fuel were abandoned. But meanwhile, the race crew had installed an extra 40 gal tank behind the cockpit, to help with the huge fuel consumption rates with alcohol. When it was decided to use gasoline, the 40 gal tank was plumbed into the water injection system, giving a total fluid supply of 115 gal for the 300 mile race. It worked out great because the gas consumption rate was barely half that of the alcohol blend and they were able to run the water injection continously if desired.

The two fuels differed little in plane performance. Both the alcohol and triptane with water injection showed a top speed of 440–450 mph at 3350 rpm and 115 in. manifold pressure. Horsepower was estimated at 2,700–2,800. It looked like an unbeatable combination. And hopes soared a notch higher when Chuck Brown qualified for the 1948 Thompson at another record 418.1 mph! This was surely going to be Cobra's year.

But once again fate stepped in. In the early laps of the race, *Cobra II* and the two Corsairs of Cleland and Becker raced wing-to-wing, with Brown showing a slight straightaway speed advantage. Then both Corsairs dropped out when their air scoops were blown loose by backfires. This left Brown far in the lead, with no close opposition. He even backed way off to save his engine. But around the fifteenth lap, the Allison began cutting out intermittently, then picking up, then misfiring. Finally barely twenty miles from the finish line, the engine quit cold—and Brown had to dead-stick in.

The problem was quickly diagnosed on the postrace inspection. A small ten-inch section of engine cowl had worked loose, exposing the back of the engine compartment to exhaust stack heat. This had overheated the fuel line to the carburetor, despite its asbestos wrapping, causing a vapor lock condition. The engine was simply being starved for fuel. When the panel was replaced, the engine ran fine and showed practically no wear when it was torn down. It was a case of the proverbial horseshoe nail that lost a war!

The *Cobra II* story ended when the plane was damaged on the landing after being ferried back to Indianapolis following the race, when it ran out of gas only a mile short of the airport. Owner Stewart didn't want to spend the money necessary to fix it up for the 1949 Thompson. It gathered dust for years in an Indianapolis hangar.

The Cleland F2G Corsairs: Mightiest of them all

Cook Cleland was an ex–World War II Navy pilot who was weaned on big radial engine carrier based fighters that literally screamed the maxim that brute horsepower could beat sophisticated aerodynamics any time. Mix this background with a boyhood fascination with all types of fast airplanes, and it was probably inevitable that Cook showed up at the first postwar Thompson Trophy race with one of the faster Navy fighters, an FG-1D Corsair. It carried a late water injected version of the R-2800 Pratt & Whitney, good for up to 2,400 hp, and Cook was confident that he had the key to the Thompson challenge.

That 1946 Thompson turned out to be a painful learning experience for Cleland. He managed to finish sixth in the race, but despite his expectations, his 2,400 hp stock Corsair was far from being one of

Cook Cleland's team of F2G Corsairs proved to be the fastest and most reliable of all postwar Thompson racers. The carburetor air scoop design was the key modification to getting over 4,000 hp. Bowers

the faster planes in the field. It became immediately obvious to our man that these big, heavy shipboard fighters would require some *real* horsepower to stand a chance against the light, sleek Mustangs and Bell Cobras.

His answer proved to be the ideal World War II fighter plane for closed course pylon racing: a big F2G Super Corsair with the 3,500 hp Pratt & Whitney twenty-eight cylinder R-4360 engine. As mentioned earlier, only eighteen of these unique planes were built before the war's end, and Cleland finagled his way to the purchase of three of the –1 land-based versions for $1,250 each, in preparation for the 1947 Thompson. These didn't include the hydraulic wing folding mechanism and arresting gear of the –2 carrier version and were considerably lighter at 8,480 lb empty.

As usual, money was short in the Cleland camp, and the big F2Gs really needed some lightening work to be at their best on the pylons. Cleland was an outgoing, fast-talking promoter type, with a line of blarney that would choke an Irishman. He was never able to land a sponsor to pay his bills, but he did manage to talk the Chance-Vought and Good-year factory people into spending some $15,000 each on reworking two of his planes, which includ-ed stripping out over 1,000 lb of equipment, check-ing all systems and repainting to a gloss finish.

The Cleland team, which now consisted of Navy pilot friends Dick Becker and Tony Janazzo, also made several modifications of their own. One involved the inlet air scoops to the carburetors. The original scoops were located at the back edge of the engine cowling and were apparently in an area of excessive turbulence at high air speeds. After Cle-land had learned how to override the automatic hydraulic boost control with a hand lever, he found to his horror that he couldn't pull much over 52 in. manifold pressure above 350 mph regardless of the throttle setting. It seemed obvious that the engines were starving for air, which, it turned out, limited top speeds to around 400 mph.

Navy engineers already had a fix for the prob-lem, in the form of large diverging air scoops with their openings right at the forward edge of the cowl. They loaned Cleland one of these expensive hand-hammered scoops, but not three. Undaunted, the team got busy and hammered out two more similar sheet aluminum ducts to fit over the top of the engine cowls. They weren't as neat as the Navy scoop, but they seemed to get the job done.

157

After installation, the pilots were able to pull over 80 in. manifold pressure at 2800 rpm and maximum blower speed (minimum slip in the fluid coupling). This was estimated to give near 4,500 hp on a super octane fuel with water injection, and air speeds jumped to 450 mph. A more normal output for race cruising was 4,000 hp at 2800 rpm on 65 in., which gave maximum straightaway speeds of 420–430 mph. Believe it or not, the big R-4360s were relatively lightly stressed at this level!

One of Cleland's more shaky modifications was to put big 100 gal tanks in the open area behind the cockpits, to carry the huge amount of ADI fluid that would be required for forty-five minutes of racing with the big engines. This extra weight of nearly 1,000 lb several feet aft of the wing screwed up the center of gravity balance of the F2Gs so much that the elevator control response would actually *reverse* for the first few laps, until some of the fluid was used up. Cleland never told NAA inspectors about that modification!

Things looked encouraging in the Cleland camp after the three planes turned in 1947 qualifying speeds ranging from 373 to 401 mph. And the planes proved to be just as fast in the race. Cleland and Becker finished one, two, with Cleland setting a new race record of 396.1 mph. But it wasn't to be for poor Tony Janazzo. On the seventh lap, his plane began to weave and wobble crazily—and almost before the horrified spectators knew there was something wrong, he plunged staight into the ground at 400 mph. The autopsy revealed that he had been overcome by carbon monoxide fumes, possibly due to one or more exhaust stacks breaking off.

The big news for Cleland's 1948 program was Shell's introduction of its exotic triptane fuel. Cleland was one of the eight or ten racers who tried it that year. His plan was to run it without water injection, thus saving the weight of the water plus helping the stability of the planes.

There was only one problem. Triptane was still basically a laboratory curiosity right after the war, and not even the Shell technicians knew that much about using it in sustained high output operation. Triptane had a slower burn rate than regular avgas, so spark timing was critical. Early in the race, when battling for the lead against Chuck Brown, both Cleland's and Becker's engines suddenly erupted with explosions blowing back through the carburetors, tearing off the makeshift air scoops and dislodging part of the engine cowling. It was all the surprised pilots could do to land their ships safely. Nobody knows to this day exactly what happened. Possibly, supercharger surge was a factor, as fuel mixture backed up in the intake system due to throt-

tling or air scoop turbulence and was touched off by the early spark timing. Who knows?

For 1949, Cleland changed to a new fuel supplier. Sohio had a new 130/170 grade that promised to be more than adequate for the big Pratt & Whitneys with or without water injection. Cook had read about some German experiments during World War II with hydrogen peroxide injection that was supposed to yield big power gains, due to extra oxygen released. So why not? He found a source in Cleveland where he could buy a stabilized mixture of hydrogen peroxide and water in barrel lots, and he planned to just pour the stuff into his ADI storage tank, rigging up a hand lever to control the injection through the existing water nozzle.

All kinds of stories grew up about this unique injection system that Cleland used in 1949. I've spent considerable effort digging out the facts. And the brutal truth is that the idea just didn't work. Cleland knew nothing about the required flow rates of the peroxide in relation to the fuel. There was no calibration of the system whatever. He just injected the peroxide through the normal ADI system and hoped that something would happen. Obviously nothing could happen, without feeding additional fuel to combine with the additional oxygen—just as is necessary to feed fuel with modern nitrous oxide injection systems.

According to teammate Becker, who first tested the idea, when the peroxide flow was turned on, there was no change in any instrument reading—air speed, manifold pressure, rpm, temperature, nothing. He might as well have been injecting pure water. The 1949 peroxide story ended right where it began: back in the barrel.

One interesting new modification that year, though, was a radical clip of some four feet off each wing tip of Cleland's No. 94 ship, with the installation of large sheet aluminum end plates to reduce vortex flow and the accompanying drag. Actually Cleland had clipped a modest 18 in. off his wing tips the previous year, apparently without effect. But he claimed the total span reduction of 8 ft in 1949, with the end plates, added 10 mph to the top speed of his plane.

The added wing loading may have hurt cornering, though, as Dick Becker in No. 74, with unclipped wings, qualified for the 1949 Thompson at 414.6 mph, compared with 407 mph for Cleland. But Becker never got to race that year. Just as he was rounding the home pylon on his last qualifying lap, the reduction gear in his big Pratt & Whitney let go. He was at full throttle, and before Becker could chop it, the engine free-revved to over 4500 rpm and threw the rod assembly apart. It was all he could do to dead-stick in with the big prop windmilling.

There was no time to fix it, and no spare engine. Becker had no choice but to sit out the 1949 race.

The Cleland story did have a happy ending. Cook went on to win the 1949 Thompson in No. 94 at a record average of 397.1 mph, with other F2Gs second and third. The big guy had proved his point conclusively: Horsepower will beat aerodynamics in pylon racing, if given even half a chance!

Charlie Tucker's clipped wing King

Ex–World War II fighter pilot Charlie Tucker was one of the few postwar Thompson competitors who preferred a P-63 King Cobra over a Corsair or Mustang for more reasons than just its bargain basement price. He was fully convinced that it was potentially and actually the fastest basic combination of engine and airframe available on the surplus market for pylon racing.

In early 1946, Tucker bought two identical C-5 models for $1,000 each, with the idea of running one in the Bendix and one in the Thompson. Initial preparation was the usual weight-strip: armor, guns, radio equipment, ammunition racks and so on. The two-stage, water injected Allison engines were left almost completely stock.

It was in wing clipping that Charlie Tucker made his mark in postwar Thompson history. He chopped a full 6.5 ft off each side of the No. 28 *Tucker Special* for the Thompson, bringing the standard 38 ft wing span down to 25 ft, and reducing gross wing area from 248 sq. ft. to an estimated 180 sq. ft. Nobody else ever came close to this much clip on a wartime fighter used for pylon racing. It was a world record!

Was it all Charlie's idea? In interviews years later, he recalled that he made the clips after discussing the technical considerations with Bell test pilot Bob Stanley and with Stan Corssin, an aeronautical engineer friend at California Institute of Technology. All three agreed that the standard P-63 had too much wing for optimum 400 mph pylon performance. The question was only, How much clip was too much? It's not known, though, if the full 13 foot clip was a unanimous committee decision!

But making this deep clip in a hangar shop with simple equipment and unprofessional know-how (just Charlie and his teenage brother) brought unexpected problems. They cut into the outboard laminated fuel cells and had to use every trick in the book to get even a ninety-nine percent seal for later

Charlie Tucker's famous No. 28 Bell P-63C had the most radical wing clip of any postwar Thompson racer: 6.5 feet off each wing. The clip was too much for stable pylon turns. Carter

high-g racing flight. The cells never did seal well, and it was leaked fuel which washed lubricant off the landing gear struts, preventing the gear from retracting in the 1946 Thompson.

Was this deep wing clip a functional success? Tucker later admitted in a moment of candor that it gained him nothing. What little top speed was gained on the straightaways by reduced wing drag was lost by mushing outward on the turns, due to the high wing loading and low aspect ratio. Also landing and takeoff became much more difficult. Landing became a delicate 130 mph mush-in, and takeoffs were limited to an easy 60 in. manifold pressure to prevent torque roll on liftoff. The overall effect was to make every flight in No. 28 an adventure!

To his credit, though, Charlie Tucker did manage to get more performance out of a P-63 than did any other postwar Thompson team. And he didn't do it with fancy engine hop-up tricks. In 1946, he qualified at 392 mph with a bone stock engine, running commercial avgas with the stock water injection system—and turning only 3000 rpm on 70 in. manifold pressure. That was the year he had to drop out of the race right after the start when his landing gear wouldn't retract.

The 1947 season was a washout when prerace experiments with alcohol fuel so goofed up Tucker's craburetor jetting that he burned pistons during qualifying on gasoline. Then in 1948, he finally gave up on No. 28, and went with his No. 30 Bendix Special, with wings clipped only 3 ft on each side. But luck was against him again. Running Shell's new triptane fuel, he pushed to 100 in. manifold pressure at 3200 rpm for qualifying—without water injection—and blew the engine. Apparently the cooling effect of the water was as much needed as the anti-knock effect of the triptane.

For 1949, No. 30, now painted a wild lavender color, got some serious engine surgery: The heavy auxiliary stage supercharger behind the engine was removed because Tucker was beginning to think that it was just dead weight at sea level, and the engine blower ratio was upped from 7.5:1, to 8.8:1. Also he installed a large 100 gal tank just ahead of the cockpit to supplement the original 25 gal water injection tank. This allowed ADI fluid flow for the full forty-five minutes or so of racing, if needed. Another interesting change was a switch to a big two-barrel Bendix carburetor from a Merlin –9 engine, which had more breathing capacity than the regular P-63 three-barrel carb.

The resulting engine combination could develop as much power as the two-stage engine on less manifold pressure, and was much more reliable with free use of water injection. Tucker proved it by qualifying at 393 mph, with top straightaway speeds

Anson Johnson's N13Y Mustang No. 45 had its belly scoop removed and cooling radiators ducted into wings to reduce aerodynamic drag to minimum. Fraites Collection

up to 420 mph, and by finishing a solid fifth in the 1949 Thompson at 378 mph. He still had the fastest King Cobra in the business.

The Story of N13Y: A very special Mustang?

Despite their clean aerodynamics and healthy horsepower potential with two-stage and intercooled Merlin engines, P-51 Mustang fighters were probably marginal Thompson racers, as shown by the saga of the Mustang licensed N13Y, racer No. 45. This racer was highly modified by knowlegeable aircraft people. And it won a Thompson race but had no clear margin of performance at any time.

The plane was originally bought just prior to the 1946 Thompson by Woody Edmundson and raced that first time in practically standard form. He took seventh place at an unimpressive 354.4 mph, running on 115/145 grade fuel without water injection. This speed seemed pretty indicative of the true potential of this P-51D model on standard fuel without injection.

Following that 1946 Thompson, N13Y was taken over by a young National Airlines pilot from Tennessee, Anson Johnson, and he began modifying and upgrading, in a small way at first. For the 1947 races, he merely chopped 2 ft from each wing tip—to a span of 33 ft—and entered the ship in the Kendall Trophy race, prior to the Thompson. Unspecified engine failure put Johnson out of that race, and there wasn't time to repair for the Thompson.

More radical modifications were in order for 1948. First, and most logical, more than 1,000 lb of equipment was stripped out, to get empty weight down from around 7,100 lb to 5,700 lb. Aerodynamics was helped by removing external accessories and by painting and polishing to a high gloss finish from nose to tail.

The big change for 1948, though, was in the engine. After much thought, Johnson came to the rather unusual conclusion that the two unique features of the Packard Merlin engine, built-in two-stage supercharging and intercooling, were really no help at all for high-speed flying at sea level. He figured that the high degree of compression only wasted engine power and that the intercooler just added dead weight. His conviction was only strengthened by the fact that his particular late P-51D model Mustang was fitted with a high-altitude –3 Merlin engine, rather than the usual medium-altitude –7. Its War Emergency rating at sea level was only 1,380 hp. It was really all wrong for low-level racing in any case.

Johnson began searching Rolls-Royce spec tables and finally pinpointed a Packard-built V-1650-25 model (–225 Rolls designation) that was used in some late British low-altitude Mosquito bombers. It had only a single-stage supercharger and no intercooler. It weighed 240 lbs less than a conventional Merlin and yet gave 1,620 hp at 3000 rpm on 67 in. at sea level. Johnson was confident that this was a more practical Merlin configuration to race with. But finding this rare –25 model in the United States took him many weeks between the 1947 and 1948 races.

Another problem, was that this –25 Merlin model wasn't fitted for water injection. But Johnson rigged up a system from an earlier Rolls engine. Water injection allowed wide open throttle operation for at least short periods. At 3200 rpm, manifold pressure went over 90 in. with the injection, and horsepower output was estimated at 2,250.

The newly modified No. 45 attracted much attention at Cleveland in 1948 when Johnson qualified at an impressive 398.6 mph, the fastest of any Mustang up to that time. But that was the year when Chuck Brown shattered all the qualifying records with his 418 mph in *Cobra II*. And the two Cleland Corsairs were well over 400 mph. Johnson knew that he would need a lot of luck to win.

And somehow he found it. Both Corsairs backfired and blew off part of their engine cowlings early in the race, and Brown's P-39 vapor-locked, dropping him out of the race only some twenty miles from the finish. Anson Johnson cruised his Mustang in from fourth place to win it all, averaging 383.8 mph for the 300 miles. He won with the simplest racing maxim of all: He was there at the finish.

An interesting postscript to the 1948 story concerned fuel. That was the year Shell introduced its exotic triptane fuel. The company wasn't giving it away, though, and Johnson signed on with Sohio for a free batch of 115/145, displaying its decal on his plane. Then when Charlie Tucker blew the engine in his P-63, he offered to sell Johnson his supply of triptane at half-price. It was an offer that Johnson could hardly turn down, especially when Tucker seemed so sold on the stuff. So it happened that Johnson won the 1948 Thompson race on Shell triptane, but with a Sohio decal on his plane.

In perspective, though, Johnson was all too aware that he had lucked out in that 1948 race with a slower plane. But winning seemed to generate extra momentum. Far from being discouraged, he was filled with ideas about how he could make his Mustang fully as fast as the big F2G Corsairs for the 1949 race. Johnson was doubly encouraged when his employers at National Airlines picked up on his much publicized 1948 Thompson win and offered him company hangar facilities and equipment to do work necessary to prepare for the next race. Further, the company chief engineer, J. D. Crane, offered technical advice, and several company mechanics offered help in modifying the plane and serving as ground crew at Cleveland the next year. It proved again nothing succeeds like success.

The most logical area for deep modification for 1949 was simply in trying to reduce the aerodynamic drag of the Mustang design to an absolute minimum. The only obvious place to work was the massive tunnel-like air scoop for the coolant radiators under the fuselage. Both Johnson and Crane agreed that it might be helpful to remove this bulky appendage entirely—to smooth up the whole underside of the fuselage—and move the radiators into the wings somehow. Theoretically, this would reduce the wing lift somewhat, but that should be no problem at high speeds and should only raise landing speeds a few miles per hour. The potential reduction in parasite drag looked like possibly as much as fifteen or twenty percent of the total.

It was easier said than done. Finding just the right size and shape radiators to fit inside the wings was a challenge. The final solution was to take four P-39 radiators, which were cubical in shape, cut them off center, weld on sealing plates and then restack them so that the overall height was reduced in relation to width. This permitted the radiators to be fitted inside the Mustang's wings without reducing core area below that of the single large Mustang

cooler. They were located just outboard of the landing gear wells. The original Mustang oil cooler was small enough to be fitted in the right wing without modification. Sheet aluminum ductwork was then fabricated to take in air at the leading edge of the wing and to vent it out in the negative pressure area on the upper wing surface, behind the radiators hinged flaps were located over the exit slots, with a lever in the cockpit to control their angle, and thus the air flow. No cooling problems were ever encountered.

Other late modifications included a second hydraulic accumulator from a DC-4 plumbed into the system, which increased the speed of landing gear retraction to just a few seconds. An attempt to cut a bit more wind drag was made by fabricating narrower exhaust stacks out of stainless steel, which didn't extend out so far into the air stream. And finally, they sent the original 11 ft four-blade propeller back to the Hamilton factory and had the blades shortened and recontoured to 10 ft. diameter. This permitted engine speed to be increased to 3250 rpm without excessive tip speed.

The Johnson team went to Cleveland in 1949 with every confidence that their "new" Mustang could race wing-to-wing with the Cleland Corsairs. This confidence was admittedly a little shaken when

The Beville-Raymond Galloping Ghost *Mustang No. 77 was virtually stock, but the owners' wide open throttle race strategy allowed them to place in all postwar Thompsons.* Bowers

another highly modified Mustang, the famous *Beguine* of Bill Odom, qualified at 405 mph. Two other F2G Corsairs, entered in that 1949 Thompson were of unknown performance potential. So Johnson only cruised around on his qualifying run, not wanting to show anything.

Nineteen forty-nine was the year of the tragic Odom crash shortly after the start of the race. Dick Becker's Corsair had blown its engine after his qualifying run and didn't start. The 1949 Thompson really boiled down to a race between the three Corsairs and Johnson. But it wasn't to be for Johnson. On the fifth lap, he began hearing loud thumping sounds intermittently. The plane didn't seem to act differently, but he apparently got cold feet and eventually came in on the seventh lap, while running in fourth place. It was found later that the thumping noises were caused by the special fabricated exhaust stacks breaking off one by one and hitting the sides of the plane.

There has always been speculation whether Johnson could have challenged Cleland and the other Corsairs if his plane had lasted. I don't think so. His 1949 airframe modifications did seem to show some small increase in speed potential over the 1948 setup, but he never gained on the three Corsairs at any time while he was in the race.

And there's one more page to the N13Y speed story. After the Thompson series was stopped following the 1949 race, Johnson got the idea of attempting to break the world 3 km landplane speed record with the Mustang; that record stood then at 469.22 mph, set in 1939 by Fritz Wendell in a Messerschmitt. Johnson had seen well over 450 mph IAS several times in flight tests and was convinced that N13Y had more speed in it. Of course, record breaking cost money. But Johnson proved to have unexpected promoting ability, and he was able to scare up three sponsors to finance the necessary official timing by the FAI for a world record attempt. Finally in June 1952, a 3 km course was set up at Key Biscayne, Florida. But from there on, it was all downhill. On one of the four fastest runs, the recording camera failed to catch the ship, making it impossible for the FAI to certify the average speed. But the time slips figured to only 435.24 mph, which wasn't anywhere near the Wendell record. Then engine problems prevented further flights at that time.

Anson Johnson always felt that fate cheated him out of that record and that the plane was really much faster than 435 mph. But I wonder if he was fooled by a faulty airspeed gauge; no evidence exists to support Johnson's claim. On the contrary, his fastest timed lap speeds on the fifteen-mile Thompson course were in the 390 mph bracket, which

would have required a peak straightaway speed of no more than 420 mph. How do you figure it?

Galloping Ghost: All out or nothing

There really wasn't anything so special about the No. 77 Mustang or about partners Steve Beville and Bruce Raymond who raced it in the four postwar Thompsons—except maybe their racing philosophy: wide open or nothing. They didn't use a game plan or any kind of race strategy. It was strictly throttle to the stop, and let it happen.

And surprisingly, their approach paid off. Beville and Raymond finished every race they entered, won fourth place in the 1946, 1947 and 1949 Thompsons and a neat second behind Anson Johnson in the 1948 race. Their prize winnings paid for the plane and expenses several times over.

The No. 77 *Galloping Ghost* P-51D Mustang, named after football great Red Grange, was procured in mid-1946 and entered in the first postwar Thompson with a minimum of preparation. Beville and Raymond lightened the plane by over 1,000 lb, blocked off the supercharger boost control on the -7 Merlin engine and invested some 600 man-hours in seventeen coats of paint, wax and polish of the exterior surfaces to create a mirror-like finish and to reduce skin friction to an absolute minimum.

Top speed was boosted a few mph by all the elbow grease, which was enough to win fourth in the 1946 Thompson. But it became obvious to the Beville-Raymond team that a better answer for future speed increases was brute horsepower.

As a result, for 1947 they concentrated on adapting water injection. Steve Beville had a friend who owned a surplus P-47 Thunderbolt fighter, and he felt that the ADI system for the big eighteen-cylinder Pratt & Whitney could be adapted to the P-51 with a little ingeniuty. It turned out to be quite a job. But the boys worked out a clever swap in which larger 40 gal fluid tanks could be located in the gun bays in each wing so that the extra weight wouldn't effect the center of gravity. Then they were able to talk the Bendix people into converting the two-barrel -7 Merlin carburetor with the necessary jetting and control valves to give just the right fuel mixture and water flow for maximum power. The resulting boost in speed was a very pleasing 20 mph, running at the same 3000 rpm and 80 in. manifold pressure, from 380 to 400 mph. It was enough to win another fourth in that 1947 Thompson race.

An additional 10 mph boost in speed for 1948 and 1949 was accomplished by merely increasing engine speed to 3200 rpm, where 85 in. was available at full throttle. By using the better fuels available and continuous water injection, the power went from 2,000 hp to 2,200 hp—not enough to throw things apart, just enough to keep up the pace and

The famous Beguine *Mustang was said to cost $100,000, with radical modifications from nose to tail. But pilot Bill Odom* lacked pylon experience and crashed fatally in the 1949 Thompson. Fraites Collection

finish in the money. Beville and Raymond followed the simplest racing rule of all: Flat out or nothing.

Beguine: **The fastest P-51?**

Some air racing historians say that the beautiful dark green P-51C Mustang known as *Beguine*—the plane that crashed in the 1949 Thompson, killing pilot Bill Odom and two civilians—was the most technically advanced plane to fly in the postwar race series. Others say that it was vastly overrated, that it showed less aerodynamic ingenuity than Anson Johnson's 1948 winning Mustang.

The major design inspiration behind *Beguine* sprang from Walter Beech, a highly successful commercial aircraft designer and manufacturer in the United States for nearly four decades. Beech wanted very much to get involved in postwar air racing, but because of family pressures he needed a "front" organization to keep his name out. This not unpleasant opportunity fell to J. D. Reed of Houston, Texas, the top Beechcraft distributor in the country, and himself a rabid race fan. Reed had just sponsored two planes in the 1947 Cleveland races. Walter Beech approached him in early 1948 with the proposal that they work together to field a potential Thompson winning P-51 for that September. Reed was to finance the project, procure the plane,

provide the facilities, pilot and so on. Beech was in every way just a guiding light.

To start, Beech wanted to use a P-51B or C Mustang rather than the more popular D model, because the fuselage had somewhat less frontal area, and he felt that the flush blending of the pilot's canopy into the dorsal hump would have less parasite drag. Also, as most other designers felt when approaching any aerodynamic refinement of the Mustang configuration, Beech wanted to somehow get rid of the large air scoop and cooling tunnel under the fuselage. Anson Johnson's solution to this problem, as outlined earlier, was to move the cooling radiators into the wings. Walter Beech came up with a much more novel solution: Put the coolers in teardrop shaped pods on each wing tip, the pods being constructed from surplus 75 gal wing gas tanks.

It will forever be argued whether or not the wingtip pods had less parasite drag than radiators embedded in air ducts in the wings. No wind tunnel tests were ever made to prove either layout. The performance evidence may furnish the answer.

Beguine was considerably heavier than Anson Johnson's N13Y. The Reed team was only able to reduce empty weight of the P-51C Mustang about 300 lb, to 6,700 lb which was some 1,000 lb heavier than N13Y. The wingtip pods themselves were quite heavy, using large round coolant radiators from a B-50 bomber (plus the original Mustang oil cooler in the right pod). They also put an extra 40 gal ADI tank under the pilot's seat, which added some weight. Finally, they added bracing between the wings and fuselage, to compensate for any structural strength lost when removing the belly cooling tunnel.

One of the more interesting modifications had to do with the wing span. The wings were clipped enough to maintain approximately the same 37 ft total span with the wingtip pods in place. But Beech insisted on having the right wing 6 in. shorter than the left. The exact rational behind this has been long lost in the maze of historical legendry.

There seems little question, though, that the Reed team got more punch out of the basic Merlin engine than anybody else in that period. They started by converting to a -9 high altitude model, which had built-in water injection and high supercharger gear ratios capable of over 100 in. manifold pressure. And they didn't hesitate to test at these racing power levels. Reed spoke of tying the plane down on a hangar apron and running the engine for over an hour at 3000–3200 rpm and 100 in. manifold pressure, by hosing cold water through the wingtip cooling pods. It's said they used a Shell triptane fuel mix for this type of strenuous endurance testing.

It was planned that the pilot could open the throttle and run the engine at up to 3400 rpm and 120 in. manifold pressure in low blower gear during a race, using triptane fuel with water injection. This was estimated to deliver in excess of 3,200 hp. And Reed even had a little extra switch in the cockpit that could cut in high blower speed for a few seconds, to give still another 8 in. pressure and 200 more horsepower. Talk about overkill!

The unusual propeller was obtained when Beech managed to talk the Hamilton-Standard people into selling him a set of experimental blades that were being developed for the P-51H program, with extremely thin sections and extra width for maximum high-speed efficiency. They were said to cost $2,500 each, and increase the top speed of the plane up to 10 mph. But their useful life was only about 100 hours.

On the subject of *Beguine's* flight performance—which was said to be the fastest of all postwar Thompson racers—I have had to depend on several reputable aviation historians who have researched this famous plane over a period of thirty years. Admittedly, most of the numbers are not certified in NAA files, and I repeat them with no guarantee of their accuracy.

In regard to the absolute top speed in level flight, the story goes that in June 1949, owner J. D. Reed had contracted with a Texas air show promoter to have his pilot, Ken Cooley, run *Beguine* at full power, 3400 rpm and 120 in. manifold pressure, for two passes in each direction over a measured mile with electric timing. The runs were to be the feature event of the show, supposedly for a fee of $10,000. The average of these four runs was reported as 502 mph.

As for pylon speed, Reed arranged with prewar ace Benny Howard to manage his efforts at the Cleveland Nationals. Benny felt it important that pilot Bill Odom fly at least one practice lap on the 15 mile Thompson course with near full power—at least 3200 rpm and 110 in.—to get the feel of *Beguine* under high-stress racing conditions, since he had no experience in pylon racing. Howard reported that one of these laps was timed at 2:06, or just under 430 mph average. So much for unofficial *Beguine* performance.

Unfortunately, very little official performance took place. As luck would have it, the team miscalculated fuel consumption on the ferry trip to Cleveland after the plane was completed in 1948, and pilot Joe Howard had to belly into a wheat field in Kansas. Damage to the plane was not extensive, but it prevented any racing that year.

Then just ten days before the 1949 Thompson, the famous woman pilot Jacqueline Cochran took a shine to *Beguine* and got her wealthy husband, Floyd Odlum, to buy it on the spot from Beech and Reed for a reported $100,000. It was a deal that they could hardly turn down. Of course, this was a bitter disappointment to Reed's pilot, who was scheduled to fly *Beguine* in the Thompson. He had even practiced pylon turns with the ship for several weeks. Instead, Jackie Cochran wanted to put her friend, Bill Odom, in the cockpit for the Sohio and Thompson races at Cleveland. And Odom had never even seen a pylon race before.

Perhaps what happened to *Beguine* at Cleveland in 1949 was inevitable. After qualifying at an impressive 405.57 mph, Odom won the preliminary Sohio Trophy race with comparative ease, though observers said his piloting was sloppy on the turns. In the Thompson, he got in trouble almost immediately, on the second lap. There's never been general agreement among race historians as to just what happened to cause that terrible crash. But the consensus seemed to be that Odom over-turned the second pylon in a steep left bank, so that he had to swing back to his right to line up for the next pylon. He apparently overcorrected on that swing, so the ship just rolled right over on its back and plunged upside down into a house. Whether the high roll

Bob Swanson used special doped fuel in his stock Mustang to win fifth place in the first postwar Thompson, when the best commercial aviation gas gave too much detonation for full power. Sunyak

inertia due to the wingtip pods had any effect is not known.

To sum up, it's probably safe to say that *Beguine* was the fastest of all early Mustang racers. But whether it was the fastest of all the postwar Thompson racers was never proved on offical clocks.

NX79161: A stock Mustang that made good

Bob Swanson was not the typical hot-blooded young ex–World War II military pilot who was attracted by the money and excitement of the first postwar Thompson Trophy race. He was a forty-year-old charter operator in Florida who wanted to try some pylon racing as part of a long aviation career. His resources were thus more plentiful than those of the typical young Thompson entrant. But his maturity told him this was strictly a fun project, not a way to get rich quick.

Swanson's first P-51D Mustang for the 1946 Thompson had the usual minor preparation: lightening, painting, polishing and so on, but he blew the engine on his qualifying run and demolished the plane on a crash landing. Swanson was uninjured. With only a couple days left before the race, several frantic phone calls yielded another D model on short notice out of New Mexico. There was just one problem: The stock 85 gal fuselage gas tank had been stripped out to fix up another plane. The team hastily installed a smaller 45 gal tank they had around. But this gave them a total of only some 200 gal of tankage for the 300 mile Thompson. There

wasn't time for other modifications, not even removal of gun bays and armor plate. They did stick in the proverbial broomhandle to block off the automatic boost control, allowing the full range of throttle operation by the hand lever. But with the undersize fuel supply it was doubtful if full throttle could be used.

And the worse was yet to come. On his final qualifying attempt, the morning of the race, Swanson noted fairly steady detonation at the War Emergency setting of 3000 rpm and 67 in. manifold pressure on the standard 100/130 grade fuel. And his lap speeds were below 350 mph. This was really a blow, with no time to rig up water injection.

But this was a time when oil company technicians who roamed the pits and hangars at Cleveland with their strange chemical concoctions really saved the day for a team. A Shell man noticed Swanson's detonation problem during qualifying. He stepped up and offered to dope his fuel load for the race with a potent triptane additive. Swanson was glad to try anything at this point.

In the race, with the limited fuel supply, Swanson decided to hang back a little, using low revs and manifold pressure, just hoping to finish in maybe seventh or eighth place on the 200 gal. But fate had better things for him. Into the ninth lap, he could see his fuel supply was going to last. So he did what most red-blooded racers would do: pushed his throttle full open, to manifold pressures over 80 in. and straightaway speeds over 400 mph—and proceeded to shock everybody, including himself, by passing Woody Edmundson and Cook Cleland into fifth place. Swanson turned the last lap faster than any other plane, at 378.4 mph! Not only did that last-minute burst increase his prize money by $2,000, but he was awarded an extra $200 for the last lap prize. For a stock Mustang it made good!

Tony LeVier's P-38: Real lightning

Tony LeVier was a veteran of prewar pylon racing who couldn't wait to get back in the saddle at the 1946 Cleveland meet. He didn't have any big money sponsor, and funds were limited, so he had to go racing in the simplest, most economical way possible.

This need to economize led him to the twin engine Lockheed P-38 configuration. But it was not just that P-38s were cheap and plentiful on the surplus market. LeVier liked the good power-to-weight ratio and reasonable wing loading for tight turning and hard acceleration off the turns. He liked the opposite rotating propellers that canceled torque effects and helped stability in tight turns. It's also not generally known that LeVier had intended that his pylon racer would double for complex stunting demonstrations at various air shows—and the P-38 was ideal for that.

LeVier didn't make radical modifications on the $1,000 P-38L model be bought in the summer of 1946. It was mostly a matter of stripping out every ounce of unneeded hardware: guns, ammunition racks, armor plate, some instruments, the engines' turbo-chargers and intercoolers and so on. In all, he dumped some 2,300 lb, dropping the empty weight of his plane to 11,400 lb. Doesn't sound like much

reduction on a percentage basis, but stripping out over 2,000 lb took some doing on any World War II fighter plane. LeVier also added two small, lightweight gas tanks to allow him to run a very rich fuel mixture for the 300 miles.

The basic F series Allison engines in the P-38L model had 8.8:1 turbo-charger gear ratios and could deliver about 1,700 hp each at 3200 rpm on 70 in. manifold pressure with full throttle on 115/145 grade fuel. Admittedly, the engines suffered detonatoin, but the extra rich fuel-air mixture helped. LeVier did not attempt to fit water injection.

As for aerodynamic cleanup, LeVier was careful to give the plane a high-gloss paint finish—fire engine red, incidentally—and the night before the 1946 Thompson, he and his crew spent hours using rolls of Scotch tape to seal over every seam between aluminum sheets on the outer skin. This stuff began peeling off from aerodynamic pressures during the race, making a rather gooey mess after the race. And the benefit was questionable. LeVier never tried the tape-over routine again.

But the plane was a reasonably good performer, considering its size and weight. Sea level top speed at full throttle and 3200 rpm (3,400 hp total) was between 390 and 400 mph, suggesting an equivalent parasite area of 6.5 sq. ft. That was a shade better than a stock P-38L.

And no one can argue with results. Tony took second place in the 1946 Thompson, fifth place in the 1947 race—and he won the 1947 Sohio Trophy race for P-38s only. His total prize winnings paid for the plane and modifications several times over. Add to this his fees for stunting exhibitions; LeVier was one of the few who made racing pay.

Prewar racer Tony LeVier had the fastest, most successful Lockheed P-38 in the postwar Thompsons. He stripped weight, cleaned up external surfaces and ran the Allison engines wide open. Bowers

167

Chapter 12

Postwar Thompson Trophy races

The 1946 Thompson Trophy race

After five years of a world war in which high-performance aircraft played a vital part, American aviation enthusiasts, and the public too, were more than ready for some racing fun and excitement on the pylons again. Fred Crawford and the Thompson Products Company were no less interested in continuing sponsorship of their famous race series, so it only remained for Crawford to huddle with a rejuvenated National Aeronautics Association to organize the first postwar National Air Races for the 1946 Labor Day weekend at the Cleveland airport. It was to be a five-day affair, with a varied program of pylon races, aerobatic demonstrations, parachuting, military fly-bys and landing contests—much like the prewar shows, but featuring a new world of war-bred aviation technology. And to assure an attractive purse of prize money, the new NAR committee was able to scare up a number of new corporate sponsors for specific events, including Kendall Oil, Sohio, Tinnerman Products, Allison Motors and others.

Those early postwar race organizers were also well aware that every phase of the program was going to be totally unlike prewar pylon racing. Just settling on a size and shape for the Thompson race

Tex Johnston won the first postwar Thompson with the highly modified Bell P-39Q Cobra II, qualifying at 409 mph. The plane was entered by a group of Bell Aircraft test pilots and technicians. Bowers

course was a major problem, considering the quantum leap in aircraft speeds compared with those in the prewar races. The last prewar course, a ten-mile rectangle generally northwest of the airport, didn't seem at all feasible for the 400 mph speeds of the postwar fighter-racers. That area was densely populated by the late 1940s. It was finally decided to lengthen the lap to thirty miles and make the course a large square generally southeast of the airport, roughly 7½ miles on a side, with the home pylon and grandstands at the northwest corner. The planes wouldn't be in sight of the spectators for only a fraction of the lap, but it was felt the longer straightaways and near 90 degree turns would be safer for the pilots. Also the area southeast of the airport was a bit less populated at the time.

The popular racehorse start was still retained, though. The planes took off in front of the grandstand and rounded the home pylon before proceeding south on the first leg of the course. The race clock was started at the drop of the flag, with planes on the ground. (Some prewar races were timed when the first plane off crossed the start/finish line in flight.) Qualifying required two consecutive laps of the race course at an average speed of at least 300 mph.

Of the twelve planes that started that first postwar Thompson, three had outstanding qualifying speeds: Tex Johnston in the *Cobra II* P-39 at 409.1 mph, George Welch in Ron Freeman's No. 37 P-51D Mustang at 394.3 mph and Charlie Tucker in a clipped wing Bell P-63C at 392.2 mph. These were easily the prerace favorites with press and fans alike. The rest of the field was a mixture of Mustangs, P-63s, Cook Cleland's F4U Corsair and Tony LeVier's brilliant red P-38. The entry of well-known prewar racing names like LeVier, Earl Ortman and Steve Wittman attracted a lot of press attention before the race, but none of them had impressive qualifying speeds.

In trying to prepare a bunch of hot-blooded young military pilots, unfamiliar with pylon racing, for the dangers of the racehorse start—and in the extra danger of hotter, higher horsepower planes—race officials asked prewar veteran Art Chester, on the NAA Contest Board, to talk to the boys just before the race. They felt that his reputation and experience would carry weight. Art did manage to calm things down a lot. Another good innovation was to use two prestart flag signals, one five minutes before the start and another one minute before. It was hoped that this would prevent the guys from revving up too soon and jumping the gun. It worked. Even though it was a noisy and exciting start for the spectators, it was probably the safest racehorse start in Thompson history!

As expected, Tex Johnston, confident that he had the fastest plane in the race, was first away and off the ground, snapping up his landing gear and pulling ahead of the field down the first straightaway. Right behind him was Charlie Tucker's powerful P-63. But Charlie didn't last long. His landing

Veteran prewar racer Earl Ortman took third in the 1946 Thompson with a stock Mustang, using his long experience in pylon racing to beat young World War II pilots. Sunyak

Cook Cleland finished a disappointing seventh in the 1946 Thompson with a stock 2,000 hp F4U Corsair. That performance showed him that he needed lots more horsepower to win future races. Sunyak

gear stuck down, and he dropped out within seconds after the start. George Welch in the fast No. 37 Mustang was slow getting away, but began gaining rapidly on Johnston after pulling onto the main course. It wasn't to be George's day either, as he started to trail white smoke from a broken cylinder head after only a few miles. Just into the second lap, he pulled around to land on the edge of the airport.

So a stunned crowd saw Johnston coming around in the lead after the second lap, cruising

Charlie Tucker was a favorite in the 1946 Thompson in his clipped wing P-63C, with a fast qualifying time. But the landing gear stuck down on takeoff. Bowers

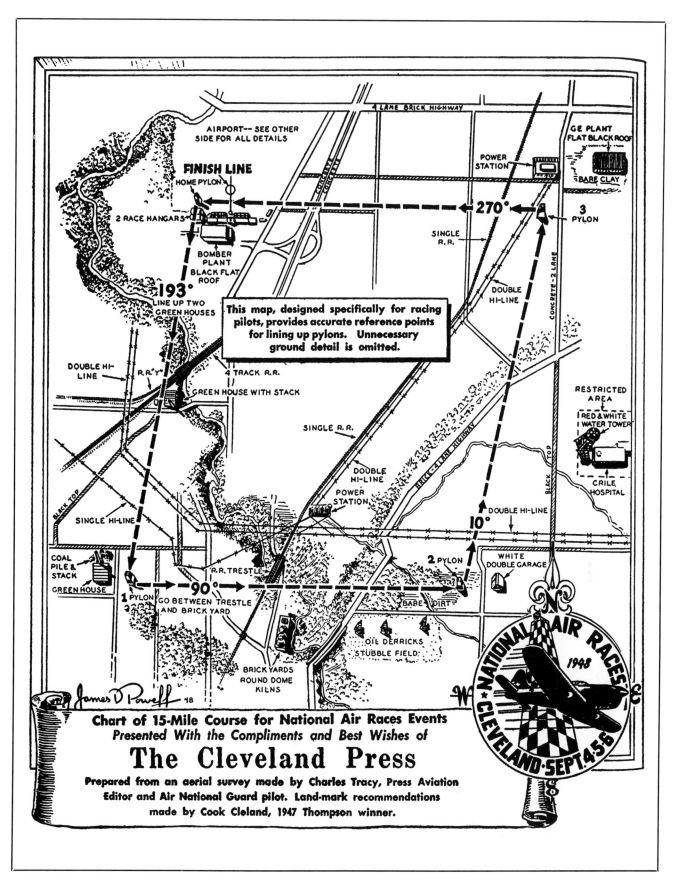

A special map supplied to Thompson pilots showed the new 15 mile course used in 1947 and 1948, with important landmarks to help the racers locate turns.

along leisurely at 3000 rpm and 62 in. manifold pressure, as the public-address system blared an unexciting lap average in the 370 mph bracket. Without radio communication, Tex wasn't aware that his toughest competitors, Tucker and Welch, had dropped out. But when nobody pulled up to pass him, he saw no need to speed up. Why stress the engine more than necessary? However, Tony LeVier had other ideas. Remembering how conservative flying had possibly cost him the last prewar Thompson, he kept the throttle of his P-38 right on the stop, moving up on Johnston several seconds each lap. When LeVier finally pulled up within a half-mile or so of Johnston, and Tex could see the little red plane creeping up behind him, he calmly increased his settings to 3200 rpm and 75 in.—which was still only eighty-five percent of his power—and motored away from LeVier like he was standing still. So long, Tony!

Perhaps the biggest surprise of the day was Bob Swanson. Through most of the race, he poked along in seventh place, behind Edmundson and Cleland, trying to conserve his fuel because his hastily prepared stock Mustang had part of its fuel tankage removed. But Swanson had a special high-octane fuel blend in the tanks, and when he saw that his fuel was going to last the race, he slammed his throttle to the stop on the last lap, passing both Edmundson and Cleland to finish in fifth place.

And that's how it ended: Johnston first, LeVier second, veteran Earl Ortman third in a Mustang, Bruce Raymond fourth in another P-51—and Bob Swanson fifth, after his exciting last lap.

It should be noted that the veteran pylon racers like Tony LeVier and Earl Ortman finished well in that first postwar Thompson, even with planes having inferior straightaway speed. They were clearly faster on the corners, and when threading through traffic. Their performance illustrated the importance of piloting teachnique and experience in pylon racing. This situation didn't occur a second time, however. By the following year, the young eagles were getting a feel for the pylons, and the prewar veterans had to earn their prize money the hard way.

The 1947 Thompson Trophy race

The 1946 Thompson race had gone off so smoothly and safely that the organizers were encouraged to shorten the course to fifteen miles for the next race, but still used the general square shape, just under four miles on a side, with the home pylon and grandstands in the Northwest corner (see map layout). They figured that this shorter race-

Teammates Cook Cleland and Dick Becker took first and second in the 1947 Thompson with nearly identical 4,000 hp F2G Corsairs. Becker's ship is shown here. Carter

The Cobra II *P-39Q was bought by an Indianapolis Kaiser-Frazer car dealer in 1947. Flown by Bell test pilot Jay Demming,* *the plane finished third behind Cleland and Becker's Corsairs.* Bowers

course would be better for the spectators because the planes would be coming around more often and in shorter elapsed time. The race distance remained at 300 miles, but now required twenty laps.

The prerace favorites were again well established from qualifying times. This was the first year for Cook Cleland's 4,000 hp F2G Corsairs, and he and teammate Dick Becker were both qualified at over 400 mph. Paul Penrose was flying Ron Freeman's fast No. 37 *Wraith* Mustang—the plane George Welch had flown in 1946—and he clocked 390.9 mph for his two laps. This plane was fitted with the refined -9 Merlin with water injection and was fast gaining a reputation among the Thompson brotherhood as a Mustang to be reckoned with. Jay Demming was flying the popular *Cobra II* P–39Q which had been bought by businessman Rollin Stewart, qualifying it at a healthy 386.8 mph. Few changes were made in the plane from 1946.

The remaining eight starters were a mixture of P-51s, a couple of P-38s (including Tony LeVier again), a P-63 and two more big F2G Corsairs—one an entry of Ron Puckett and the other Cleland's backup plane flown by Tony Janazzo. (Janazzo has been erroneously identified as "Ben Jacoby" in some accounts of the 1947 race.) There was even a thirteenth plane that started that race, a late Curtiss P–40Q flown by Joe Ziegler. He never qualified, but slipped into the lineup in the confusion at the start, apparently determined to bluff his way into the race.

Officials never flagged him out, so he took off and raced with the rest of the field.

At the drop of the starter's flag, Jay Demming in the lightweight *Cobra II* was away and into the air first (just as the year before) building up a substantial lead over the rest of the field down the first straightaway. The others were a little slower away, but without incident—all except Ron Puckett. He couldn't get the big R-4360 Pratt & Whitney started in his F2G Corsair, and he didn't get started and rolling until the leading planes were in sight at the end of their first lap. This put him behind nearly four minutes before he even got off the ground.

Meanwhile, Dick Becker in his big Corsair was gaining rapidly on Demming, passed him shortly into the second lap and led laps two, three and four. Cook Cleland was pulling up, too, after a slow start and passed Demming and Becker into the lead on lap five.

But Paul Penrose had his own plans. After getting his Mustang cleared out and the fuel mixture settings right, he gradually put on more revs and manifold pressure. On the sixth lap, he turned an impressive average of 404 mph and passed a surprised Jay Demming into third place. But he had apparently shifted the -9 Merlin engine into high blower ratio and developed a violent supercharger surging condition when he throttled back on the next lap. Penrose was forced to bring the plane in a few moments later.

173

But this was only a small part of the attrition in that memorable 1947 Thompson. Charles Walling had already dropped out on the second lap with fuel feed problems in his P-38. On the seventh lap, Tony Janazzo, in the third Cleland Corsair, was gradually overcome by carbon monoxide fumes behind the huge R–4360 Pratt & Whitney, and plunged into the ground at 400 mph before a stunned crowd at the edge of the airport. Apparently part of the elaborate exhaust plumbing on the four row radial engine had fractured.

Still more mayhem visited the pack. It was Woody Edmundson on the eleventh lap. His engine exploded coming around No. 3 pylon, and he rode the plane down, escaping with cuts and bruises from the fiery crash. On the thirteenth lap, the Allison engine in Joe Ziegler's P-40 quit over open country, and he bailed out, as the plane crashed to the ground.

By this time, only seven of the thirteen starters were still flying. Ron Puckett, after his delayed start, finally got in the air, but with an obviously sick engine. He sputtered along, though, eventually passing Bill Bour's P-63 into sixth place. But then, on the nineteenth lap and only a few miles from the finish, his engine quit cold, and he had to land on the airport. He was awarded $500 as a special consolation prize, for a plucky catch-up race that had the crowd cheering him on.

The finishing order was Cleland, Becker, Demming, Beville and LeVier in the first five places.

Cleland turned a new record average of 396.13 mph for the 300 miles.

Race historians have always wondered if Penrose might have caught up with Cleland, if the No. 37 Mustang hadn't dropped out with engine trouble. Both planes had turned laps at 404 mph. But the bottom line is that Cleland's big 4,000 hp Corsair was really just loafing at 400 mph, while Penrose had to let it all hang out to exceed 400. Maybe that's why Cleland finished and Penrose didn't.

The 1948 Thompson Trophy race

The 1948 Thompson was flown over the same fifteen-mile square course as was the 1947 race. The pilots and spectators alike had been quite satisfied with the layout, and there seemed no pressing need to change.

As always, three or four planes stood head and shoulders above the rest of the field on a basis of qualifying speeds. Those speeds were proportionally faster than ever before for one very significant reason: Shell's new triptane 200/300 grade fuel. All four top qualifying planes were using the stuff, which permitted considerably higher manifold pressures than would have been possible the year before on regular 115/145 grade fuel (with or without water injection).

Allison test pilot Chuck Brown was now flying *Cobra II*, with a much more powerful engine, and he surprised everybody with a record qualifying average of 418.1 mph. This only challenged Cook Cle-

Prewar veteran Tony LeVier brought his P-38 in second in the 1946 Thompson and fifth in 1947. The plane was not highly modified, just consistent and reliable. Bowers

Ron Freeman's No. 37 Mustang, Wraith, *was flown by Paul Penrose in the 1947 Thompson. The plane turned the sixth lap* *at 404 mph, then dropped out with supercharger surge.* Fraites Collection

land to push the revs and manifold pressure of his F2G Corsair beyond usual limits: He clocked only a few ticks slower at 417.4 mph. The qualifying trials were becoming a kind of sideshow by then, with piloting and tuning pride at stake and plenty of media hype to keep things boiling. A top spot on the

time trial list was almost as prized as winning the race.

Even Dick Becker got carried away in the qualifiers and came in with a two-lap average of 405.9 mph. Anson Johnson turned 398.6 mph with the strong N13Y Mustang. The popular No. 37 Mustang

Anson Johnson won the 1948 Thompson in a nearly stock Mustang *when Chuck Brown's hot* Cobra II *had engine trouble near the end.* Kohn

Bruce Raymond finished second behind Johnson in the 1948 Thompson in the stock Mustang, Galloping Ghost. Partners

Raymond and Steve Beville finished in the money in every postwar Thompson with this plane. Sunyak

that had done so well in 1947 with Paul Penrose at the controls had been sold to J. D. Reed of Houston and was now flown by Chuck Walling under the name *Jay Dee*. He clocked a 381.5 mph for his two

laps. The rest of the ten plane starting field included two P-51s and three Bell P-63s.

The early laps of that 1948 Thompson race proved to be the fastest, noisiest and most competi-

Chuck Brown turned his fastest lap at 413 mph in the 1948 Thompson with the re-engined Cobra II, but was forced down

near the finish when a vapor lock cut off the fuel supply. Fraites Collection

tive in the history of the series. As usual, *Cobra II*, with probably the best power-to-weight ratio in the field, was first off and away down the front straight. The two F2G Corsairs of Cleland and Becker were not quite as quick away, due to their tremendous weight; but they started to gain on Brown once in the air. Then the race was strictly a matter of horsepower, weight and aerodynamic drag. Apparently Brown had the better numbers that day. He turned a record average speed of 413 mph on his second lap, then backed off just a tad to see if the two Corsairs had the beans to pass him. On the third lap, Becker's Corsair backfired on the slow burning triptane fuel, blowing off the air scoop and part of the engine cowling. He was forced to land. One down and one to go. On the fourth lap, Cleland pushed to 410 mph, but gained only a few feet on Brown. Then the backfire bug hit Cleland too. It blew his cowl away almost exactly as on Becker's ship. The engine kept running, but there was no way he could continue.

With his toughest competition out, Chuck Brown then backed off some more and led the race easily from lap five, with Anson Johnson second and Charles Walling third in No. 37 Mustang. But it wasn't over yet. Sometime around the fourteenth lap (as deduced later), a ten-inch piece of engine cowling shook loose from Brown's plane, exposing a fuel line to close exhaust heat. This started a vapor lock condition—fuel boiling in the line to the carburetor—which caused the engine to start to misfire and cut out intermittently. Brown began to slow down by 30–40 mph.

It didn't take long for the Johnson and Walling ground crews to see that Brown was in trouble and swing into action with signals for their pilots to pour on the coal. They were then more than eight miles behind Brown, with only five laps to make it up. But both had plenty of revs and manifold pressure in reserve, and they used them. Johnson hit one lap at 394 mph in the chase. But all the effort of the chase got Walling was another terminal case of supercharger surge, probably from again shifting to high blower ratio with the -9 high altitude Merlin. He had to shut down and drop out.

In the next two laps, the crowd could see that Johnson was not going to be able to catch the faltering *Cobra II*. Then Lady Luck gave him a boost. On lap nineteen, only forty miles from the finish, Brown's engine quit cold, and he had to dead-stick in. It was a terrible shock to him when he found later that he had not won the race. He had miscounted the laps, and thought he had just finished the twentieth lap when his engine quit. As it was, Johnson

Cook Cleland was forced out of the 1948 Thompson when slow burning triptane fuel caused a huge backfire that blew off the air scoop and part of the engine cowling. Sunyak

177

Texan J. D. Reed bought the No. 37 Mustang in 1948 and renamed it Jay Dee. *Although the plane was still very fast,* recurring supercharger surge put pilot Charles Walling out of the 1948 Thompson. Carter

cruised in at a cool 383.77 mph average for the full 300 miles. He was almost a full lap ahead of second place Bruce Raymond in another Mustang.

Looking back at that 1948 Thompson melee, the major topic of those perpetual bench racing sessions among air race historians has been: Could Cleland have beaten Chuck Brown if both planes had been able to run at full power for the 300 miles? With their qualifying speeds within one mph of each other, such a race would have surely been one wild scramble. The engine troubles that put both planes out weren't really related to pulling excessive power. Brown was felled by vapor lock when a loose cowling panel exposed a fuel line to exhaust heat. And it is felt that Cleland's big Pratt & Whitney wouldn't have backfired on the triptane fuel with a bit less spark advance. With the proper spark timing, Cleland might have been able to run the 300 miles at

Cook Cleland clipped his Corsair's wings sharply for 1949 Thompson, which didn't help speed a bit. But he won anyway, at record average of 397.1 mph. Bowers

The beautiful dark green Beguine *Mustang was the crowd favorite in the 1949 Thompson. But pilot Bill Odom's lack of* *pylon experience led to a fatal crash on the second lap.* Aldrich Collection

4000+ hp output and to average up to 410 mph. But we'll never know.

The 1949 Thompson Trophy race

For the 1949 Thompson race another major change was made in the shape of the course, though the fifteen-mile lap length was retained. Instead of a four-sided course with near 90 degree corners, the officials decided to try an unusual seven-sided shape, with shorter straightaways and much less abrupt corners of around 50 degrees. The course was almost like a huge circle, and the faster planes were expected to be in a shallow bank all the way around. Officials felt that this might be a safer situation than the sharper 90 degree corners, which generated g-load factors of eight and nine in some of the faster planes, making high-speed stalls a constant danger.

It was also decided to shorten the race length to fifteen laps or 225 miles. This was done primarily to reduce the amount of fuel required and thus reduce the wing loading of the planes on the early laps—hopefully as a safety measure on early pylon turns. The shorter race length might also increase spectator excitement by keeping more planes in contention right up to the finish line. Race officials had been appalled by the rate of attrition of planes in earlier Thompson races. Only three planes had finished the 300 miles the year before.

The reaction of the pilots to the new conditions varied from enthusiasm to strong objection. Some were relieved that the stall danger was reduced by the easier turns. But others were uneasy about trying to pass slower planes with the very short straight sections and multiple pylons. Passing was always easiest on long straightaway sections, especially because the rules required passing at least 150 feet to the right of another plane. Some pilots of the faster ships that did a lot of passing felt that the multiple shallow turns would require them to fly wider radius turns and to lose a couple of seconds per lap. But the seven-sided course layout stood.

The Sohio people created another new race condition. Sohio had a new 130/170 grade high performance fuel at Cleveland in 1949 and was giving 500 gal of it to any team who would display its decal. This fuel didn't seem to have the backfiring tendencies of triptane, and most teams signed up to use it (though it couldn't handle quite as high manifold pressures as triptane).

As usual, before the race a handful of planes stood out as favorites on the basis of qualifying times. Dick Becker turned the highest qualifying speed of 414.6 mph in one of Cook Cleland's F2Gs, but his reduction gear stripped coming across the finish line, and the plane had to be scratched. Cleland timed 407.2 mph in his other Corsair. Ben McKillen got a good average of 396.3 mph out of his new F2G, with little experience in flying or tuning it. Ron Puckett had to be satisfied with 373.5 mph in the fourth Corsair; he was still working on the engine. But Bill Odom was impressive at 405.6 mph in the beautiful new *Beguine* Mustang, and his win in the earlier Sohio race further established him as a favorite, despite his lack of experience in pylon racing. Anson Johnson was barely up to expectations at 383.5 mph in his 1948 winning No. 45 Mustang, which was sporting radical new aerodynamic modifications for the 1949 race. Charlie Tucker was faster at 393.3 mph in his old Bendix P-63 with less wing clip, now running a single-stage Allison at 80 in. manifold pressure. The remainder of the ten plane starting field consisted of four P-51s.

At the drop of the starter's flag, Ben McKillan was away first in his big Corsair and led through the first lap. It was during the fateful second lap that Bill Odom crashed into the house at the No. 2 pylon, apparently rolling over in a high-speed stall. Pilot inexperience was listed as a major factor. After the crash, Cleland and Ron Puckett eased by McKillan, both turning lap speeds in the 390–400 mph range. But Cleland was just baiting Puckett, trying to see how fast he could go. Puckett had rigged up a makeshift carburetor air scoop similar to Cleland's, which should have given him at least 20–30 mph more potential straightaway speed. And Cleland heard via the grapevine that Puckett had learned the trick of slipping his blower drive with a hand lever for more manifold pressure. Cleland wanted to find out just how much punch his competitor had.

Puckett didn't take the bait, continuing to trail Cleland. Finally on the fifth lap, Cleland opened up a little and pulled away from Puckett, turning the highest race lap speed of 406 mph. Puckett still didn't, or couldn't, accept the challenge. He just settled down into second place. Cleland backed off a little then, just enough to keep Puckett well behind him, led the last eleven laps and finished two miles in the lead. McKillen finished third, another two or three miles behind Puckett.

Looking back on that 1949 Thompson, it seemed obvious that neither Puckett nor McKillen had any intention of really pouring it on and racing Cleland for 150 or 200 miles. Both ships probably had considerably more speed than was used. But the owners may have been as unsure of their piloting as of their planes. Charlie Tucker looked fast in qualifying, but he obviously felt it was futile to try to keep up with the Corsairs. Anson Johnson's plans were thwarted when his specially fabricated exhaust stacks began burning off one by one, exposing him to carbon monoxide. He came down on the ninth lap. Steve Beville finished fourth in a near stock Mustang. Until better evidence comes along, we'll have to credit Cook Cleland with the fastest of all the postwar Thompson combinations. He was the unquestioned Champ.

Ben McKillan copied the Cleland formula for winning with brute horsepower and bought a Corsair F2G for the 1949 Thompson. He finished third behind the F2Gs of Cleland and *Puckett. Note the diverging air scoop designed by Navy engineers.* Bowers

Epilogue

The reasons behind the demise of the Thompson Trophy race series after the 1949 event have excited speculation and lively debate among air race historians.

The most obvious reason—and the one almost always given as *the* reason—was the tragic crash of Bill Odom. Odom crashed into a house in the nearby town of Berea, killing a mother and her thirteen-month old child. A number of pilots had been killed during the Thompson series. That was almost to be expected. But none had involved either spectators or residents near the airport.

The protection of public rights and safety was less developed in the 1940s. Today a high-speed, low-level air race over a populated area would be unthinkable. No liability insurance carrier would touch it. And the public outcry over something like the Odom crash would resound across the country within hours.

On the other hand, don't get the idea there was no public reaction to the Odom crash in 1949. The Cleveland newspapers, radio and civic groups had plenty to say. Their reactions ranged all the way from proposals to ban all future forms of air racing

to a complete overhaul of rules on pilot qualifications and routing of the race course.

Certainly, the Odom crash figured as one important factor in the demise of the Thompson races at Cleveland. But it was by no means the only factor, nor was it necessarily the key factor. If the Odom crash had been the only consideration, there might very well have been a Thompson race in 1950. The race committee was going full speed ahead with preparations and, in response to the 1949 crash, was making major changes in rules and regulations. And there were several serious proposals for race sites other than Cleveland on the table.

No, perhaps a more important factor in stopping the Unlimited air races after 1949 was the infamous "police action" in Korea, which started in June, 1950. Even though that war didn't threaten the nation's survival, as had the Japanese attack on Pearl Harbor nine years earlier, it had much the same effect in mobilizing the nation's military and industrial machines. Many of the young Thompson pilots, in fact, were called back into active service in

that summer of 1950. It's very possible that a race two months later would have had a small field of entries. The Korean war was a major factor in the demise of the Thompson Trophy races at Cleveland.

It must be noted, though, that when conditions settled down in the United States in the 1950s and there was no longer a national military emergency, no one rushed to return high-speed, closed course air racing to the metropolitan areas. Most organized closed course racing in the fifties involved tiny 200 mph midgets on 2½ mile courses laid out within airport boundaries. And when 400 mph closed course racing was finally revived in 1964, it was done over open desert at Reno, Nevada, or over water near various large coastal cities. Never again did high speed racing take place over populated land areas.

So perhaps the truth lies somewhere in the middle here: The Odom crash did not end the Thompson Trophy races. But if there had been a 1950 or later event, it would not have been held at the Cleveland airport.

Race results

1930 Thompson Trophy Race Results

Place	Pilot	Plane	Engine	Average race speed	Remarks
1	Speed Holman	Laird *Solution*	Pratt & Whitney Wasp Jr.	201.91	Last biplane winner
2	Jim Haizlip	TravelAir R	Wright Whirlwind	199.80	Lost 100 rpm due to fuel
3	Benny Howard	Howard *Pete*	Wright Gypsy	162.80	Small 90 hp engine
4	Paul Adams	TravelAir *Speedwing*	Wright Whirlwind	142.64	Commercial sport biplane
	Arthur Page	Curtiss XF6C-6	Curtiss Conqueror	—	Crashed lap 17, overcome by fumes
	Errett Williams	Wedell 92	Wright Whirlwind	—	Out lap 8, fouled spark plugs
	Frank Hawks	TravelAir R	Wright Whirlwind	—	Out lap 3, restricted fuel

Race distance: 100 miles; 20 laps of the 5 mile course
Fastest race lap: Page, 219 mph

1931 Thompson Trophy Race Results

Place	Pilot	Plane	Engine	Qualifying speed	Average race speed	Remarks
1	Lowell Bayles	Gee Bee Z	Pratt & Whitney Wasp Jr.	267.34*	236.24	Engine upped to 535 hp
2	Jim Wedell	Wedell No. 44	Pratt & Whitney Wasp Jr.	221.05**	227.99	Stock engine, 450 hp
3	Dale Jackson	Laird *Solution*	Wright Whirlwind	201.91**	211.18	1930 winner improved
4	Robert Hall	Gee Bee Y	Pratt & Whitney Wasp Jr.	213.87*	201.51	Commercial sport plane
5	Ira Eaker	Lockheed Altair	Wright Whirlwind	220***	192.82	Commercial mail plane
6	Benny Howard	Howard *Pete*	Wright Gypsy	175.68*	163.51	Small 90 hp engine
7	William Ong	Laird *Speedwing*	Wright Whirlwind	190***	153.05	Commercial biplane
	Jimmy Doolittle	Laird *Super Solution*	Pratt & Whitney Wasp Jr.	255.35*	—	Out lap 7, broken piston

Race distance: 100 miles; 10 laps of the 10 mile course
Qualifying: 175 mph minimum straightaway speed

Optional proof of speed:
* Shell Straightaway Dash, 1 mile
** Previous closed course average speed
*** ATC certified top speed
Fastest race lap: Bayles, 241 mph

1932 Thompson Trophy Race Results

Place	Pilot	Plane	Engine	Qualifying speed	Average race speed	Remarks
1	Jimmy Doolittle	Gee Bee R-1	Pratt & Whitney Wasp	296.29	252.69	Power to 770 hp
2	Jim Wedell	Wedell 44	Pratt & Whitney Wasp Jr.	277.06	242.50	Power increased to 535 hp
3	Roscoe Turner	Wedell-Turner	Pratt & Whitney Wasp Jr.	266.67	233.04	Modified Wedell 44
4	Jim Haizlip	Wedell 92	Pratt & Whitney Wasp Jr.	266.44	231.30	Stock engine, 450 hp
5	Lee Gehlbach	Gee Bee R-2	Pratt & Whitney Wasp Jr.	247.34	222.10	Designed for Bendix race
6	Robert Hall	Hall *Bulldog*	Pratt & Whitney Wasp	243.72	215.57	Restricted air inlet
7	William Ong	Howard *Ike*	Menasco B6	213.86	191.07	180 hp unsupercharged
	Ray Moore	Rider R-1	Menasco C6S	237.74	—	Out lap 2, engine

Race distance: 100 miles; 10 laps of the 10 mile course
Qualifying: Shell Speed Dash, 3 km; 200 mph minimum
Fastest race lap: Doolittle, 266 mph

1933 Thompson Trophy Race Results

Place	Pilot	Plane	Engine	Qualifying speed	Average race speed	Remarks
1	Jimmy Wedell	Wedell 44	Pratt & Whitney Wasp Jr.	278.92	237.95	One lap at 254 mph
2	Lee Gehlbach	Wedell 92	Pratt & Whitney Wasp Jr.	251.93	224.95	Sour engine
3	Roy Minor	Howard *Mike*	Menasco B6S	241.61	199.87	Supercharger added to B6, 230 hp
4	George Hague	Rider R-2	Menasco C4S	210.13	183.21	Midget version of R-1
5	Z. D. Granville	Gee Bee Y	Pratt & Whitney Wasp Jr.	DNQ	173.08	Last-minute entry
	Roscoe Turner	Wedell-Turner	Pratt & Whitney Wasp	280.25	—	Disqualified, cut pylon

Race distance: 100 miles; 10 laps of the 10 mile course
Qualifying: Shell Speed Dash, 3 km; 200 mph minimum
Fastest race lap: Turner, 265 mph

1934 Thompson Trophy Race Results

Place	Pilot	Plane	Engine	Qualifying speed	Average race speed	Remarks
1	Roscoe Turner	Wedell-Turner	Pratt & Whitney Hornet	295.46	248.13	Hornet rated at 825 hp
2	Roy Minor	Brown B-2	Menasco C6S	243.14	214.93	Refined C6S, 320 hp max
3	John Worthen	Wedell 92	Pratt & Whitney Wasp Jr.	248.91	208.38	Engine rough
4	Harold Neumann	Howard *Mike*	Menasco B6S	239.62	207.06	Winner of Greve race in 1934
5	Roger Don Rae	Rider R-1	Menasco C6S	235.33	205.36	Power limited by detonation
6	Art Chester	Chester Special	Menasco C4S	229.71	191.60	Supercharger added to C4, 185 hp